# New Testament Alive

## the gospels:
## matthew. mark. luke. john.

Christopher P. Meade, Ph.D.

www.NewTestamentAlive.com

Volume 1

# CONTENTS:

## The Gospel of Mark

## The Gospel of Luke

# TO MY CHILDREN

## LUKE, MEGAN, & ALLISON

Thank you for who you are and for all that you teach me.

# ABOUT THIS BOOK

As a young boy, I often dreamed of scaling Mount Everest, running a sub-four-minute mile, descending to the bottom of the Pacific Ocean to explore the Mariana Trench in a submarine, and diving from the jagged rock cliffs of Acapulco. I've always loved adventure, challenge, and the thrill of discovering the unknown.

As I've grown older, that desire has never left me; it has only intensified. What has changed is the means in which to experience that reality. I no longer desire to climb the highest peak or plunge to the bottom of the ocean floor, but to experience Jesus in and through every area of my life. My passion is the same, but it has now become directed away from inanimate objects and goals and focused fully toward a person—Jesus. My boyhood zeal remains intact, but my life's journey is now fueled by a truth that is encased within a simple, yet powerful prayer, penned by the apostle Paul.

And I pray that you, being rooted and established in love, may have power, together with all the saints, to grasp how wide and long and high and deep is the love of Christ, and to know this love that surpasses knowledge—that you may be filled to the measure of all the fullness of God. (Ephesians 3:17-19)

Thank you for picking up a copy of this book. I'm honored that you would read what I have to say and to consider what I think. My prayer for you is that as you read the words and ideas from these pages that you will give honest consideration to your life, your goals, your aspirations, and your identity as a person. I hope this book will be useful to you as both a "mirror" for inward reflection and spiritual discovery, and as a "window" to look through and gain new perspectives about God, Jesus, the Holy Spirit, other people, grace, and truth.

This book is written as an informative and inspirational devotional that focuses on the person and teachings of Jesus Christ. It's filled with many of my personal stories, analogies, insights, and failures. Places in this book are raw, honest, and uncomfortably transparent (for me). I share with you the lessons I've learned and the lessons I'm still learning along my spiritual journey as a follower of Jesus.

It's been said that we gain wisdom from the books we read and the people with whom we hang out. Wisdom is the ability to make right choices in life. Wisdom comes to us from the Bible, from our experiences (good and bad), and from other people's experiences that we choose to listen to and learn from. I hope to be a resource and encouragement to you by sharing some of my own insights and life lessons, as well as some of the insights and lessons that others have graciously shared with me in my walk as a Christ-follower. I hope this book will be a conduit of wisdom into your life and that it will ultimately draw you closer to Jesus.

This book is the first of four volumes and begins with the gospels (Matthew, Mark, Luke, and John). It's laid out in such a way that it provides both a general overview of each chapter in each gospel as well as practical applications for daily living. Each chapter follows a similar format: (1) brief observations from the chapter, (2) unpacking one portion of scripture, (3) suggestions for an area of personal application, and (4) an honest prayer.

There are several ways you could read this book. Of course, it's possible to sit down and power-read through it in a day or so if you choose. My recommendation would be to use it as a daily devotional. I think you will get more out of it if you do it that way. Read one chapter a day from this book along with one chapter from your Bible. (If you don't have a Bible, e-mail me and I'll send you one at no charge). Follow the sequence I've laid out in the book. Begin with Matthew, then proceed to Mark, Luke, and finally John. Because there are 89 chapters in the gospels (Matthew 28, Mark 16, Luke 24, John 21), if you read one chapter a day, you will have read through all four gospels in less than three months.

So, in essence, I'm suggesting a 90-day reading plan. Right now, there are lots of infomercials advertising 90-day exercise plans to get you ripped, and ripped fast. I've learned that what you pay attention to in your life usually gets better. If you pay attention to your health, you get healthier. If you pay attention to your relationships, they get better. If you pay attention to your finances, things get worked out. If you pay attention to your spiritual life, it deepens. Let me encourage you to take the 90-day challenge to build up your spiritual life and grow deeper and stronger like never before. Choose to pay attention to your relationship with God. See what He can do in and through your life when you set aside 90 days to be with Him. I really believe you'll be happy that you did.

I've written this book with three kinds of people in mind. First, I want to inform the spiritual truth-seeker about the God of the Bible, and in particular, Jesus Christ.

Second, I want to encourage those of you who find yourself in a season where you've grown tired and weary in your faith journey. I want to encourage and comfort you in God's grace and truth as well as inspire you to serve Him anew as you discover His amazing plan for you and His immense love for humanity.

Finally, I hope to challenge those of you who consider yourselves seasoned Christ-followers. I'm endeavoring to present Jesus to you in an authentic, relevant, prophetic, and biblically accurate manner. I hope you are stirred to deeper faith, stronger love, and full-hearted action.

Shall we?

Christopher Meade, Ph.D.

## Acknowledgements

I'm very grateful to my friends and colleagues at Grace Chapel in Boise, Idaho. It's an honor to serve the Lord with each of you. Thank you to the faculty and student cohorts at George Fox University. I love being part of this learning community. A special thank you to Mary Meade, Allison Meade, Luke Meade, Megan Meade, Cherie LaPorte, Kevin Piazza, and Brian Boone for your proof reading, sound engineering, and design work. Finally, thank you to the many friends, teachers, and mentors, both near and far, who have deposited in me rich life lessons through your wise words and inspiring examples.

## Matthew Chapter 1

# JESUS: GOD WITH US

*And you shall call his name Jesus, for he will save his people from their sins. All this took place to fulfill what the Lord had spoken by the prophet: "Behold, the virgin shall conceive and bear a son, and they shall call his name 'Emmanuel' which means, 'God with us.'" When Joseph woke from sleep, he did as the angel of the Lord commanded him: he took his wife, but knew her not until she had given birth to a son. And he called his name Jesus. (Matthew 1:21-25)*

## Book of Beginnings

The book of Matthew is first of the four gospels. Like Genesis, it's a book of "beginnings." This gospel account is written to a primarily Jewish audience. It links many of the promises found in the Old Testament scriptures to their fulfillment in the New Testament. Matthew, the author of this book, was also an eyewitness of Jesus, a former Roman tax collector, and one of the 12 apostles.

The gospel of Matthew presents Jesus as the Messiah (God's anointed one). The Jewish people were promised a leader that would come one day and set up a new kingdom. They had hoped it would be like King David's. The Jewish people believed that their new king (the Messiah) would be a triumphant political leader who would lead their nation to freedom. They thought the Messiah would liberate them from political oppression (which during the first century was the Roman Empire), and establish a righteous government. Jesus was, in fact, the Messiah, but He established a different kind of rulership and kingdom than they had expected.

## Birth of Jesus Christ

Chapter one contains the genealogy and birth of Jesus Christ. Genealogies were important to many societies, including the Jewish people. "Family trees" were not only a matter of historical record, but gave each family a strong and clear sense of identity and calling. Matthew lists Jesus' genealogy because it shows His legal claim to the throne of David, which was a prerequisite of the coming Messiah. Matthew is suggesting that Israel had been waiting over 2,000 years for the fulfillment of God's promise that was being fulfilled now in the person of Jesus Christ.

The chapter concludes with the details of the dramatic story surrounding the birth of Jesus. Luke's gospel describes the birth story through the eyes of Mary. Matthew's gospel describes it through the eyes of Joseph. As the story unfolds, the angel announces Jesus' conception by the Holy Spirit. Mary and Joseph are engaged at the time. Joseph considers divorcing Mary, as he thought she had committed adultery. Joseph is warned by an angel not to divorce her. Rather, he's told to take Mary as his wife and name the child Jesus. The angel quotes the prophecy from the book of Isaiah that says, "Behold, the virgin shall conceive and bear a son, and they shall call his name Emmanuel - which means, God with us." (Matthew 1:23)

## Emmanuel: "God with Us"

In these ancient times, names were given to people as descriptions of who they were. That's why you often find in scripture that when a person met God face-to-face that their name was changed because that person's nature and purpose was forever altered due to their encounter with God. So when the prophet Isaiah declared that another name for Jesus is "Emmanuel," he is trying to tell us something about His nature and His great plan for each of us. Matthew's gospel opens in the first chapter and concludes in the last one with this very theme: Emmanuel, the God who is with us (Matthew 28:20). Because the name Emmanuel means "God with us," the scriptures are revealing something unique and wonderful about God's nature and intentions. God desires to be "with us" and alongside us to help us in our lives. That's one of the reasons why Jesus came: to put a face on the invisible God, and to extend His embrace to humanity.

## The Holy Spirit

In the book of Genesis, the first question God ever asked man in the Garden of Eden was, "Where are you?" Even from the beginning, God has always desired to be with us in loving relationship. Jesus described the Holy Spirit as the "helper," which is derived from the word *paraclete,* which means "one alongside to help." This is one of the themes found within the grand narrative of scripture: God loves us and wants to be with us. He pursues us and extends His reach toward us with an invitation to come near.

## The Whisper Test

Mary Ann Bird, in her book *The Whisper Test,* illustrates this thought well as she describes an experience she had with a teacher when she was a young child. She writes:

> I grew up knowing I was different, and I hated it. I was born with a cleft palate, and when I started school, my classmates made it clear to me how I looked to others—a little girl with a misshap-

en lip, crooked nose, lopsided teeth and garbled speech. When schoolmates asked, "What happened to your lip?" I'd tell them I'd fallen and cut it on a piece of glass. Somehow it seemed more acceptable to have suffered an accident than to have been born different. I was convinced that no one outside of my family could love me. There was a teacher in the second grade we all adored. Her name was Mrs. Leonard, a sparkling personality. Annually, we had a hearing test. Mrs. Leonard gave the hearing test to everyone in the class, and finally, it was my turn. I knew from past years that as we stood against the door and covered one ear, the teacher sitting at her desk would whisper something, and we would have to repeat it back. Things like, "The sky is blue," or "Do you have new shoes?" I waited there for those words, similar to what God must have put into Mrs. Leonard's mouth…those seven words that changed my life. Mrs. Leonard said, in her whisper, "I wish you were my little girl. I wish you were mine. I choose you."

## I Choose You

This story reminds me how Jesus time and again impacted people's worlds by "whispering" a very similar message. It was simple, sincere, and life-altering. It was the message of "Emmanuel." Jesus walked around saying to the forgotten, "I choose you." He called out to the lonely, "You are mine." He declared to the troubled, "My peace be with you." Jesus was and is the God who is with us. He promised that in times of difficulty and sorrow, He would extend His grace to meet us and sustain us, even in our darkest valley.

## God With Us

"God with us" is central to the gospel message. Jesus came to earth and lived among people. And before He was crucified and resurrected, He promised that He would send the Holy Spirit to help us, comfort us, teach us, guide us, and live inside us to transform us into His image and likeness. We are not alone! We are not forgotten. It was Jesus' intention that this "whisper" would spread over all the earth and seep into the heart of every human being.

## The God Who is Near

My prayer for us is that we too would echo the "whisper" of good news, and declare the message of "Emmanuel, God is with us" to the watching world. God has come near, and His invitation is still going out to the world.

## Emmanuelize

Let us "Emmanuelize" the gospel of Jesus. Let people see that as Christ-followers, we don't claim or pretend to be perfect, but rather that God is working in us and through us, not because we are good, but because He is good and He is with us. Let our lives be authentic, open, and honest. Let the world see Jesus' grace working in us in spite of our weaknesses, sins, and failures.

Today the Holy Spirit promises to walk with us and transform us from the inside-out. God the Spirit carries on the ministry of God the Son, Jesus Christ. Who do you know that needs to hear God's whisper? Who needs to be reassured that God is near and available even today?

Matthew Chapter 2

# LESSONS FROM A HAPPY MEAL

*And behold, the star that they had seen when it rose went before them until it came to rest over the place where the child was. When they saw the star, they rejoiced exceedingly with great joy. And going into the house they saw the child with Mary his mother, and they fell down and worshiped him. Then, opening their treasures, they offered him gifts, gold and frankincense and myrrh. And being warned in a dream not to return to Herod, they departed to their own country by another way. (Matthew 2:9-12)*

## First Century Spiritualists

Chapter two begins with the wise men inquiring as to the where-abouts of the newly born Jesus. These "magi" (as Matthew calls them) were wealthy, intellectual, first century spiritualists. These guys were a mix of astrologer and astronomer. We could call them "astrolomers!" These wise men were also familiar with the religious literature of their day, including the Old Testament writings and prophecies concerning the promise of Israel's coming Messiah who would rule the world in justice and peace. Like many people in the ancient East of that time period, they believed strange "star happenings" and "planets aligning" indicated something very important in the earthly realm. So, these "spiritual truth-seekers," noticing a heavenly phenomenon in the sky, connected the prophetic dots (Numbers 24:17, Micah 5:2), and launched out on an arduous quest to locate the promised Messiah.

## Herod Reacts

At the same time, Herod, the corrupt and spiritually impotent king of the Jews, gets word of these wise men's intentions to find this promised king and "Messiah." The thought of any other king in the making was a direct political threat to Herod and his cronies. So, Herod reacts like any wicked, paranoid, narcissistic dictator would: with violence and atrocity for all. Herod attempts to trick the wise men and fails in the process. He then launches an all-out brutal genocide on a population of young boys in the hopes of murdering Jesus.

Joseph is warned in a dream to take Jesus and flee the country. He gathers up his family, gets out of town, and lays low for a period of time. After some time passes, Herod dies. Joseph and the family return and they settle in Nazareth. Jesus, a homeless refugee, has escaped death this go-around. But the threat of death will follow Him off and on His whole life until He dies on the cross as the Messiah, God's anointed and appointed one for all mankind.

## Truth Seekers

Whenever I read this story, I'm always drawn back to the story of the wise men who were spiritual seekers in pursuit of truth. I love the dichotomy that's found in these "magi." On one hand, you have a cadre of guys who are smart, autonomous, gutsy risk-takers who are bent on spiritual adventure, intrinsic exploration, and the search of truth. They'll stop at nothing to find what they are looking for. They'll invest their own resources, time, energies, and talents to find what really matters in life. They study up, saddle up, and set out on an Everest-like adventure of a lifetime.

Yet, on the other hand, when they find "truth," they recognize it and fall on their faces in submission and worship before the God of the universe (even if this god's current form is still just as a baby). They offer extravagant gifts fit for a king and a savior (gold, frankincense, and myrrh). These guys give not only their best material and financial gifts, but their posture indicates they offer their lives to His service as well (Romans 12:1).

## Christmas at McDonald's

I remember one of the first Christmases my family and I celebrated together after we first moved to Boise to start Grace Chapel. Someone in the church called me about a week before Christmas and said that they had some gifts that they wanted to bring over to my children, who were at that time eight, six, and three-years-old. I said, "Sure, come on over." When the doorbell rang, my kids bolted out of their bedrooms to join Mary and I as we all opened the front door to our "gift-bearing Christmas visitor." We welcomed her in. She handed us two large plastic grocery sacks filled to the brim with what appeared to be gifts. She looked at the kids, winked at them and said, "There's something in here for everyone." My children's eyes were wide and bright. I have to admit even I was getting excited for them. She then looked at me and said, "Here's a little something for the church, too." She handed me a brown paper grocery bag stuffed to the brim. I thanked her and she scurried out the door.

We then gathered in the living room to unpack the two plastic bags of gifts for the kids. My children asked me why she had come over to give us gifts if she didn't know us. I said, "Well, she told me that she loved to give gifts to her pastor's family each year, and she was new to our church. This is her way of saying 'Merry Christmas.'" As we sat around on the floor in a small circle, I unpacked the gifts for each of the children. Silence filled the room. The gifts for the kids turned out to be broken Happy Meal toys that this woman's child didn't want any more. I thought to myself that this kid must have eaten at McDonald's everyday for the last two years! Every little plastic toy in the bag was broken, or pieces from the toy were missing (an arm, a head, or leg, or a wheel from a little car, etc.).

At first we didn't know if it was joke, but it turned out that it wasn't. My kids looked at me for some sort of interpretation. I didn't know what to say. I then opened the gift in the brown bag that she had brought for the church. I guess because I was the pastor, I was the "designated representative" to receive the church's Christmas gift. It too, was junk from her closet that she was discarding. It was a collection of weathered and mismatched clothes and old bed sheets. I told the kids that maybe someone in the church could use the old sheets, and I then offered to fix some of the broken Happy Meal toys for them. They were a bit bewildered, but fine. I was angry.

## The Church is More Than a Charity

Later that night, I realized that the "gifts" this lady brought over to my kids and the church were really not intended to hurt our feelings. She was only doing what she was taught. To many people, the church is nothing more than a charity. Many are cynical of the church today (and some have good reason). Because of a charity mindset and a deep-rooted cynicism, many often give the church their leftovers, be it money, time, or involvement. Even though Jesus said that He would build the church and the gates of Hell wouldn't prevail against it, many in our culture view the church as just another "extra" to add to their already busy lives.

## Bringing Him Our First Fruits

The gospel cost Jesus everything. Often, we bring Jesus our broken Happy Meal toys—our extras and the things we don't need or want anymore. Instead of bringing Jesus our first fruits, be it our finances, our service, or our talents, some bring sets of old bed sheets in hopes that their conscience will be appeased and their human goodness validated. The gospel calls us to a lifestyle of sacrificial worship and surrender. We are called to live beyond ourselves. Life isn't all about us, it's about God and others. Sometimes I've wondered if we are more interested in tax write-offs than we are in honoring Jesus with everything that we are and everything that we have in all-out worship of Him.

Opening those gifts that evening many years ago was a defining moment for me. I realized that I too gave Jesus my "extras" rather than my very best. I too gave out of my abundance rather than my sacrifice. That night I became conscious, in a new way, that Jesus was worthy of my very best (and yours, too) in every area of my life. No, I don't always live that way, but it is the aim and intention of my heart.

The lesson of the wise men still speaks to us today. They gave Jesus their best gifts. They offered Him gifts fit for a king. These Magi presented Him gifts that cost each of them something from their own treasury. When they had nothing else left to offer Him, they got down on their knees and presented their very lives before Him in extravagant and honest worship.

## God Deserves Our Best

Jesus is worthy of our best gifts, not our broken Happy Meal toys. He's worthy of the best of our time and service, not our leftovers. Jesus' cause and mission on the earth is worthy of my "best" finances, talents, and skills, not my leftovers. Yes, this is lived out in our families and in our jobs. But we are told in scripture to make sure and give high priority to the household of God (the local church) in each of our lives.

Let's take our cue from these wise guys on how to really love and honor God with the entirety of our lives. There's a lot more going on in this chapter than three dudes dressed in Christmas garb, riding camels and giving away presents to a baby in a barn.

My prayer for us is that we too will offer all that we are and all that we hope to be to the Creator of the universe, Jesus Christ. God gave us His very best by sending Jesus to the earth where He lived a perfect and sinless life, then died a sacrificial death on the cross in our place so we could be forgiven of our sins and forgiven for choosing to live life out from under the leadership of Jesus and God's value system. Because of this, He is worthy of our very best in return. No, we don't do this to gain His favor or receive salvation. Salvation is a free gift, by grace, through faith in Jesus Christ. But once I've accepted that gift, I offer Him a gift in return: my entire life.

## Matthew Chapter 3

# OBEYING THE WHISPER OF GOD

*Then Jesus came from Galilee to the Jordan to be baptized by John. But John tried to deter him, saying, "I need to be baptized by you, and do you come to me?" Jesus replied, "Let it be so now; it is proper for us to do this to fulfill all righteousness." Then John consented. As soon as Jesus was baptized, he went up out of the water. At that moment heaven was opened, and he saw the Spirit of God descending like a dove and landing on Him. And a voice from heaven said, "This is my Son, whom I love; with him I am well pleased." (Matthew 3:13-17)*

## John the Baptist

Chapter three begins with the story of John the Baptist, the forerunner of Jesus Christ. John sets the stage for Jesus' public ministry. John preaches a fiery message that connects God's Old Testament work to the person and work of Jesus. John urges the crowds to remove the obstacles between themselves and God. His message of "repentance," (changing one's mind and direction) is core to experiencing the "kingdom of heaven." John rallies many people to the shores of the Jordan River with a passionate plea to get right with God, to experience life God's way, and to identify with God's call by experiencing water baptism.

The word "baptize," or *baptizō*, in Greek means, "to dip, plunge, or immerse." Baptism is a public identification of an inward decision to follow Jesus. "Going under the water" for John's followers symbolized God's cleansing of sin and forgiving work in their lives.

John also tells the crowds that one (Jesus) is coming after him who will baptize them with fire and with the Holy Spirit. Fire symbolizes Jesus' work of purifying and cleansing in the life of a Christ-follower. It also typifies judgment for the unrepentant. Jesus gives the Holy Spirit as a gift to all those who believe in Him and His message.

## Understanding Jesus' Baptism

Finally, the chapter ends with John baptizing Jesus. This is the inaugurating act that launches Jesus' public ministry. John is uncomfortable baptizing Jesus because he knows that Jesus has no sin and has no need to repent. Jesus insists. He tells John that He wants to "fulfill all righteousness." John concedes and baptizes Jesus. The Spirit of God descends upon Jesus and God's voice from heaven speaks out words of commendation and love over Jesus.

This portion of scripture reveals one of the foundational qualities of Jesus' character. Jesus made a conscious decision to "fulfill all righteousness," which means doing what's really right before God and others. Jesus didn't have to get baptized. He was God. He was sinless. He was perfect. But even though Jesus did not need to be baptized as a step of repentance (like we do), He did want to completely identify with John's message. He wanted to show continuity with all that God was doing. A decision for righteousness is a decision to do what's right and to what's best. It's not looking for a way to take spiritual short-cuts or find the easy way. It's valuing God's grace rather than taking it for granted and using it for our own advantage.

## Fulfilling All Righteousness

I remember years ago when I first read this passage of scripture. It penetrated my heart. I was a brand-new Christian, newly married, and living in Tyler, Texas. I was an aspiring guitarist/songwriter with lots of new recording gear, microphones, guitar, and other miscellaneous musical equipment.

One night while I was praying, I remembered how I had participated in a nighttime burglary of a Tucson music store, with some friends when I was 14. We took some guitars and amplifiers. While I was praying, I thought I had heard God speaking to my heart telling me that I was to "fulfill all righteousness," by selling all of my current recording equipment, microphones, and guitars and giving all of the money that I could raise from the sale to the owner of the store that I had burglarized as a gift of restitution (we had sold the stolen equipment soon after we took it).

I felt God speak to me, saying, "You hurt and stole part of a man's dream for his future. You were a source of great discouragement to him many years ago. Chris, you too think about having a future in music. I would like you to give up your dream for now. Sell all of your equipment and give the store owner all of the money. And Chris, tell him that I asked you to do this."

I told my new pastor what I sensed God was asking me to do. I told my young wife, Mary, too, and I asked for her counsel. For the next few weeks, when I would come to church and worship on Sunday morning, I would feel this impression in my mind and heart. I couldn't escape it. I would hear, "Chris, are you ready to make things right? What are you waiting for?" To be honest, I was very afraid. I thought if I obeyed God that I might get in trouble for my past misdeeds if this man was still angry with me (which I assumed he was).

## A Fork in the Path

At the same time, I felt it was a fork in my path concerning my new-found faith in Christ. Was I going to take the easy way out? Was I just looking for a short-cut in my faith? I knew what I had done as a teenager was terribly wrong, but at the same time I knew that I was forgiven of my past sins. In my mind, I didn't have to do this. I could just sweep it under the carpet (of grace), tell no one, and move forward. God would forgive me because I was genuinely sorry. I knew that I could still go to heaven and ignore this voice in my heart. But I wanted Jesus, more than anything, to be the centerpiece of my life. I wanted to grow, to follow, to trust, and to experience His presence in my life. I wanted a new kind of life.

Long story short, I sold as much equipment as I could over the next few weeks. I took all of the money and all of the rest of my recording equipment and guitar and packed them in my car and headed out to Tucson. Once in Tucson, I called the owner of the music store and asked to meet him. When we arrived at the music store, I asked Mary to wait outside in our car just in case something unexpected or violent happened in the exchange. (She was pretty concerned).

I walked in and the owner was waiting for me with four other men. I asked if the men could help me unload my car. We brought in several boxes of recording equipment and piled them up in the middle of the showroom floor. I then reached into my pocket and took out all the money and gave it to him. I told him that I was one of the teenagers that had burglarized his store years ago. I asked for his forgiveness. I told him that I had just recently become a follower of Jesus, and that while I was praying to God one evening, He had asked me to sell all of my music equipment as restitution and to try to make things right.

I was scared and shaking. You could have heard a pin drop in that store. No one said anything. Finally, the owner began to tremble. Tears filled his eyes. Then he broke down weeping. The four big men that surrounded him were speechless. He told me that he too was a follower of Jesus and that he had drifted away from his faith over the past few years. He told me that now he knew for sure that God was real. He rededicated his life to Christ. He accepted my money and equipment as restitution. He forgave me and thanked me. He told me all was good. We shook hands and I left.

## Responding to God's Whisper

That day was a defining moment in my 25-year-old life. I look back now and I'm so happy that I responded to the whisper of the Holy Spirit. Yes, I made a past wrong right, but something else happened, too. The trajectory of my future forever changed that afternoon. Something was deposited in my life that words cannot explain. God would ask me again over the next 25 years to trust Him and to take risks for the sake of the gospel; to do the right thing before God. No, I'm not perfect. Anyone who knows me knows that well. I've failed along the way. But I also have done my best to "throw deep" and never punt when I hear God whisper to me, "Step out. Risk. Fulfill all righteousness."

## Take the Plunge to Obey

My prayer today is that whether you have just made Jesus your Lord and Savior, or if you have been a Christian for a long time, that together we make "a decision to fulfill all righteousness" in our lives. What might God be whispering into your soul that He wants you to make right? Is it with Him? Someone else? Let's take the plunge and obey God's promptings to initiate the next step of spiritual growth in our lives by doing what's right before God and others.

Never choose the easy path; choose the God path. Obey what God is saying to you. Let's trust God deeply. Let's walk in genuine repentance daily. Let's live out the authentic Christian experience. When we do, we'll see God work in us, through us, and all around us in incredible ways. Let's make Jesus' name famous to a watching world!

Matthew Chapter 4

# BLOOMING IN THE DESERT SEASONS OF LIFE

*Then Jesus was led up by the Spirit into the wilderness to be tempted by the devil. And after fasting forty days and forty nights, he was hungry. And the tempter came and said to him, "If you are the Son of God, command these stones to become loaves of bread." But he answered, "It is written, 'Man shall not live by bread alone, but by every word that comes from the mouth of God.'" Then the devil left him, and behold, angels came and were ministering to him. (Matthew 4:1-4, 11)*

## Temptation in the Desert

Chapter four opens with Jesus being tempted by the devil for 40 days. Satan hatches a sinister plot to destroy Jesus and sabotage His calling to be the Savior and Redeemer of humanity by enticing Him to sin. If Jesus had sinned, it would have disqualified Him from living a perfect and sinless life, which was a prerequisite of the sinless Messiah (Christ). Jesus triumphed and obeyed God victoriously. Although God never tempts anyone to sin, He does use our circumstances to test and strengthen our character. God doesn't test us to see us fail; He tests us to see us succeed. Let me explain.

## Tempting Versus Testing

There is a difference between "tempting" and "testing." The goal of tempting is to destroy. Tempting has a motivation within it that pushes and pulls on something with the hopes of breaking it. On the other hand, the goal of testing is to certify. The Greek word for testing means "to document." Testing is putting something or someone through a purifying process with the hope of getting a "seal of approval" or a "stamp of certification" that something has passed, or has been approved, and/or validated as "trustworthy."

## The Master Craftsman

Imagine a master craftsman who places his hands on his newly designed wooden chair and begins to lean on it with his weight. He tweaks it here and pulls on it there by putting pressure on the legs, the seat, and then on the back. His goal is to ultimately offer his custom-built chair to an elderly guest to sit in. The craftsman's goal is not to break his chair. Rather, it's to find any weak places in its design or construction. As he runs his hands along the chair's frame, it's only to see if there are any loose hinges, uneven legs, or jagged splinters protruding from the seat. If he happens to find anything that is loose or uneven, he will gladly fix it or shore it up. He's happy to find something that needs just a bit more of the master's touch and polish. The pushing, the pulling, and the applying of pressure on the chair is only intended to make the chair safe, strong, and able to sustain heavy weight. The craftsman wants to be able to say to the elderly guest, "I've tested and inspected it myself. It's solid to the core."

## God's Workmanship

This is a picture of what God wants to do with our lives as well. He wants to shore us up, to strengthen us, and ultimately, to add weight (responsibility, ministry, influence, affluence, etc.) to our lives. The Bible says, "For we are his workmanship, created in Christ Jesus for good works, which God prepared beforehand, that we should walk in them." (Ephesians 2:10)

God doesn't want us to break or splinter in the process. So, what does He do? He tests us in order to show us what's inside our hearts. As we own up to those weak places that need to be shored up, strengthened, or purified, we can invite the Holy Spirit to work in and through us. Remember: Jesus never speaks to us in words of condemnation, but in words of invitation. He invites us to allow Him to work in us through this purifying process called "testing."

## Authentic Christianity

One of the secrets of the authentic Christian experience is knowing that we can't fix ourselves by ourselves. We need a power greater than ourselves to shape and transform us into the image and likeness of Jesus. Sure, we can make some progress on our own if we "will it" hard enough, but we can never get to the place that we desire deep down.

Attempting to "fix ourselves by ourselves" is what religion is all about. Religion is man's attempt to get right with God. Religion is about people trying to do something for God in hopes of making Him happy (or at least to get Him off their backs). Christianity is different than religion. Christianity begins and ends with God, not man. Christianity is God's attempt to reach down to humanity and offer the free, unmerited gift of love and forgiveness through what Jesus did on the cross. Christianity invites us into a relationship with Jesus, not into a religion.

## A New Kind of Revolution

The chapter continues with Jesus ministering and preaching to great crowds. His message is one of repentance (changing our minds and direction) and showing how the sovereign rule of God was now birthed and coming upon the land. The Jews of His day heard this rallying cry and immediately thought, "Revolution and military resistance!" Yes, Jesus was talking in the language of revolution, but a revolution of a different kind, and a subversion that was sourced in a different place (heaven). Jesus' message was about bringing God's spiritual light into a lost world of darkness. It was a message of establishing peace and justice in a society surrounded by war and steeped in lawlessness. It was a message of hope in an era that was sustained by violence. Jesus' message was one of healing and forgiveness in the midst of a world ensnared by greed, hatred, and racism. Jesus came to set in motion the beginning of God's great reversal. The process of righting every wrong had now begun.

## Following His Call

Finally, Jesus calls His first disciples to follow Him. One-by-one, Jesus pursues them and invites them to join Him in life's greatest adventure. These guys were ordinary, working-class dudes who came from diverse backgrounds. They gave up everything to follow Him. For these guys, Jesus' calling was dramatic. It appeared to come out of nowhere. That still happens today. For some God intersects lives and speaks suddenly. For others, God works and calls more through a process; it happens over time. The point: Both are valid. When you hear or sense God calling you forward to trust Him and follow, say yes.

## The Gift of the Desert

My prayer for us is that we would recognize God's testing, perfecting, and calling in our lives. Seasons of testing can be hard, painful, and lonely like Jesus experienced in the desert. But always remember: God loves us so much that He is committed to developing us, rather than just giving us what we want in the moment. His plans for our lives are good.

Today, if you find yourself in a season of "desert testing," let me encourage you to surrender to God anew, listen for His voice, and be willing to change when you feel His touch on your life. God has beautiful gifts, deep life lessons, and gems of wisdom that He wants to deposit into our lives, but they often come wrapped in "Desert Paper." If we're not careful, we can miss what God has for us. So, welcome the lessons. Let His words affect you and impact your life.

Matthew Chapter 5

# MIRROR WRITING:
# JESUS' BIG TALK ON THE HILL

*"Blessed are the poor in spirit, for theirs is the kingdom of heaven. Blessed are those who mourn, for they will be comforted. Blessed are the meek, for they will inherit the earth. Blessed are those who hunger and thirst for righteousness, for they will be filled. Blessed are the merciful, for they will be shown mercy. Blessed are the pure in heart, for they will see God. Blessed are the peacemakers, for they will be called sons of God. Blessed are those who are persecuted because of righteousness, for theirs is the kingdom of heaven. Blessed are you when people insult you, persecute you and falsely say all kinds of evil against you because of me." (Matthew 5:3-11)*

## A New Kind of Value System

Jesus begins this chapter with the big talk on the hill. "The Sermon on the Mount," as this famous sermon is called, is grounded in a new kind of ethic that is geared for everyday Christians living in any era. God is at work in a fresh new way. Jesus is not only calling men and women to follow Him as whole-hearted disciples, but He also promises to enable and empower them by the Holy Spirit to live out this new way of living that He is declaring.

This chapter describes the new set of kingdom values that are to become the "new normal" and moral compass for the people of God. At first glance, these new values appear opposite and juxtaposed to what we commonly think of as "normal" within our current contemporary culture.

## Mirror Writing

Leonardo da Vinci was famous for writing his personal notes in a mirror as a way to hide his innovative ideas from others. To the regular reader, his words on paper would appear confusing and mere gibberish. But if you put Leonardo's writings up to a mirror, and then read his writing through the mirror's reflection, his words and ideas would then appear clear, understandable, and compelling. (This was called "mirror writing," which was a form of writing in reverse.) The most common contemporary use of this can be found in the front of ambulances where the letters of the word "AMBULANCE" are written in mirrored letters so people that hear the approaching siren can look in their rear-view mirror, read the word, and then get out of the way.

## God's New Normal

Like mirror writing, it appears Jesus is espousing, in the Sermon on the Mount, the very opposite of what we think of as normal and natural as human beings. At first glance, it appears Jesus' new teaching is reversed; it doesn't make sense. Why? For starters, our society teaches that meek people aren't blessed; they get squashed. Nice guys don't win; they finish dead last. People who mourn aren't happy; they are just a bunch of crybabies and need to get over it and buck up. You're not blessed when people insult you and take advantage of you because you're doing the right thing; rather, you hire a lawyer, sue the snot out of them, and plan your payback.

## Incarnating Jesus' Value System

As Christ-followers, we are called to not just believe in Jesus, but to walk in the new value system that He birthed. These are heaven's values and we are encouraged to live them out even though we still live here on earth. At times, it may feel like "mirror living," but in reality, it's a worldview sourced in truth and aided by the Holy Spirit and it's all part of the authentic Christian life.

Jesus is proposing a different reality in this sermon; it's a new way to think, work, love, and live. As we embrace these values and new perspectives, the ripple effect of God's kingdom becomes a reality in our lives. Things like love, hope, mercy, self-control, faithfulness, peace, compassion, righteousness, forgiveness, and justice become the norm. This is more than a philosophy. Rather, it's part of Jesus' proclamation of the good news where God has begun a new thing in the world. It's not just a hopeful ideal, but it has already been birthed and it has been set in motion through Jesus.

## Eight Core Realities

As the chapter continues, Jesus touches on eight core attitudes (beatitudes), about being salt and light to the world, and how He's come to fulfill the Old Testament law and promises. He also addresses anger, lust, divorce, promise-keeping, retaliation, and loving your enemies. Again, at first glance, Jesus' response to each of these will appear "mirror-like" to our natural reasoning.

Jesus opens His sermon with eight "realities" that produce happiness in our lives. I find that interesting because everyone I've ever met (including myself) wants to be happy, and of course, some will do just about anything to achieve it. Now that I think of it, I've never met anyone whose goal was to be miserable in life. I have known miserable people, but they didn't want to be that way. Jesus tells us the secret of true happiness, and it's found in the "red letters" (His actual words) of scripture.

## Sustaining Happiness

*Psychology Today* conducted a study where they asked 52,000 Americans "What would it take to make you happy?" The researchers tallied the results and reported their findings: social life; job; being in love; recognition and success; sex; personal growth; good financial situation; having a house or apartment; being attractive and beautiful; "the city I live in"; religion; recreation and exercise; being a parent, marriage; and partner's happiness. If you'll notice, most of the answers were all external in nature, rather than internal. The popular idea of happiness is that it's contingent on having the right circumstances. It's having the famous, "when and then" thinking.

- "When I get a boyfriend or girlfriend, then I'll be happy."
- "When I get out of school, then I'll be happy."
- "When I get a job that pays well, then I'll be happy."
- "When I get married, then I'll be happy."
- "When I get a house that's my own, then I'll be happy."
- "When I have children, then I'll be happy."
- "When the children leave home, then I'll be happy."
- "When I retire, then I'll be happy."

## Webster's Take

As you can see, "popular happiness" is an external, never-ending cycle. Webster defines "beatitude" as "a state of utmost bliss," in other words, true happiness. It's a kind of joy that is self contained and completely unrelated to circumstances. It's a joy that bubbles up from within, rather than from without. That is the picture of this happiness that Jesus is portraying. Our English word "happiness" comes from the root "hap," which means chance. For most people, happiness is when everything in life is going well and when there are no ripples. But when there's a change in fortune, a failure in health, the collapse of a plan, the disappointment of a relationship, or even a change in weather, happiness can disappear overnight.

## Jesus' Take on Happiness

The good news of the Bible is that the happiness that Jesus is talking about in this passage is a joy that no one can take away from us. It's a joy that rises above every circumstance, difficulty, and trouble. It has nothing to do with chance or happenstance. For brevity's sake, here are Jesus' eight perspectives (Beatitudes) that promise to make us truly happy. I've phrased them as action statements because part of being a person of faith is about movement towards God rather than just postulating and being trapped in circular thinking.

1. Pursue a genuine and authentic relationship with Jesus.
2. Lean into God when life is overwhelming.
3. Trust God to provide for you.
4. Walk in God's instructions.
5. Practice forgiving.
6. Maintain a clear conscience.
7. Cultivate healthy relationships.
8. Approach everything with an eternal perspective.

## Happiness Begins as We Follow Jesus

When God is the center of our life and we begin to live out these eight principles, we'll experience true happiness. God has made us with a vacuum in our hearts that only Jesus can permanently satisfy. The culture's remedy for happiness is at best just a short-term fix and at worst unable to deliver at all. Happiness is not a result of our current circumstances; it's a choice. It begins when we choose to follow Jesus and walk by faith and not by sight.

"For now we see in a mirror dimly, but then face to face. Now I know in part; then I shall know fully, even as I have been fully known." (1 Corinthians 13:12)

Matthew Chapter 6

# UNMASKING THE GREAT ILLUSION

*"Do not store up for yourselves treasures on earth, where moth and rust destroy, and where thieves break in and steal. But store up for yourselves treasures in heaven, where moth and rust do not destroy, and where thieves do not break in and steal. For where your treasure is, there your heart will be also. No one can serve two masters. Either he will hate the one and love the other, or he will be devoted to the one and despise the other. You cannot serve both God and Money."* *(Matthew 6:19-21, 24)*

## Being Rich in the Things That Matter

Jesus continues His teaching of the Sermon on the Mount. He unpacks the topics of giving to those who are under-resourced, explaining the principles contained in the Lord's Prayer and fasting. Jesus talks about our devotion to God and the lure of loving money in place of God. He encourages us to be rich in the things that will outlast our earthly lives: treasures in heaven. Jesus concludes this chapter with reassuring words of God's care and faithfulness to us. Therefore, we can trust Him in everything and not be anxious.

Jesus reminds us to keep our worship of God foremost in our hearts and priorities. Too often in our contemporary society, the pursuit of money becomes deified and morphs into an object of worship and devotion. Today, just like in Jesus' era, the love of money (some translations say *Mammon* instead of money) can become a god of sorts that even trumps God as our object and focus of worship.

Let me be clear: There's nothing wrong with money. Some of the most amazing people I know are people of means and affluence. Rather, I'm talking about the love and the obsession over money. Remember: We can get so busy making a living that we fail to make a life. It's always a tragedy when well-meaning people unknowingly kneel at the altar of Money sacrificing their children, relationships, integrity, health, and faith on it.

## Culture Shift

Over the years, there has been a dramatic shift in what defines the American Dream. What once was a philosophy of hard work, industriousness, integrity, and the drive to become a better person has now morphed into an axiom of instant gratification and fast cash. If Hollywood is any indicator of what the American society wants and values, look no further than some of the recent television shows such as *Who Wants to Be a Millionaire, Who Wants to Marry a Millionaire,* and *Deal or No Deal.* These shows (and I'm sure, more to come) are indicative of this societal shift.

## The Power of Illusion

I have a friend in Tucson who, years ago, used to work with the famous illusionist, "The Amazing Kreskin." He once told me how Kreskin would pull off some amazing illusions in his show. I later learned that illusionists try to misdirect your focus off the important and onto the unimportant.

In essence, this is what the devil and popular culture attempt to accomplish (no offense intended, Mr. Kreskin). Both would love to lure us into thinking that acquiring lots of money and possessions will allow us to attain happiness, and ultimately aid us in arriving at a place of self-sufficiency where we won't need to depend on anyone, including God. That's why Jesus cuts through and clarifies when He says, "You can only serve one master: God or money. You can't serve both." There's no in-between; it's either one or the other. In a world that values relativism, Jesus, in this instance, talks the language of absolute truth.

## The Lie of More

Today, so many believe the axiom that "more will one day be enough." We're taught that when we have more, we'll then be successful and happy. Many people believe that when they have more money and more material possessions that will equal happiness. One reason why Madison Avenue marketers work so hard to package and present their products is to sell "happiness" through their advertisements. The scriptures say that happiness cannot be bought; that's an illusion. Listen to the words of King Solomon:

> "Those who love money will never have enough. How absurd to think that wealth brings true happiness! The more you have, the more people come to help you spend it. So what is the advantage of wealth – except perhaps to watch it run through your fingers!" (Ecclesiastes 5:10-11 NLT)

## Tragedy at Home

One of the saddest examples of money not equaling happiness comes from my own family. My dad was raised in a very tough home. His mom (my grandmother) was married seven times, which meant my dad had seven stepfathers. Of all the men in his life, the last stepfather, Phil Meade, was like a real father to my dad, so much so that Phil adopted him, and my dad took the last name Meade as his own. They loved each other very much. As a young college grad, my dad joined Phil Meade in his insurance business as a salesman and business/owner intern. Phil not only owned his own insurance company in Philadelphia, but on the side, Phil was also a fast-hustling venture capitalist. He loved money, the fast life, and gambling in Las Vegas. He fell prey to the illusion that "more money will one day be enough."

My grandfather's quest for money and happiness soon turned into a downward spiral where he ended up owing hundreds of thousands of dollars to others. Threats were made against him, my dad, my mom, and my brothers and I if he didn't pay up. Coupled with alcohol abuse, my grandfather, Phil Meade, committed suicide when I was four-years-old. My dad found him dead in his bedroom a few days later with his suicide note. Soon afterward, my parents and all four of us boys moved out west to restart our lives.

## Money Alone Can't Satisfy

The notion that "more will one day be enough" isn't true; it's a mirage. And for some, it's a deadly one. Money never buys happiness. That's why Jesus told us to not store up for ourselves treasures on earth, where "moth and rust destroy, and where thieves break in and steal." (Matthew 6:19)

Jesus lovingly reminds us in this verse that when we intensely crave money and earthly things to always remember three words: moths, rust, and thieves. These are words that help snap us out of the hypnotic trance that our culture spins around us. These words are anchored in truth and reality.

## Moths, Rust, and Thieves

First, "moths" reminds us that our possessions will one day wear out and get old. Our material assets will most probably end up in scrap yards or, at best, be recycled into something else and then sold on a shelf in some store across town. Second, "rust" reminds us that our belongings will one day soon lose their glitter and glamour. Our stuff will corrode and ultimately deteriorate right in front of our eyes. Finally, "thieves" reminds us that so many things in life can be taken or stolen from us. We can lose not just our money and possessions, but we can lose our jobs, our relationships, and even our health. And of course, the ultimate thief is death, which waits for all of us.

## Invest in Eternal Things

Jesus offers us wise counsel: Invest in the things that will outlast your life. Invest in the things that will not wear out, rust away, or that could be stolen. Jesus calls those things "heavenly treasures." What are heavenly treasures? They are simply God, other people, and what Jesus calls "good works."

Jesus invites us to invest in our relationship with God; it's a treasure that is eternal and that will last forever. He challenges us to love Him above anything and anyone. When it's all said and done, we'll be so happy that we did.

Invest in people. Men and women are made in the image and likeness of their Creator. They are eternal beings and will live forever…somewhere. We should help those who are far from God discover His love for their lives. Eternity is at stake.

## Heavenly Treasures

Finally, good works and helping others are heavenly treasures. Feeding the hungry, speaking up for the marginalized, contending for justice, extending mercy and compassion, protecting the unborn, supporting financially the furthering of the gospel, educating the illiterate, helping those who are sick, visiting the prisoners, and rescuing those who are in harm's way are the kinds of works that bless God and help people. Jesus tells us these actions have an eternal facet to them and their results will be seen in heaven. The time to act is now, because once we're in heaven there will be no more opportunity to invest; it'll all be over. So, start small, but start now. Timing is everything! My prayer for us is actually the apostle Paul's words to his fellow Christ-followers:

> Therefore it says, "Awake, O sleeper, and arise from the dead,
> and Christ will shine on you." (Ephesians 5:14)

So then let us not sleep, as others do, but let us keep awake and be sober. (1 Thessalonians 5:6)

## Breaking the Grip

May we awake and be spiritually sober. May Christ's light illuminate the shadows and excuses in our hearts that keep us captive. May God's Word snap its fingers together and break Mammon's hypnotic grip that tries to lull us into the swinging watch of cultural conformity. May we instead be transformed by the power of the Holy Spirit. The cultural landscape is filled with many spiritual illusionists and imposters. Like an experienced magician, Mammon masquerades itself as happiness, success, and freedom. May God grant us penetrating discernment to see beyond Mammon's slight-of-hand, and instead turn toward the one true God and His Son, Jesus Christ.

Matthew Chapter 7

# SANDCASTLES AND SNOWMEN: BUILDING FOR ETERNITY

*"Everyone then who hears these words of mine and does them will be like a wise man who built his house on the rock. And the rain fell, and the floods came, and the winds blew and beat on that house, but it did not fall, because it had been founded on the rock. And everyone who hears these words of mine and does not do them will be like a foolish man who built his house on the sand. And the rain fell, and the floods came, and the winds blew and beat against that house, and it fell, and great was the fall of it." (Matthew 7:24-27)*

## Finishing Up the Big Talk On the Hill

Jesus finishes up His Sermon on the Mount in this chapter. He cautions about judging people and tells why it's important to always remember to begin the judgment-making process about attitudes and behaviors of others by first looking at ourselves. Although we should strive to hold high morals and values for ourselves and the world, Jesus encourages us to be careful not to look down on people's failures and shortcomings, and by all means, to not fall into the trap where we set ourselves above others and "play God."

## Asking, Seeking, Knocking

Next, Jesus explains the prayer principle of asking, seeking, and knocking before God. God loves the qualities of passion and confidence in our relationship with Him. He's a good Father and always responds to us in ways that are best for us. He's always working for our good even when we can't see it. Because we're human, we all have moments of doubt where we wonder if God really does answer our prayers when we pray. I like this quote from Archbishop William Temple: "When I pray, coincidences happen; when I stop praying, the coincidences stop happening." Ask. Seek. Knock. He's listening. He cares about you. Talk with Him and tell Him how you feel.

## Jesus' Brand

Jesus sums up much of the Old Testament law and the writings of the Israelite prophets by saying, "So whatever you wish that others would do to you, do also to them." Today we call that mantra, "The Golden Rule." It gets to the very heart of God: treating people the way God would treat them. Jesus goes on to discuss how, when we live in a genuine relationship with God, we become fruitful and effective in life. Jesus explains the organic process of spiritual health, wholeness, and multiplication through an illustration of trees, roots, and fruits. He also explains some concrete ways to discern true Christ-followers from those who only talk the talk, and in reality, don't have an authentic relationship with God.

## Building Sustainable Foundations

Finally, Jesus concludes this chapter by talking about the importance of building your life on the right foundation and with the correct presuppositions regarding truth and reality. We do this by listening and thinking about Jesus' teaching, but also by putting it into practice in our lives. In the book of James, we're cautioned to make sure and not just be hearers of the Word but doers of it. Otherwise, we fall prey to a form of deception that is shrouded in religion.

Jesus tells us the scaffolding (belief systems and life teachings) that we position around our life is critically important, especially in times of difficulty and trouble. The strength and potential of our life often depends on it. When storms, hurricanes, and earthquakes come, how a building was constructed determines whether or not it will remain standing. Jesus uses the analogy of rocks and sand to illustrate His point of building a strong foundation.

## A Lesson in Rocky Point, Mexico

As I reflect on this biblical truth, I want to share two stories that underscore the importance of building your life on Jesus' teaching and with an eternal perspective. The first story took place when my kids, Luke and Megan, were small children. We once spent a summer weekend on a Mexican beach, in a town called Rocky Point in the Baja. We decided to build a giant sand castle down by the water's edge. With pails and shovels in hand, we began building our elaborate sand fortress in the moist, hard-packed white sand. The tide was still out, but we knew that it would soon be coming back with a vengeance. We were racing against the ticking clock.

Once constructed, our sandcastle had a three-foot high reinforced wall and a one-foot deep moat that was dug out in the front and sides of the wall that protected the castle. Like a canal drainage system, our plan was to capture and funnel away the incoming water that would soon be smashing in on us. We even had a contingency plan ready to go if the waves breached the walls sooner than we expected. We were ready! I then lifted Luke and Megan up over the walled fortress and put them down next to our beloved sandcastle to protect it from the incoming waves of foaming salt water.

They would protect the inside, and I would protect the outside. We were both ready to bail out the incoming water from the ocean waves.

Like we expected, the seawater began to rise and come back in. It methodically gained ground as it moved up the beach line until it was teasing us with bursts of its mist and spray. Within a short time, small waves turned into large waves, which eventually flooded our moats, broke through and over our walls, and demolished our sand fortress to smithereens. In just a matter of minutes, our sandcastle was washed away right before our eyes in spite of our best efforts.

## Storms Will Come

Jesus tells us that the waves and storms of life will happen to all of us; no one can escape this reality. No matter how high we build our walls, how deep we dig our moats, or how well intentioned we plan for the unexpected, life will at times, break through, topple over, and come crushing down on each of us.

Jesus is saying that the people who build their sandcastles (homes, relationships, lives, and futures) out of sand will be overtaken by the waves; they will not escape unscathed. They will miss out on eternal life in heaven, and they will miss out on the peace, assurance, joy, and confidence that Christ offers in the midst of such difficulties in this life. Jesus encourages us to listen to His Words and apply what He tells us. Because He loves us and wants the best for us, He warns us up-front about the dangers of living life out of our own well-intentioned mental constructs, rather than from the long-standing spiritual truths presented in the scripture. Jesus invites us into His way of living and encourages us to anchor our lives into the bedrock of His eternal truths. When we do, His promises produce a strength and a hope that won't disappoint.

## Building Snowmen

The second story took place several years later when my youngest daughter, Allison, taught me this same truth about this "wise building of one's life," but with a different twist. We had just moved to Boise and a huge snowstorm had dumped a foot or so of snow on us. Our backyard possessed all the ingredients necessary to make a great snowman: tons of fresh snow. I remember watching Allison systematically build a little snow-man. Her fingers were frozen stiff, cheeks red flushed, nose running, and her eyes sparkling from the biting cold breeze of the early morning air. What really captured my attention was when she burst through the sliding glass door, into the kitchen, and enthusiastically told me, "This snowman is going to be my treasure!" Then she turned and ran outside where she stayed for at least two hours diligently constructing this project with all the gusto a four-year-old could muster.

As Allison was building her snowman, I remember thinking, "As adults, we do what you're doing all the time. Many people give their talents, time, and treasures to build 'snowmen' all their lives." I wanted to tell her what I was thinking, but I knew at the time she wouldn't understand.

## Invest Your Life Wisely

I continued thinking, "Allison, as you grow older, you're going to find that you will have numerous choices to build things with your life. There will be many opportunities and countless endeavors that will gladly wel-come the sacrifice of your time, or receive the investment of your hard-earned resources, or accept the deployment of your energies and God-given talents. But remember, my sweetheart, to make sure that when it's all said and done, that your time, your resources, your efforts, and your talents won't be built on something that will melt away. Make sure you build your life on something eternal. Invest your future in something that will last the long haul. Many well-intentioned people give their hearts and lives to building snowman, but only later will find it melts right before their eyes."

## Think it Through

After thinking awhile, I looked up and saw this little girl racing against the late morning sun. I thought, "People are like that, too. They get going so fast in life that they too get caught up in the moment. Life takes on a 'frenzy' of activity. Many will one day discover that their 'snowmen,' their 'treasures,' the things that they spent their whole lives building, will disin-tegrate right before their eyes."

## Build Your Life On Jesus

What kind of house are you building? What kind of life are you constructing? What "spiritual magnetic pull" grounds your compass? God's Word invites each of us to build our lives on the Rock; it's a firm foundation that lasts forever. Investing our lives on the Rock (Jesus) assures us that our foundation will never wash out to sea or melt. The Rock is not a philosophy, a religion, or set of behaviors. It's not about trying to be a good person or ascribing to a set of noble principles to live by. Those are all great things that make us nice people to be around, but the Rock is a person and that person's name is Jesus.

## Cultivate, Invest, and Be Strategic

Let me encourage you during this season of your life to cultivate your relationship with God. Build a heart that cares about people. Move beyond hearing and reading Jesus' words, but live them out. Choose to invest wisely in your future in order that your efforts will not "melt away" when the heat comes. Be strategic in how you use your time, your talents, and your financial treasures.

My prayer for us is that we will see and learn this secret of building wisely. Build your life on a foundation that will never fade away. Apply the teachings of Jesus into your personal life, your faith, your family, your work, your marriage, your church, and your future. It's your decision what you give your life's efforts to. Let me challenge you to give your efforts and your energies to God, to people, and to the causes that really matter. When the storms come, and when the end of your life finally arrives, investing in heavenly treasures will be a decision that you will never regret.

Matthew Chapter 8

# LIFE'S STORMS:
# BLESSING IN DISGUISE?

*And when he got into the boat, his disciples followed him. And behold, there arose a great storm on the sea, so that the boat was being swamped by the waves; but he was asleep. And they went and woke him, saying, "Save us, Lord; we are perishing." And he said to them, "Why are you afraid, O you of little faith?" Then he rose and rebuked the winds and the sea, and there was a great calm. And the men marveled, saying, "What sort of man is this, that even winds and sea obey him?" (Matthew 8:23-27)*

## Jesus' Word in Action

Jesus' teaching on the Sermon on the Mount was the focus of the previous three chapters. They described the things that Jesus "said." This particular chapter shifts and captures Jesus' words in action. It catalogs the miraculous deeds Jesus "did." Both Jesus' teachings and His actions point to His authority and assignment as Israel's long-awaited Messiah.

Jesus demonstrates His Messianic healing power by restoring the leper, making healthy the Centurion officer's servant, and alleviating every kind of sickness and disease among the multitudes. Isaiah 53:5 is referenced: "But he was wounded for our transgressions; he was crushed for our iniquities; upon him was the chastisement that brought us peace, and with his stripes we are healed."

Jesus reaches out in compassion to the fringes of society that are disillusioned, disenfranchised, and discarded by the general population. God's new kingdom has finally been birthed in and through the person of Jesus Christ. It's here! God's Son has arrived, but in a way that confused many people of the day because Jesus chose peace not war, forgiveness not revenge, healing not destruction, compassion not judgment, and the cross not rebellion.

## Jesus Heals

As the chapter continues, so do Jesus' miracles. He not only heals people, but now He demonstrates His power and authority over nature and the physical world by calming a raging storm. The disciples' fear transforms into confidence. Nothing seems out of His grasp or control. Awe and wonder fill the air. God's "good news" travels throughout the countryside.

Not only are physical forces reversed, but so too are evil ones. Demons are cast out of people. Upside-down lives are restored. Oppression is turned into optimism, and pain is converted into new beginnings. Life thrives in the presence of God's Son.

If Jesus can heal the sick, rule over the physical world, and overturn evil, He most certainly is worthy of our full devotion and trust. Our lives are in good hands when we surrender and follow the Master. Anything life throws our way can be absorbed by God's goodness through the person of Jesus.

## The Truth About Storms

As I reflect on the passage of scripture that I selected for this devotion, I'm drawn again to the story of Jesus calming the storm. Storms come in all shapes and sizes. They are symbolic of the difficulties, hardships, disappointments, failures, and problems that we face from time to time. Storms are inescapable. They visit everyone. I wish it wasn't true, but it is. Storms test us, stretch us, stress us, scare us, and for some, unfortunately, can kill us.

At the same time, storms have the ability to mold and produce something beautiful, life-giving, and powerful within us. That's why two people can go through virtually the same thing and come out completely different. Some people get better and others get bitter. One thing is certain: Storms will change us. But the question is "how?"

There is an old Arab proverb that says, "Sunshine alone only produces deserts." I believe that. God uses the storms in our lives to shape our inner character by etching more of His character into the fabric of "who we are." Someone once said, "Life is like a tube of toothpaste, you don't know what's inside until it's squeezed!" It's in the midst of storms that our lives are "squeezed" and we come face-to-face with what's inside us.

## Inside-Out

God is just as concerned with who we are becoming on the inside as He is with what we are doing on the outside. God uses trials and difficulties in our lives as a way of turning our weakness into His strengths. He takes our impurities and converts them into something of His untaintedness through His divinely orchestrated refining process: storms. God desires to work in our lives in such a way that will reflect His radiance to a watching world.

## Lessons from a Silversmith

One of the ways God accomplishes this is likened to how the old-time silversmiths used to purify and refine silver, gold, and other precious metals. They would take the silver products in the rough and place them in cauldrons that would then be put under intense heat for a certain period of time. As the silver in the raw underwent this heating process, its impurities would separate away from the silver and rise to the top of the boiling caldron. The silversmith would then scoop them off. He would repeat this refining process again and again until no more impurities would surface to the top. Finally, he would be left with only "pure silver" in the cauldron.

God does the same thing in our lives, too. He allows us to undergo seasons of "intense heat" where the character impurities in our lives surface to the top, so to speak. Often, we're disappointed in ourselves when we see some of those "character pollutants" that are inside of us, but we shouldn't be. In fact, we should be excited. Why? Because the impurities are no longer under the radar of our lives, but out in the open. We can now ask for God's help, healing, and intervention in our lives. The apostle Peter said it this way:

> "You have been distressed by various trials, that the proof of your faith, being more precious than gold which is perishable, even though tested by fire, may be found to result in praise and glory and honor." (1 Peter 1:6-7)

Peter is reminding us that God does some of His finest work in us by allowing us to encounter "storms." Strong character is sculptured within us as we undergo pressure and encounter various challenges and hardships. This is how the disciples' fear was converted to confidence in the story. The disciples didn't realize that fear was even resident within them, but the storm revealed that it was, in fact, embedded deep within them. Once we are aware of the problem, we can go after the right answer and seek God's assistance.

## Understanding Divine Process

Even though God uses storms in our lives, it's important to remember that He isn't the author of all of them. But He does promise to walk with us in the midst of each one that comes our way. Nothing touches our lives without His awareness and His permission. God knows that there are certain character qualities and habit patterns that need to be chiseled out of our lives. If there was another way to produce the character that He desires within us, I'm sure He'd use that method, but there isn't.

Storms produce something beautiful in us like nothing else can. Storms refine our character. Storms test us. Storms build our confidence and faith in God. They prepare us to be used by God. God has every intention of doing wonderful things in and through our lives. His plans for us are always good.

## Look for God's Evidence

My prayer today is for those of us who find ourselves in the midst of a storm. Let God's Word help you navigate the turbulent waters. It's His desire for us to come through the refining process looking more like Him. Don't give up; look up. Yield to His divine process in your life. Celebrate what He is revealing to you through His refining touch. Look for the evidence of what God is doing in you and not His absence. You'll always see what you are looking for.

Matthew Chapter 9

# FROM THE FIELD TO THE FATHER'S HOUSE

*And Jesus went throughout all the cities and villages, teaching
in their synagogues and proclaiming the gospel of the kingdom and
healing every disease and every affliction. When he saw the crowds,
he had compassion for them, because they were harassed and helpless, like sheep without a shepherd. Then he said to his disciples, "The
harvest is plentiful, but the laborers are few; therefore pray earnestly to the Lord of the harvest to send out laborers into his harvest."
(Matthew 9:35-38)*

## Jesus Front and Center

Jesus returns to His hometown in Capernaum where He cures a man of paralysis. Jesus not only supernaturally transforms this man's physical life, but He reconstructs his spiritual future by forgiving him of his sins like only God can do. The Scribes get ticked off with Jesus and resist Him because they think He's dishonoring God by putting Himself in the place of God (forgiving sins). Little do they know, that later Jesus would say, "To see Him was to see the Father." (John 10:30,14:7-9)

Jesus demonstrates in full color His extraordinary authority. In the early chapters of this book, Jesus establishes His authority through His teachings in the Sermon on the Mount. In the previous chapter, He displays His authority over disease, demons, and the physical properties and laws of the universe. In this passage of scripture, Jesus triumphs over paralysis, sin, blindness, and even death itself.

## The Power of the Cross

Because Jesus is Israel's divine representative (the Messiah), and because He's God's one and only Son from heaven, when we put our trust and faith in His authority, many wonderful things can take place. Jesus has the authority and power to heal our ailments and forgive our sins, but those who are touched are those with faith.

Jesus came to close out the Old Testament religious system of how a person was once made right and acceptable before God. Instead of going through the venue of human priests, who offer the appropriate sacrifices on behalf of the people, we can now go directly to God ourselves, through the person of Jesus, because of His sacrifice on Calvary's cross on our behalf. Jesus has become God's "once-and-for-all priest" who makes us clean and provides a bridge to God and the stairway to heaven. Here's what Hebrews says:

> "Day after day every priest stands and performs his religious duties; again and again he offers the same sacrifices, which can never take away sins. But when this priest (Jesus) had offered for all time one sacrifice for sins, he sat down at the right hand of God." (Hebrews 10:11-12)

## Surprise Endings

As the chapter continues, Matthew tells of his own calling and conversion to Christ. He explains how Jesus not only added oomph back into his step, but how Jesus opened wide a brand new life and a bright shiny future for him. The good news of the gospel is that God desires to do the same for you and me. Jesus came to earth to usher in a new thing God had promised throughout the ages. Even today, God still loves to do new things in us and through us. He specializes in writing surprise endings to the storylines of our lives. Again, Jesus has the authority and power to spiritually revolutionize our lives, but those who receive it are those with faith.

## Miracles and Healings

Jesus ramps up again with more astounding miracles and healings. In an ancient world where the blessings of modern medicine were basically nonexistent, and in a culture where human suffering and widespread disease was the norm, you can see why crowds would flock to Jesus with such a sense of urgency. As Jesus would cure them, awe and wonder would pervade the city streets, local markets, and family conversations. Word of Jesus' compassionate ministry and loving leadership spread like a prairie fire.

## A Call to Pray

The chapter wraps up with a call to prayer. There are just a few times in the gospels where Jesus actually tells His disciples how to pray; this is one of those times. He encourages His followers to pray that God would raise up men and women who have hearts for "the harvest." Jesus uses an agrarian illustration of the "Lord of the Harvest" to convey God's deep passion and concern for people to be brought in from the fields and into the Father's house.

## Life is About Relationships

Life is about relationships: first with God and then with others. To be out of relationship with God is to miss out on a very important dimension of life. I know that firsthand. I experienced a life "outside of the Father's house" for many years when I was younger. Like the song, "Carry On My Wayward Son" by Kansas, I was spiritually searching and looking for truth. The only problem was that I couldn't find "peace when you are done" or a place to "lay my weary head to rest," as the song said. But when I finally made a decision to trust Jesus, to seek His forgiveness, and to ask for His help to align my life with the things He said were true in the scriptures, my life began to change.

## God is Pursuing You

Our world is overflowing with smart, well-meaning, yet spiritually lost people. Many have looked far and wide to things like religion, the church, and various positive philosophies to find peace, meaning, and connection with God, but they've come up empty. Unfortunately, many are disillusioned because they've been let down in their search for God. But the good news is that God is alive, and He is pursuing you. He's closer to you than you might think. Let me encourage you to not give up in your pursuit of truth. Keep searching. Keep seeking. Keep pursuing. You will find Him (or should I say, He will find you).

For those of you who are still exploring your spirituality and have yet to make a decision either way, let me suggest a simple prayer to pray each day that helped me in my journey. I actually prayed this prayer for several weeks, on each day of my confusion: "God, please reveal truth to me. Help me discover You in my search. There are lots of options out in the world. I want to follow the real truth. If You show it to me, I'll go that way."

## Chose Wisely

Let me also encourage those of you who consider yourselves followers of Jesus, to join Jesus' great cause on earth. We've been invited to help Him in fulfilling His mission of bringing lost people into an authentic relationship with God. Remember: God sent His Son. The Son sent His Spirit. The Son and the Spirit send us into the world to tell others about God's great news to humanity. Jesus came for the down-and-out as well as for the up-and-out. We're told in the Bible that "God's harvest" will never self-reap, but it will self-destruct if left on its own.

We only have one life to live for Jesus on this earth. In about 50 or 60 years, most everyone reading this right now will no longer be alive. Our lives will soon be over. James calls life a "vapor." He says it's here today and gone tomorrow. Job says that our life is but "breath." The psalmist calls our life a "sigh" and it's finished. It's so important that we don't forget why we are here on planet Earth. It's important to finish well.

## Finish Well

I love the story about John Stephen Akhwari, who was a Tanzanian marathon runner in the 1968 Mexico City Olympics. I remember as a kid watching him run on television. It was spell-binding. Akhwari entered the stadium in the dark of night after running 26 agonizing miles. He was in last place and hours behind the winner. Akhwari hobbled the final moments around the track with a bandage on his leg as he winced in pain. After the race, he was interviewed by a sports announcer who asked him why he didn't quit. His answer was compelling. Akhwari said, "My country did not send me 5,000 miles to start a race. They sent me 5,000 miles to finish a race."

## The Eternal Race

The same is true with us as well. God has called us into a co-mission with Him; an eternal race of sorts. It's very easy in this life to become distracted and preoccupied with non-eternal things. That's why it's important that we, too, keep focused and finish well. We must lock in on the things in life that are eternal and really matter. God has called us to join Him in life's great race: the harvest. The reason Jesus began this race was to search out those who are lost and those who are far from Him. He's called us to finish what He started 2,000 years ago. People's eternity is at stake.

My prayer is that God would renew our hearts and inject new compassion and a catalyzing energy into our priorities. May we partner with God in helping those who are far from Him find their way out of the field and into the Father's house. This mission is not for the faint of heart, but it is our calling and assignment. Let's run our race while we still have breath, life, and ability!

Matthew Chapter 10

# FINDING NEW STRENGTH IN THE FACE OF DIFFICULTY

*"Behold, I am sending you out as sheep in the midst of wolves, so be wise as serpents and innocent as doves. Beware of men, for they will deliver you over to courts and flog you in their synagogues, and you will be dragged before governors and kings for my sake, to bear witness before them and the Gentiles. When they deliver you over, do not be anxious how you are to speak or what you are to say, for what you are to say will be given to you in that hour. For it is not you who speak, but the Spirit of your Father speaking through you."*
*(Matthew 10:16-20)*

## Jesus' Second Big Talk

Jesus calls His disciples together and shares His second big talk about the new thing that God is doing in the land. He introduces a fresh and unique way of "being the people of God." Jesus shares with the 12 both the short-term mission to reach the Israelite community, and the long-range global initiative to reach the entire known world with the good news.

## The Commission

For the first time, the disciples are given the opportunity to take the message of the gospel out and into the surrounding communities without Jesus being present. They are given clear instructions, empowered with spiritual authority, promised supernatural ability, sent with relational encouragement, and cautioned with prophetic warning as they prepare to engage the world as ambassadors for Christ. The 12 apostles ("apostle" means "people who are sent out") are to go forward in faith and to take no money with them on their journey. They are to expect those who hear and receive the gospel decree to feed them and meet their financial needs, while the gospel message itself is always free.

## Being a Disciple Costs

Jesus tells the disciples to not take it personally when people reject them and their message because, in reality, they are really rejecting Christ Himself. Those who dismiss God's gracious invitation and who instead prefer a life without God will, in fact, receive what they ask for: a life of separation from God both now and in eternity. God forces Himself on no one but offers Himself to everyone.

Even though God's new day was dawning, Jesus' followers were cautioned that the future for a Christian disciple wasn't always going to be easy. In fact, Jesus forewarns them that they will encounter family misunderstandings, difficulties, opposition, bullying, violence, persecution, and even death for their beliefs. Today, in the United States, we often take for granted the religious freedoms protected in the First Amendment and the religious tolerance that is a tenant of postmodern culture, but in the days of the early Church, Christ-followers suffered greatly for their beliefs and for publicly identifying with Jesus and His message.

## My Nepali Friends

In my own church, I've been privileged to hear the stories of the men and women, who have come from Nepal and Bhutan, who have suffered greatly and endured both physical and emotional abuse at the hands of former tribal elders and other community leaders simply because these women and men were Christ-followers and were willing to step outside the Hindu caste system. As a pampered Westerner (that's not how I see myself, but on a global scale, that's really what I am), I have been humbled by their bravery, stature, and commitment to Christ. They don't go around bragging or drawing attention to themselves. Rather, they choose to focus on the grace of God and they live out their Christian faith authentically, peacefully, unobtrusively, and with a sense of gratefulness for the privilege of simply being known as followers of Jesus.

## Lessons on a Loading Dock

I can't say that I've encountered real persecution like my Bhutanese friends, but I do remember a season when I was a new Christian that I was harassed for several months at work. At that time, I worked at an East Texas hospital on a loading dock in the shipping and receiving department. Several old-timers tried hard to get me fired because I would bring my Bible to work and read it over my lunch break. They couldn't understand why I didn't want to sit around in the break room with them and pass around the porn magazines and engage in fabricated fish tales of one another's late-night escapades that supposedly took place the evening before at the local club.

Pornography was part of my diet before I came to Christ, I would tell them. But after becoming a follower of Jesus, I had chosen a different direction for my life and that stuff wasn't part of it anymore. I explained that Christ was helping me live out a new kind of stewardship over my mind and sexuality. I was a new person. That fueled my nickname on the loading dock: "Chris, the virgin Bible boy." It was hurtful then, but kind of funny now. Several of the truckers told me to not only get out of their faces, but that I should consider being a preacher-boy.

In the end, I was brought into the purchasing director's office, and while behind closed doors, I was threatened with termination if I mentioned Jesus' name again during work hours. So, for a few months during my lunch hour, I would go to an unoccupied portion of the hospital basement in order to read my Bible. Of course, over time, personnel changed around the hospital, and by the time I left to pursue another job, I had made friends with many of those who were left who had opposed my faith.

## God Wastes Nothing

Looking back over that season of my life, I think God had a good sense of humor allowing those guys, and that unique situation I was in, to be one of the ways He was orchestrating deep character development and spiritual formation within my life. I only wish that I had known then what I know now. I would have had a whole lot more fun with everything and not worried so much. Maybe that's why Jesus tells us to fear not and to instead trust Him in the face of every difficulty, large and small. God wastes nothing. He uses everything (both positive and negative) in our lives in such a way as to shape us, form us, and grow us into His image and likeness.

## God's Got it Covered

There is nothing so imposing or ominous in our lives that God cannot intervene and work wonders. If God can create the universe, form Adam from the dust of the ground, part the Red Sea, take down kingdoms, and raise Jesus from the dead, He can surely work the impossible on our behalf if He so desires. If for whatever reason, God chooses not to intervene, then our responsibility as children of God is to trust Him. Let me encourage you that if you find yourself in a similar situation today, pray, believe, and trust (and if you can, laugh at some of it now, because it might be funny later).

There is also nothing too small to go unnoticed or that is too menial a concern to ask for His help. He loves us and is committed to us more than we can humanly comprehend. God wants to have an honest and healthy relationship with us. Good relationships talk about the day-to-day issues just as much as they do the big challenges. Not only does God want to be like a counselor or parent in our lives, but He also wants to be a kind of friend. Friends talk. They listen. Sometimes they say nothing but are just "there." If God cares about the tiny sparrows and knows every hair on our heads, then He wants to listen and be a part of the smaller, personal, daily things of our lives, too.

## God's Lens

My prayer today is that we will allow God to change us anew as He brings us closer to Himself in loving relationship. My hope is that we can see life through God's lens. The scriptures will help us do that. God is still doing a new thing in the world and He extends His invitation to all of us, through the person of Jesus, to experience this new life on a personal level. May you reach out to Him and experience fresh grace, strength, and perspective. God's plans for you are good—that's a promise from heaven.

Matthew Chapter 11

# A BRAND NEW WAY OF BEING AND LIVING

*"Come to me, all who labor and are heavy laden, and I will give you rest. Take my yoke upon you, and learn from me, for I am gentle and lowly in heart, and you will find rest for your souls. For my yoke is easy, and my burden is light." (Matthew 11:28-30)*

## A Firebrand Preacher

After Jesus sends His 12 disciples out on their first solo ministry trips into the village areas, a conversation takes place between some of the followers of John the Baptist, Jesus' cousin and ministry counterpart, and Jesus. John, finds himself in prison for offending King Herod by denouncing his immoral behavior with his own brother's ex-wife. John the Baptist was a firebrand preacher with a sizzling message of repentance and holiness toward God, which, of course, helped land him in the slammer. John spoke the truth and wasn't intimidated if you were affluent, influential, or powerful. John was a what-you-see-is-what-you-get prophet, and John told you what he saw—politically correct or not.

Jesus Himself said some pretty complimentary things about John's character and ministry. Even though John the Baptist was amazing, he was still a human being who found himself in a difficult season of life that squeezed down on his soul like the jaws of a vise. While sitting in the king's dungeon awaiting execution, John was discouraged and disillusioned in his faith. So, John sent his disciples over to talk with Jesus in hopes of clearing up some questions and concerns that plagued him.

## The Messiah

John, like others, thought the Messiah would come as a spear-wielding revolutionary who would ultimately overthrow the Roman regime. I remember watching the movie *Braveheart* and listening to how the inspiring patriot, William Wallace, challenged and rallied together his ragtag group of Scottish kinsmen in an epic battle for freedom against the English. Wallace's famous cry for "freedom!" while bravely raising his sword into the air was the kind of image that John the Baptist, and others, had hoped that Jesus would ultimately embody. But instead of teachings laced with undertones of subversion and overthrow, Jesus instead preached about forgiveness, healing, mercy, and justice. Not only did He teach these things, but He did them as well.

John was confused and so were others. Many people of the day thought that Israel's Messiah would be a kind of "supernatural William Wallace" of sorts: charismatic, warrior-like, and a passionate revolutionary. He would be one who would fight violence with violence, an eye for an eye, and ultimately execute God's righteous judgment on the oppressive government of the day through rebellion and overthrow. That's why it was baffling to many when Jesus seemed to be doing the exact opposite.

## God Was Doing a New Thing

John, like many others, did not completely understand that Jesus was not only birthing a new way of being God's people, but was introducing a new sort of life altogether. God was breaking into the world in a brand new way through Jesus, and Jesus was demonstrating the kind of life and value system that existed and operated in heaven. That's why Jesus encourages us to pray, "Thy kingdom come, Thy will be done, on earth as it is in heaven" (Luke 11). This is what Jesus meant when He talked about the "kingdom of God."

Jesus goes on to challenge people to think twice before dismissing His teachings as some out-of-touch, antiquated, irrelevant, and misguided religion. Every decision reaps consequences, including no decision. Jesus cautions the townspeople to not get caught up in the age-old patterns of excuse-making, blame-placing, and responsibility-shifting that people use just so they don't have to believe, and can instead justify within themselves the lifestyle that they want.

## God Speaks in Words of Invitation

The chapter ends with God's personal invitation to come close to Jesus. Like a warm breeze rustling through the multi-colored autumn leaves in a grove of trees, so too God's spirit beckons and bids men and women of all backgrounds and all cultures to experience the authentic God-life. This Christian life, when lived out of a simple and genuine relationship with God, is one of joy, peace, confidence, inspiration, and rest, even when surrounded with difficulty.

## Whosoever Will, Come

My prayer for us is that whatever situation we face, we know for sure that Jesus invites us to experience His love, peace, and forgiveness. I love the story that Ernest Hemingway tells about a young man named Paco who ran away from home and wandered the streets in Madrid, Spain. His relationship with his father was strained and broken. His dad was heart broken and did all he could to find his son. Finally, in desperation, Paco's dad placed an ad in the local newspaper *El Liberal*. The advertisement read: *"Paco, meet me at the Hotel Montana at noon on Tuesday. All is forgiven! Love, Papa."* The next day the father went down to the hotel and was shocked to find 800 young men had responded to the ad.

In some ways, we're all "Paco," estranged from our heavenly Father; that is, until we receive Jesus into our lives. Jesus came to earth, died on a cross, and rose from the dead in order for you and me to come home to God. Jesus forgives our sins, and because of Him, we are made right before God. God wants you and me to come home to Him. It doesn't matter who we are, what we've done, who we've done it with, or how long we've done it. God loves us, accepts us, forgives us, and longs for us to respond to His gracious invitation. Open your heart anew to Him. His way is gentle, and you will find rest for your soul.

Matthew Chapter 12

# PEOPLE MATTER MORE
# THAN INSTITUTIONS AND RELIGIOUS RITUALS

*At that time Jesus went through the grainfields on the Sabbath.
His disciples were hungry, and they began to pluck heads of grain to
eat. But when the Pharisees saw it, they said to him, "Look, your disciples are doing what is not lawful to do on the Sabbath." He said to
them, "Have you not read what David did when he was hungry, and
those who were with him: how he entered the house of God and ate
the bread of the Presence, which it was not lawful for him to eat nor
for those who were with him, but only for the priests? Or have you not
read in the Law how on the Sabbath the priests in the temple profane
the Sabbath and are guiltless? I tell you, something greater than the
temple is here. And if you had known what this means, 'I desire mercy,
and not sacrifice,' you would not have condemned the guiltless. For the
Son of Man is lord of the Sabbath." (Matthew 12:1-8)*

## The Pharisees on the Rampage

Like rabid, self-appointed paparazzi, the Pharisees once again pursue Jesus with a vengeance over the technicalities of the Sabbath. They turn over every rock and lurch around every corner hoping to bring Him down. The Pharisees aspire to discredit His character, dispute His message, and thereby destroy His movement. They accuse Jesus of not only violating the commands of scripture, but of working alongside the devil and making divine claims without the miracles to back it up. Jesus clearly and concisely refutes each accusation with authority and grace.

As the chapter begins, Jesus explains the heart behind the notion of "Sabbath keeping," for which He's been accused of violating by healing someone on the Sabbath day. Before I address the specifics of what Jesus was explaining to the Pharisees, let me first say that God instituted the Sabbath as a way to ensure that human beings would not allow their work to keep them away from a relationship with Him. There's a natural proclivity for people to get caught up in the frenzy of life and in the business of making a living to survive and succeed. People can easily drift in their relationship with God as they become consumed in their work. What once was a "hot" relationship with God can drift to "warm" and even "cool" before you know it.

## The Spirit of the Sabbath

God instituted a system in the Israelite community where one day each week was to be set aside to worship (no work), to remember God's faithfulness, and to reflect on the things that really matter in life: loving God and loving people. This weekly rhythm of refilling and regeneration aids in spiritual renewal, emotional rejuvenation, and physical re-catalyzing, which benefits all human beings who take advantage of it. It was a built-in spiritual system to help people stay calibrated in their life-long pursuit of God. This principle is true and applies even today. When we set aside regular time to reflect on God's goodness and who we are as God's beloved children, we gain a renewed and eternal perspective of who God is and who we are as people. If we're not careful, we can forget God and even forget who we are in the process, and if or when that happens, that should concern us.

## Don't Forget Who You Are

I remember once when that happened to me: I forgot who I was and it scared me. I was 14 and hanging out after school with some buddies where we were shooting some pool at a friend's house. There was a makeshift chin-up bar lodged up high in between the door jam in a back bedroom. Trying to show off my "amazing athletic prowess" to a watching female bystander, I started sprinting down the hallway and leaped for the chin-up bar like a trapeze artist in a Barnum and Bailey circus event. I was going to do some "high-flying acrobatics" for my audience. Instead, the bar snapped and I tumbled head first onto the cement floor. I cracked my head like an egg and was knocked out cold for almost an hour. I woke up in my friend's bedroom with paramedics shining a penlight into my eyeball while I was lying on my back drifting in and out of consciousness. The EMT kept asking me, "Who are you and what are you doing here?" For several hours I couldn't remember my name or who I was. I was transported by ambulance to a hospital where I stayed for four days. I did eventually regain my memory and my sense of identity, but it was a frightening experience.

That can happen to us, too. We can lose our bearings of who we really are and why we are here on planet earth. We can sometimes lose our way and drift from the things that really matter: loving God and loving people. The purpose of life can become complicated. At times, we can even get disillusioned about our faith and the whole point of life. Obsessive busyness can cause us to forget the things that really matter.

## Reflect, Remember, Recharge

We live in a world that is stuck on "fast-forward." If we heed the wisdom found in the scriptures, we'll build wise boundaries around our spiritual liberties. Setting aside a weekly time to reflect, remember, and recharge will aid us in not only cultivating a loving relationship with God and others, but it can be an impetus behind relieving stress, increasing creativity, and solving difficult problems more effectively. In principle, the Sabbath is a good idea and contains healthy principles of renewal that convert into personal and spiritual fruitfulness. The goal of the Sabbath was and is a principle to aid us in connecting with God.

## People Matter

At the same time, in the above passage of scripture, Jesus is not saying that the Sabbath was not important, or that we shouldn't frame our lives around it. He was saying that the Sabbath principle doesn't supersede God or is an end in itself; it was a means to an end. What was the end? Again, it's loving God and loving people. Jesus is teaching the Pharisees that people matter more to God than anything. People are incredibly valuable. God demonstrates this value by sending Jesus to the earth to die for our sins. People matter enough to God that He would have His son die in our place, so we could be in relationship with Him when we trust our lives to Christ and receive the gift of His forgiveness. People matter more than things, principles, and spiritual systems. People matter more than well-intended religious rituals. So, to make His point, Jesus heals again, on the Sabbath.

Even today, people are valuable to God and their concerns and needs should matter to us as well. This is at the heart of what Jesus was teaching. People and their needs should be elevated above our church institutions, our government systems, and our religious rituals that sometimes, unintentionally, become the "end" instead of the "means." Like many things in scripture, God's counsel to us would be to learn to do both things in balance:

1. Admit we're human and take full advantage of the Sabbath principle which has been created for our health and benefit.

2. Love God and people above principles, systems, and religious rituals.

My prayer for us is that we would learn to do both: incorporate the Sabbath and love God and people above the Sabbath. If you are one who finds yourself drifting a bit, and your love for God and people has moved from hot to warm, make it a priority this week to push away from your work and find a good local church where you can worship God and connect with other Christ-followers. We get life from the things we connect to. The Sabbath principle has been created for our benefit. Take advantage of it. It will aid you in achieving personal and spiritual fruitfulness. Embracing the Sabbath principle will help draw each of us to God and it will aid us in not forgetting who we are and why we are here.

## Matthew Chapter 13

# GOD'S RIGHT-SIZING:
# THE PROMISE OF A NEW NORMAL

*"The kingdom of heaven is like treasure hidden in a field. When a man found it, he hid it again, and then in his joy went and sold all he had and bought that field. "Again, the kingdom of heaven is like a merchant seeking fine pearls, and upon finding one pearl of great value, he went and sold all that he had, and bought it."*
*(Matthew 13:44-46)*

## Unpacking Spiritual Truth

The gospel of Matthew contains five of Jesus' major discourses. This chapter is the third such teaching. Jesus unpacks spiritual truths surrounding the topic of the "kingdom of God." He uses parables (small allegorical stories) to explain mysteries and insights from a "heavenly perspective." This chapter contains several stories:

- The Sower and Soils
- The Wheat and Weeds
- The Mustard Seed
- The Yeast
- The Hidden Treasure
- The Pearl
- The Net

Jesus is using these parables as a way to explain some of the unique characteristics of God's kingdom and the transformational change that occurs when it's activated in our lives. He also gives us a glimpse of how portions of the spiritual world operate.

## Longing for God's Promises

Many of Jesus' listeners yearned for the day when God's long-awaited promise of a new kind of world would become a present-day reality. They anticipated a final judgment that would establish justice, peace, and equity for all. They dreamed of freedom and the day when God (through the Messiah) would once and for all triumph over evil and rescue them from political oppression and racial abuse. They hoped for the day when every wrong would be made right and all that was bad would be made good.

It is no wonder crowds followed Jesus wherever He went. Not only did He cure their ailments and heal their vexed spirits, He elevated hopes and inspired people's deepest aspirations for a new kind of life and a bright future. But just like people today, Jesus' listeners got some things right and were way off in other areas.

## Still the Same Today

One of the things I find intriguing in this chapter is that even today, we long for many of the same things that the listeners of Jesus' day wanted.

We desire peace, justice, and equity in the world. We yearn for communities that are free of violence and racial abuse. We wish for political systems and forms of governance around the globe that are others-oriented rather than self-serving. We hunger for a world where evil is nonexistent, and where health, joy, compassion, and right-living are the norm. But where many go astray is not in "what God wants to do," but in the "how, where, and when" of God's fulfilling of these longings.

Many hoped that Jesus (the Messiah) would establish God's kingdom (a new way of being and living as the people of God) through violence and armed resistance. But God's plan (the how) was for Jesus to die on the cross (the where) as the sacrifice for all mankind. God's new reality was inaugurated through Jesus' sinless life, crucifixion, death, and resurrection.

Not only did Jesus defeat sin, evil, the devil, and death through His sacrifice on Calvary's cross, but He birthed a new era for God's people and for God's way to expand in the earth. As we will see later, because many misunderstood God's plan and process, they turned against Jesus and rejected Him.

## God's Rule

Like the many beautiful colors contained in a pack of crayons, Jesus explores the unique shades and facets of God's kingdom. The terms "kingdom of heaven" and "kingdom of God" are interchangeable. They are phrases that mean God's rule or God's reign in the lives of people, both now on earth and eternally. The kingdom of heaven is not referring to the afterlife or a location that we go to once we die. Rather, it's a heavenly governing system of rulership that we are encouraged to live under as followers of Jesus here on earth. As we live under this new kind of rulership (God's rule), transformational change begins to take place in and through our attitudes, behaviors, relationships, values, and goals. Jesus and His teachings begin to guide and govern every aspect of our lives.

## A Values-Driven Life

The focus today in many organizations and businesses is about being "values-centered" or "values-led" or "values-driven." Values are invisible, and at times intangible, yet they have clear and concrete attitudes, behaviors, and outcomes that are associated with them. These outcomes are tangible, and in many ways, measurable. Companies can measure how and if their "core values" are being adopted. Values have both intrinsic and extrinsic elements to them. Today, organizations of all kinds are dialed in to the importance of how their brand adds value to the customer or stakeholder.

In some ways, the kingdom of God is like a values-focused organization, too. Inside things affect outside things. God's kingdom is invisible, yet has clear external attitudes and behaviors connected to it. In a sense, it's intangible, yet it intersects and impacts our world in observable physical ways. The kingdom of God has a "values element" to it. Kingdom values are the normal operating system in heaven, even as we speak. One day, they will be the accepted values for all of humanity.

## A New Way of Living

Jesus came to earth to proclaim a new system of governance in and over the human heart. As the heart changes, so do relationships, families, communities, and nations (Proverbs 4:23). This process begins by turning over the leadership of our lives to God and yielding to Him through the person of Jesus Christ. When we respond to Jesus' invitation to enter into a loving yet submissive relationship with Him, something catalyzes spiritually in us, and through a process of spiritual transformation, our spirit begins to inform our hearts, which begins to inform our behavior. The Bible calls that phenomenon being "born again" or being "made new" in our spirits.

As we allow Jesus to take over the leadership of our lives, some circles call that "letting Jesus be Lord." When Jesus is Lord of our lives, He becomes ruler over our values. His Word becomes our map and compass. His Spirit becomes our mentor and guide. Our new map, compass, and guide affect our values, and of course, our values manifest themselves in our attitudes and behaviors.

## Mystery and Ambiguity

God's kingdom also contains mystery. Some of us do just fine with unanswered questions, ambiguity, and cliffhangers, but some don't. Understanding God and His timetable can be daunting. Many of the parables in this chapter warn people that even though we can't always see God's kingdom with our natural eyes, God is nevertheless doing something profound in the world. He is alive and working. A harvest is coming. Hard work and patience are required.

Yes, God's kingdom has been birthed, but it's also a process that is unfolding over time. Like an early morning sunrise that crests the eastern skyline and grows brighter and stronger each hour until it's completely overhead, so too God's kingdom is expanding. And one day, it too will come to complete fulfillment and a new reality.

## Following His Lead

My prayer for us is that we would joyfully place our lives under the leadership of Jesus and the authority of His teachings. His ways are wise and loving. Even when we don't understand, He always has our best in mind. His future for us is bright. Being a Christ-follower is being someone who not only believes and trusts in Jesus, but obeys Him. Jesus taught us that God is our Father and we are His children. Therefore, obedience is part of our relationship with God.

## Integrating "Lord" and "Savior"

We are God's servants, and obedience is part of that relationship. That is what Jesus was getting at when He said, "Not everyone who says to me, 'Lord, Lord,' will enter the kingdom of heaven, but only he who does the will of my Father who is in heaven." (Matthew 7:21) Jesus is telling us that we have to do more than just call Him "Lord," that we must treat Him as Lord, and treating Him as Lord infers obedience. One of the misconceptions that is floating around in contemporary Christian thinking is that Jesus can be someone's "Savior" but not their "Lord"; in other words, a person isn't planning on obeying Him, but they are planning on going to heaven (being saved).

Being "Lord" and "Savior" is in some ways one and the same. Let me explain it this way: Imagine a lone hiker gets hopelessly lost deep within a dense and massive forest in the Alaskan wilderness. He knows it's just a matter of time until he dies. Then, out of the blue, a park ranger appears across the valley. At first, the hiker rushes up to the park ranger and hugs him, saying, "Thank God you're here. I'm lost. Can you help me find my way out of the forest and back to safety?" Calmly and confidently, the park ranger responds, "Absolutely. I know this forest like my backyard. I also have a GPS and know what to do."

The lost and desperate hiker breaks down crying and says, "You're my savior and rescuer! Thank you." After sharing some food and water, the park ranger says, "Okay, now follow me. Let's go." Suddenly, the hiker glares into the eyes of the park ranger and quips back, "Who made you Master and Lord? Nobody tells me what to do. I'm the leader of my own life and the captain of my own ship." Humbly, the park ranger responds, "Okay, suit yourself." And he walks off.

## The Joy of Obedience

What the lost hiker didn't understand was that the park ranger couldn't be his savior without being his lord. The park ranger couldn't rescue the hiker and lead him to safety if the hiker wasn't willing to follow. Obedience is a natural part of our relationship with God, and it's an expression of our faith in Jesus. Again, we don't obey Jesus just because we have to—we obey Him and His teachings because we want to and because we love Him. Jesus told His disciples, "If you love me, you will obey what I command" (John 14:15). When you love someone, you want to please him or her. When you trust someone, you obey him. That's because you know that person has your best interest at heart.

## Connecting Faith and Trust

Faith is not only accepting Christ into your life as Savior and forgiver of your sins, but it's also trusting Jesus and His teachings in such a way that He becomes the leader and Lord of your life. When we allow His rulership to begin to take place in our lives, spiritual transformation begins and we change. My hope is that we move beyond thinking about God's kingdom to living out the God-life, which is, in fact, the "good life" that we all deep down really long for.

Matthew Chapter 14

# RECIPE FOR THE MIRACULOUS:
# A LISTENING EAR AND AN OPEN HEART

*Now when it was evening, the disciples came to him and said, "This is a desolate place, and the day is now over; send the crowds away to go into the villages and buy food for themselves." But Jesus said, "They need not go away; you give them something to eat." They said to him, "We have only five loaves here and two fish." And he said, "Bring them here to me." Then he ordered the crowds to sit down on the grass, and taking the five loaves and the two fish, he looked up to heaven and said a blessing. Then he broke the loaves and gave them to the disciples, and the disciples gave them to the crowds. And they all ate and were satisfied. And they took up twelve baskets full of the broken pieces left over. And those who ate were about five thousand men, besides women and children.  (Matthew 14:15-21)*

## Grace, Fame, and Criticism

As chapter 14 unfolds, Jesus' Messianic identity comes into greater focus. Word of His miraculous deeds and grace-filled teachings have traversed the countryside and even wiggled its way into Herod's royal court. Jesus' fame advances. Criticism continues from the religious elite at every turn. Miracles flourish. Danger amplifies. It's not by accident that this gospel writer, Matthew, has us briefly step back into the past with a short discussion about John the Baptist (who has already died). He wants us to understand where the storyline is headed: the cross. As Jesus' notoriety increases, so too does the animosity and aggression from the religious gatekeepers of the day. Jesus' newly proposed kingdom way of being and living threatens them at their core because the gospel proclaims that their places of power and positions of prestige will change. The role of the religious "big Kahuna" is coming to end and being fulfilled by Jesus' sacrifice on the cross. People will no longer need to go through another priestly human being as their mediator to God in order to receive forgiveness for their sins.

## Herod Resurfaces

Herod, the Tetrarch, re-enters the story. Remember, it was in Matthew chapter two that Herod the Great tried to murder Jesus as an infant. Years later, Herod the Tetrarch (one of the many sons of Herod the Great) is on the same rampage again, but in stealth mode. Herod is beginning to put the pieces together of Jesus' new kingdom teaching that is the centerpiece of contemporary conversation: If there is a new kingdom coming, then there is a new king as well, and that king ain't Herod! Therefore, Matthew wants us to know that plans for Jesus' murder are already being drafted in the hearts and minds of the religious and political elite.

## Jesus Presses On

As the chapter finishes, Jesus courageously moves forward in the face of stiff opposition. He continues to teach about the new things God wants to do in people's lives. Jesus draws life lessons from the past, lives in the moment, and promises a future that is bright for those who will believe in Him and follow His teachings. Jesus heals the sick, cures the disillusioned of heart, and rescues the spiritually lost. His invitation is to all people.

At the end, the scene shifts and the disciples find themselves panicking in the midst of a raging storm. Jesus comes to them, walking on the water. They see the power and divinity of Jesus demonstrated. We see the disciples' humanity. Of course, Peter does example a heart of faith as he steps out of the boat to pursue Jesus, but soon sinks. As the readers, we're left with an honest picture of the Christian life: moments of faith and confidence and moments of doubt and hesitation. As we keep our eyes on Jesus and not on our circumstances, things always go better.

## Feeding the 5,000

Reflecting on the entirety of this chapter, I'm again drawn to the story of Jesus feeding the 5,000 with the five loaves of bread and two fish. This miracle of provision is demonstrative in scope, yet simplistic. It teaches us about Jesus' supernatural ability and His compassionate concern for meeting our daily needs. It also reveals how Jesus asks each of us to partner with Him in meeting the needs of others that are around us. He didn't do it alone, and even today He still doesn't. Just as the disciples only had a few loaves of bread and fish, we too can feel we don't have the ability or means to meet the entirety of someone's needs. If we're not careful, we can over-analyze things and end up doing nothing. Jesus asked the disciples, and He asks us as well, to do what we can and use what we have. He'll take care of the rest. Jesus gets excited when we as Christ-followers look for creative and bold ways to meet the needs of others.

## A Recipe for the Miraculous

When God's timing and our listening ears come together, very special moments can take place. Never underestimate what can happen when God, a receptive ear, and a ready heart come together. It's a recipe for God to do something marvelous in both the giver and the receiver.

Years ago, there was a wonderful "miracle of provision" that took place in my own life. At the time, I was living in Tyler, Texas, with my wife and 18-month-old son. We were working hard trying to make ends meet, but found ourselves at the end of a pay period without food to eat or milk for our baby. After staring into the empty refrigerator one morning, my wife looked at me and said, "What are we going to do? We don't have any food and we don't get paid for four days." "I don't know," I replied. We were stressed, depressed, and afraid for our son.

About an hour later, our doorbell rang. When I opened the door I saw a little white-haired elderly lady named Ava Lee Gentry gently smiling at me. "Good morning, Chris," she said. Although I had recognized this lady from church, I really didn't know her yet. I remember thinking to myself, "What's she doing here?" Kindly, she said, "Chris, I have some bags of groceries in my car. Would you please help me carry them into your home?" She turned and walked back to her car. Shocked, I didn't know what to say. I followed her out to her car.

Seeing the puzzled look on my face, she said, "I was praying last night when I heard in my heart God saying to get up early this morning and go buy ya'll some groceries and milk for your baby. That's why I'm here." I tried to hold the tears in, but they started dripping from the corner of my eyes, even though I tried as hard as I could to remain stoic and strong. Mary and I will never forget unloading bag after bag after bag until we had to put the grocery bags on the floor, as our small tabletop could hold no more. She humbly said to us, "Have a really good day. I must go now." Off she drove.

## Becoming a Partner with God

Mary and I stood around the overflowing table and just looked at each other. I went into the bedroom and found a camera so I could take a picture in order to show my children one day how God saw our need and answered the cry of our hearts when we were young parents. Amazingly, God spoke in the middle of the night and put an impression into the heart of a little old lady who was willing to partner with God in a miracle of provision. Ava Lee passed away last year, but she has left a lasting legacy and lesson of faith in my heart: God's timing, a listening ear, and a ready heart equals a recipe for the miraculous.

Although that happened more than 20 years ago, I still have the picture that I snapped of all that food on our tabletop. It remains on my desk by my computer as a daily reminder of what God can do in us and through us when we partner with Him.

## God is Listening

That day was a very special moment in my life. Ava Lee's willingness to listen to the Holy Spirit and follow that simple prompting that God placed in her heart to meet one family's need serves as a constant reminder that God cares, listens, and intervenes when we least expect it. Sometimes, God's way of supernaturally intervening in the life of others is by involving and using us as the conduits of His provision.

Never underestimate God's timing, a listening ear, and an obedient heart. When they come together, amazing things always transpire. My prayer for us is that we would be willing this week to use what we do have to meet the needs of others. Let me encourage you to turn your ear toward heaven and listen to the whispers of God's Spirit. He just might be speaking and directing you to meet a simple, yet important, need in a young struggling family that will take a picture of their answered prayer and cherish you and God's faithfulness even after you are gone.

Matthew Chapter 15

# UNDERSTANDING THE DIFFERENCE BETWEEN STYLE AND SUBSTANCE

*Then Pharisees and scribes came to Jesus from Jerusalem and said, "Why do your disciples break the tradition of the elders? For they do not wash their hands when they eat." He answered them, "And why do you break the commandment of God for the sake of your tradition? So for the sake of your tradition you have made void the word of God. You hypocrites! Well did Isaiah prophesy of you, when he said: 'This people honors me with their lips, but their heart is far from me; in vain do they worship me, teaching as doctrines the commandments of men.'" (Matthew 15:1-4, 6-9)*

## Jesus is the Same Yesterday and Today

Jesus continues His ministry of teaching God's Word wherever He goes. His followers experience a new sense of God's presence, power, and promise in their lives and futures. In this chapter, Jesus introduces some of the new things God wants to do in and through people of all ages and backgrounds. These people are invited to be a part of His story. Jesus teaches, rebukes, heals, feeds, and inspires. He explains the difference between God's commandment and human tradition, purity versus impurity, and authenticity versus hypocrisy.

The Pharisees and scribes keep looking for ways to put a kibosh on Jesus' newfound movement that is gaining momentum. They believe that if they discredit the messenger and His message, then the movement will fail. Unbeknownst to them, their human traditions, modified temple practices, and re-jiggered religious customs have been superseded by the scriptures, as well as God's original desire toward His people. In essence, their religious systems have morphed and become useless idols in place of God.

## Visualizing Grace and Truth

Even today, Christians of all sorts can unintentionally go astray as we begin to elevate our human traditions and our postmodern philosophical worldviews over the supremacy of the scriptures. In order to not fall into the "Pharisee trap," I think it's wise when it comes to conversations around doctrine, culture, preferences, traditions, lifestyles, politics, and behaviors to frame the discussion of tradition versus innovation or denominational style versus biblical substance by using the "closed hand/open hand" analogy that many have used to make the point. Let me explain.

Imagine a person standing in a room with their arms outstretched. They extend their left hand and right hand toward you. With their left hand, they clinch their fist and make a closed hand. For illustration's sake, allow this closed hand to symbolize the non-negotiable tenets of the Christian faith: Sin is the problem, the devil is the adversary, forgiveness is the invitation, the cross is the solution, Jesus is the answer, and the Bible is absolutely true to the core (to name a few). Held tightly in this left hand are the things that never change. They are not matters of style or personal taste. Rather, they are the core truths (substance) of our faith. They are the biblical commandments that are black and white and clearly found in scripture.

With the closed hand on the left, this person stretches out their fingers on their right hand wide open until you see the palm of their hand as they make an "open hand." The open hand symbolizes the other side of the pendulum that makes room for differences when it comes to secondary matters of our faith: worship styles, a glass of wine at dinner or not, political affiliation such as Republican, Democrat, or Independent, use of tattoos, vegetarian or carnivore (to name a few).

## Liberty, Conscience, and Convictions

It's important to allow people to always have the freedom of conscience and to enjoy the liberty provided by grace in their decision-making and lifestyle choices where the Bible is silent. Other biblical principles, wisdom, and the Holy Spirit will guide us into all truth where the Bible is quiet. It's important to remember that this is God's design. He did this on purpose. Therefore, we must strive to be people with our own strong convictions. At the same time, we must live out that conviction or expression of faith in a spirit of openness, tolerance, and generosity toward others. Of course, living this way produces a kind of dissonance inside us. It's always easier to surround your life with sameness. But just as unhealthy genetic mutations spawn from reproductive sameness (inbreeding), so too does unhealthy spiritual mutation transpire when we surround our lives with people who are just like we are and who think just like we do. Slowly, the world becomes smaller, one-dimensional, and boring.

Yes, we must have our own convictions, but we must always ooze with graciousness and acceptance of others. This is one of the main beefs many young people (Christian and non-Christian) have with the extreme Religious Right movement. Many young people perceive it to be a bunch of angry, judgmental, hypocritical Christians, and these young postmoderns want nothing to do with it. When I see Jesus in this chapter of scripture, I see a person that people loved to be around. Jesus was loving, accepting, and fun to be with, and yet He possessed an extremely high set of standards and convictions. He hung out with people very different than Himself. And of course, He was criticized for it.

## Living with Gracious Tension

Both principles (closed hand/open hand) must coexist in people's lives in order for spiritual health and biblical balance to be present. This is harder to do than it appears, especially when we are talking about a diverse community of people relating to each other in gracious and civil ways (the church) while attempting to live out Jesus' teachings. Nevertheless, this is God's challenge to us.

Many people want things to be black and white in every category of life (sometimes I do too). They believe that approach makes life easier to navigate. Of course, life doesn't work that way. God loves freedom, diverse cultural expression, individuality, creativity, and nuance. Just look at the magnificent spray of a summer sunset or the shifting lights of the Aurora Borealis and you'll see a multiplicity of light and color that seems to dance in the sky above.

## Fear Blinds Us

Second, fear causes people to want to legislate certain "open-handed" areas and choices in life. When life moves out of the "clearly defined," uncertainty appears, and the feeling of control diminishes which often produces anxiety. For example, sometimes well-intentioned parents (me included), because of fear that their children might misuse or misappropriate an "open-handed" liberty, or might respond with a different "conscience or conclusion" over a particular issue different than theirs, present this "liberty of choice" as an immutable truth and a "closed-handed commandment," which it isn't. At the same time, those who enjoy certain liberties are encouraged to be very thoughtful of whom they are with and of their surroundings so as not to offend or be a source of struggle for others who have convictions and a conscience that is different.

## Misdiagnosing My Own Fear

Looking back in my own life, there were instances where I should have taken more time to explain this "liberty" (whatever it might be), along with the appropriate boundaries, consequences, and responsibilities that were associated with it. But for me to do that would have meant that I first understood this principle and that I would not allow fear to subtly creep into areas where it had no business. I know in some cases I didn't want my kids to experience some of the painful consequences that I experienced from taking a liberty and abusing it (misuse of alcohol, for example). When I was a young parent, I didn't recognize my fear. It was easier at that time to just repackage it as black and white. So, I presented some things "closed-handed" to my children that were really "open-handed."

## St. Augustine

I love the words of St. Augustine (354-430), who said, "In essentials, unity. In non-essentials, liberty. In all things, charity." My prayer for us is that we would learn to better discern the difference between style and substance, tradition and scripture, and liberty and biblical command. May God give us strong and unyielding biblical convictions in this relativistic world in which we live. At the same time, I pray for an attitude of tolerance and openness toward others that honestly communicates God's loving heart to a searching and cynical world. May God grant us wisdom in such a way as to figure out how to allow both principles to operate within our lives.

## Keep Growing

May we take the time to listen more, learn always, and ask lots of honest questions from others. It might be easier to surround ourselves with sameness and operate within the borders of a black and white life, but God desires for us to be people who are fully alive and who experience the God-life abundantly. It's a life that is full, multi-dimensional, and limitless. May we impact our world for Christ as we become a clear and gracious voice of persuasion, rather than a contentious voice of protest.

Matthew Chapter 16

# LIVING THE GOOD LIFE
# (WHICH IS THE GOD-LIFE)

*Then Jesus told his disciples, "If anyone would come after me, let him deny himself and take up his cross and follow me. For whoever would save his life will lose it, but whoever loses his life for my sake will find it. For what will it profit a man if he gains the whole world and forfeits his soul? Or what shall a man give in return for his soul?" (Matthew 16:24-26)*

## The Desire for Signs

This chapter begins with the Pharisees and Sadducees working together (which was odd) hoping to bait Jesus to "prove himself" by producing a "sign" from heaven. In actuality, they were trying to trap Him and hoped that they could accuse Him of either being a false prophet who was bent on leading the people of Israel astray, or by being in cahoots with the devil himself. Jesus refuses to play into their deceptive lure and refuses to dishonor God by reducing Him to the likes of a street-corner-magician doing tricks for the local crowd.

## Signs Point Us Toward Something

Yes, Jesus performed signs all the time, but they were motivated out of love and compassion for people, not to boost His popularity or to defend Himself to a group of critical, arrogant, and mean-spirited intellectuals. Signs were never intended to be an end in themselves. Rather, signs were always pointing toward something else. They were the means to the end. Signs direct you toward a final destination just like a mile-marker on the side of a highway leads and directs you toward an upcoming city. In Jesus' case, the end destination was His imminent crucifixion and resurrection from the dead.

Today, like in Jesus' day, people often camp out around "signs" and other unexplainable spiritual phenomena, rather than realizing that, for the Christian, signs were and are to point toward Jesus. Signs are not the goal or the final destination; Jesus is, and He always will be. Signs are cool. Jesus is cooler.

It's interesting to note that the Pharisees and Sadducees weren't exactly best friends. But when it came to entrapping Jesus in some form or fashion, they gladly worked together. Throughout history, not only has a common goal united people, but having common enemies has, too. Both the Pharisees and Sadducees were in positions of power and influence and were threatened by Jesus and His fast-growing movement. They didn't want to lose their positions of stature and notoriety or other cultural, religious, and economic benefits. So, they hoped to discredit Jesus at any cost.

## The Pharisees and Sadducees

In Jesus' day, the Pharisees were a group of Jewish legal experts who were bent on bringing all of Israel into close observance of Jewish law (as set forth in the Torah). They created many of their own traditions, developed their own commentary surrounding theology and practice, and fashioned their own spiritual disciplines around prayer and religious life.

On the other hand, the Sadducees were a group of Jewish aristocrats that adhered to the Pentateuch (the first five books of the Old Testament) and adopted many of their own self-created religious traditions. They resisted the Pharisees' practices and traced their religious pedigree back to King David's high priest, Zadok. The Sadducees did not believe in any form of afterlife (including resurrection). Again, these two diverse groups working together said a lot about how they felt about Jesus.

As the chapter continues, Jesus warns the disciples about the watered-down teaching (leaven) and practices of the Pharisees and Sadducees. He then asks Peter who the multitudes say that He is. Peter responds and says, "Like one of the prophets."

## Perceptions of Jesus

It's clear that many of the ancient Israelites saw Jesus quite differently than we do today. Many in our culture view Jesus as a soft-spoken, effeminate, frail, Anglo, religious teacher. In Jesus' day, He was viewed like other big-hitter prophets of old: a strong, brave, fearless communicator of God's Word to a wayward culture that was filled with a corrupt political and religious system. God's prophets were messengers, on behalf of God, who stood up and spoke up, no matter what the consequences were, against injustice, spiritual waywardness, and social inequity.

## Who Do You Say That I Am?

Jesus then asks Peter who he, personally, thinks Jesus is. Peter replies, "You are the Christ, the Son of the living God." Peter identifies Jesus as more than a brave and bold prophet, but as the Messiah, God's anointed true King. It's not clear at this stage if Peter really knew everything about Jesus, such as how He would die and rise from the dead, that Jesus was actually the second person of the Trinity, or how Jesus would assert a kingly leadership role. Many scholars believe that although Peter knew Jesus was the anointed Messiah, he wasn't sure on the specifics of how and when Jesus would move into this Messianic role publicly. If Peter thought like many of the folks in his day, he would have believed that the Messiah, whoever he was and whenever he appeared, would eventually plan an all-out takeover and political overthrow in order to right every wrong and establish God's rule, peace, and justice of the earth.

The chapter finishes with Jesus forecasting His own death. He promises a reality that is fast approaching where God's kingdom will be established. It will grow, expand, and multiply. But Jesus won't be establishing God's new way of living and being with violence or force. Rather, it will be birthed by sacrifice, suffering, and death on a cross.

## The Disciples' Call

Jesus challenges His disciples to take up their crosses and follow Him. The cross was an instrument of death. Following Jesus cost everything. It was all or nothing. Sink or swim. Jump off or go home. There was, and is, no in-between. The disciples' call is still going forward. We are not called to a mental philosophy, or a nice religion to espouse, or an intellectual faith to hold close like an old blanket or teddy bear. We are called to follow Jesus. We are to put our faith in Christ (Who He is and What He said) and allow it to affect our lives. As we do, He'll give us the strength and motivation to want to live out His teachings. Today, Jesus is still calling people to follow Him. He tells us that if we try and hold on to our lives, we actually lose them; but if we lose our lives in Him, we actually will find life. This is one of the great paradoxes of Christianity. All of God's promises are fulfilled in Jesus Christ.

## Step Up and Step Out

I remember the first time that I jumped off of a 10-meter platform into a swimming pool in Tucson, Arizona. To call it a huge rush was an understatement. As a kid, I prided myself on my ability to do flips and twists on a low-level diving board (one meter), but standing on the edge of the

10-meter platform was truly daunting. I felt vulnerable, scared, and a bit disoriented. I started to second-guess myself and began talking myself out of jumping into the pool. Over-analysis of the situation began to paralyze my confidence and ability.

The same is true with faith. When we come to points of decision, we can over-analyze to the point where "constant analysis" becomes our worldview. We fail to act because we are always analyzing. We can fall into a trap where we pride ourselves on our own ability to anesthetize ourselves (and others) from a true and meaningful spiritual life. Our intellect, which was designed to enhance spiritual discovery, can actually, if left unchecked, hinder spiritual life. Life is more than analysis; it's about following God and serving others.

My prayer for us is that we will step off the platform and leap over the barriers that keep us from the God-life, which is the good life. Yes, following Jesus costs, but the rewards far surpass any sacrifice or discomfort that we will ever experience. Divers dive. Disciples follow. And Jesus promises that He will help us, through the person of the Holy Spirit, and lead us along the way. Let's live the good life. It's our choice and it's a choice I believe we'll never regret. Let me encourage you to jump! I did, and after that, it was easy to keep going back for more.

Matthew Chapter 17

# THE APPLAUSE OF HEAVEN

*After six days Jesus took with him Peter, James and John the brother of James, and led them up a high mountain by themselves. There he was transfigured before them. His face shone like the sun, and his clothes became as white as the light. Just then there appeared before them Moses and Elijah, talking with Jesus. Peter said to Jesus, "Lord, it is good for us to be here. If you wish, I will put up three shelters—one for you, one for Moses and one for Elijah." While he was still speaking, a bright cloud enveloped them, and a voice from the cloud said, "This is my Son, whom I love; with him I am well pleased. Listen to him!" (Matthew 17:1-5)*

## The Transfiguration

Chapter 17 begins with the Transfiguration of Jesus on Mount Hermon. His divine glory is supernaturally manifested in front of a small cadre of His closest disciples. This small band of followers are now aware, beyond a shadow of a doubt, that Jesus is God's one and only Son. God the Father verbally affirms His love for Jesus in their midst. Jesus is the Messiah. He's the hope of the whole world. His death is imminent. The cross awaits Him. Jesus is God's suffering servant who will willingly surrender His life for the sake of others (Isaiah 53). God's love and power will triumph. The Resurrection victory is just around the corner, and it will soon change the course of human history forever.

This extraordinary encounter on the mountain is one of the great climatic moments where Jesus is clearly connected to God's grand storyline and divine plan of redemption that has been prepared for since the beginning of time. In this supernatural encounter, both Moses and Elijah stand with Jesus. Moses was Israel's lawgiver. Elijah was one of Israel's all-time great prophets. Moses and Elijah represent the Old Testament law and the prophets that were indicative of the old covenant and all its promises. With Moses and Elijah present and alongside Jesus, a symbolic portrait of truth and grace is captured for all to see. Jesus is not only the fulfillment of God's old covenant to humanity, but He is God's new and better way.

## The God Who Pursues

Throughout history God has been in passionate pursuit of people who will join Him in a loving and committed relationship. He's always been in love with people. It started way back in the Garden of Eden with Adam and Eve and continued forward with the nation of Israel. God has always hoped to make His relationship with His people a source of blessing to the whole world. He has always taken His relationships with people very seriously. God is not flippant or fickle. Because of His great love for humanity He initiated a relationship (covenant) with the people of God (Israel). That covenant is called the Old Testament law. It describes the promises and expectations of God's relationship with His people before the new work that was taking place in and through Jesus.

## The New Covenant

Because of Israel's repeated disobedience to the agreements, expectations, and boundaries of God's covenant promises, their relationship with Him suffered and, at times, ceased to exist. Because God is both loving and just, He chose to make a new covenant with humanity. It would be a new kind of agreement, one for which He would take full responsibility as covenant initiator and keeper. This time, the relationship would not be based on the Old Testament law, but on God's grace and undeserved favor that He would extend toward all people through the person of Jesus. Now, instead of a relationship based on the expectations and promises of the Old Testament, God was instituting a new agreement with people everywhere. It's called the New Testament, or the new agreement.

Rather than going through the law and the words of the prophets to get to God, God-seekers now go through Jesus directly because of His sacrifice on the cross (which makes believers in Jesus right with God because we are forgiven of our sins and can now be friends with God). The promises of God can now be ours, through Jesus, rather than through keeping the Old Testament law. This is what Jesus was getting at earlier when He said, "I am the way, the truth, and the life. No one comes to the Father except through me." (John 14:6).

Like runners in a relay race, who pass the baton within the exchange zone of their lane, so too the Transfiguration is that wonderful picture of that "transitional coming together," where God's old agreement is about to pass the baton to the New Covenant in Jesus. The Transfiguration is a live, prophetic drama announcing God's fulfillment of one set of promises and expectations to people and instituting a brand new set through the person of Jesus Christ.

As the chapter continues, Jesus again predicts His suffering, death, and Resurrection. He is God's sacrifice for our sins. He's the Redeemer of mankind. The disciples are troubled to hear Jesus' prediction that He will be crucified. Jesus explains to the disciples what a delight it is to be in close fellowship with a loving God when we accept His invitation of grace and forgiveness.

## Unconditional Love

This story reminds me again that God loves us because of who we are not because of what we do. God is a loving Father and He loves us because we are His kids. There is nothing we can do to incite more love out of God. He loves us twice: First, because He made us. Second, because He purchased us back from sin through Jesus. God loves us just as we are and loves us too much to allow us to stay the same.

God accepts us based on Jesus' performance not ours. It was Jesus who lived a perfect and sinless life on earth and is thereby qualified to be our Savior. It was Jesus who died on a cross for us so that we could be forgiven of our sins. When God looks at Christians, He looks through the lens of what Jesus did for us on Calvary's hill. Yes, we do good works for God, but not in order to gain love, acceptance, or salvation. Rather, we do good works in Christ because we are saved, and it is a response of gratefulness and worship of God. We don't earn God's love; that's called religion. Jesus didn't die for a religion. He died so that we would have a relationship with the Father.

God sent His own Son to free us from the various religious systems of the day that tied our performance with His love. He loves us—period. To know love is to know the cross. To please God is simply to be in a loving and honest relationship with Him.

## Applause From Heaven

I remember when my daughter Megan was a small child and was part of a T-ball team in Boise. If you have never witnessed one of these Little League games with children five and six-years-old playing a form of baseball for the first time, you've got to be there in person to appreciate it. These children can't play a lick of baseball! Most kids don't know the rules or don't care. It's pure baseball chaos at it's finest! Kids run the wrong way around the bases. No one catches the ball, if it's ever even hit. Outfielders watch birds and butterflies and play with their ponytails or stare off into space. Batters cannot strike out, so kids are up to bat for what seems like an eternity. But you just wait and see what happens when, if by accident, some kid does hit the ball. There will be standing ovations, screaming parents, and cameras flashing! It's amazing...the parents, that is!

If you would ask these parents why they are going ballistic they would all tell you the same thing. Their applause is not based on the performance of their kid (they can't play baseball), it's based on their relationship. Each parent applauds their kid because they are "their little girl" or "their little boy." I know that's why I applauded my Megan, and why I still applaud her today. She's my little girl.

That's why God applauds us, too. He does so, not based on the basis of our accomplishments, but because we are His son or His daughter. We may accomplish magnificent things in this life, but we will never earn God's approval because of those things. He loves us because of who we are and His relationship with us (thank God for the New Covenant).

## Come Experience Jesus

My prayer for us is that we wouldn't waste a moment, and that we would boldly enter into this full and wonderful relationship with God through Jesus. Let me challenge you to not be a person who has a second-hand relationship with God. It's been said that God doesn't have any grandchildren, just kids. We can't have a second-hand relationship with God through a believing parent, spouse, or close friend. We all need to experience Jesus for ourselves. The psalmist said, "Taste and see that the Lord is good." (Psalm 34:8)

Maybe you are one who feels it's hard to be a Christian. If so, let me encourage you back to the cross. Ask Jesus to show you His hands and feet that were pierced for you. Let Him show you His side that was lanced for you. Ask Jesus to "rewind the video," so to speak, and show you how many times He's picked up the tab for you. Ask God to refresh your memory. Like the disciples, ask the Holy Spirit to show you who Jesus is in all of His power, beauty, and majesty. I've found that changing is not hard at all when you experience His love anew. Choose to enter by grace, through faith, into a loving relationship with God. You'll be glad you did. He's already applauding you. Can you hear Him?

# Matthew Chapter 18

# STAYING FREE TO FOLLOW GOD'S CALL

*"If your brother sins against you, go and show him his fault, just between the two of you. If he listens to you, you have won your brother over. But if he will not listen, take one or two others along, so that 'every matter may be established by the testimony of two or three witnesses.' If he refuses to listen to them, tell it to the church; and if he refuses to listen even to the church, treat him as you would a pagan or a tax collector." Then Peter came to Jesus and asked, "Lord, how many times shall I forgive my brother when he sins against me? Up to seven times?" Jesus answered, "I tell you, not seven times, but seventy-seven times." (Matthew 18:15-17, 21-22)*

## Healthy Relationships

This chapter in the gospel of Matthew contains Jesus' fourth great mega-sermon. It emphasizes the importance of a healthy and biblically functioning community of faith. Jesus establishes a broad foundation that depicts how the God-life affects our everyday relationships as well as our relationships with those outside the Christian faith. Jesus prescribes practical ways to not only nurture healthy relationships and solve personal offenses when they come, but also how to repair broken relationships when they fall into ruin. Jesus' solution involves honest truth-telling, courageous and loving relational confrontation, and forgiveness.

Over the years, I've watched many people (and at times, myself) attempt to deal with relational difficulties in every conceivable way except the way Jesus has prescribed. The end result is always the same: hurt, broken relationships, and relational alienation. Jesus' solution is always geared to an end result that brings about health, wholeness, personal growth, and God being glorified.

## The Power of Forgiveness

Forgiveness is one of the most overlooked, yet powerful, spiritual weapons in our arsenal. Forgiveness is not a suggestion; it's a command from Jesus. It's not a gift we give to people who we feel are deserving. Forgiveness is first and foremost a gift we give to ourselves because it keeps us free from other people's sins. It also allows us to stay free as we follow God's call for our lives.

Sin really doesn't destroy God's people, but unresolved sin does. The devil doesn't care what side of the boat we fall off of in life. We can fall off the right side, left side, or backwards. We can fall off because someone pushed us, or because we fall off ourselves through our own ignorance. The devil doesn't care. He just wants us to fall off of the boat and drown. The same is true in life. The devil loves to use unresolved offenses people have with each other in order to stop them from following God's call in their lives. The devil cackles when people choose to sever relationships with each other rather than sit down and seek biblical resolution as the scriptures teach. He snickers when people refuse to forgive their differences and misunderstandings and, instead, bail on each other, and at times, even bail on God. Remember, the devil's personal mission statement declares that he has come to steal, kill, and destroy. Jesus has come to give us life to the full. (John 10:10) We are exhorted to vigilantly contend for healthy relationships, maintain the unity of the Spirit, seek to resolve rather than bail, value the right thing to do rather than who is right, and forgive as many times as you need too in order to stay free. Health, wholeness, personal growth, character development, and God being glorified are always the fruits that follow.

## Child-Like Characteristics

Also in this chapter, Jesus uses the example of a child to teach His disciples a valuable life lesson. He explains that true God-followers must never lose the qualities that children so naturally embody: vulnerability, trust, humility, simplicity, purity, and joy. Jesus tells us that living a life that emulates these characteristics is the litmus test to becoming great in God's eyes. No, we are not to live lives that are childish. Rather, we are to inculcate a characteristic of child-likeness in our faith toward God.

Jesus goes on to explain that although bad things do happen to good people (because of the depravity of sin), consequences will come to the one who takes advantage of others, especially the innocent child, the vulnerable, the powerless, the helpless, and the marginalized. God watches out for these people in ways that we often don't understand in our culture. Jesus describes horrific and graphic consequences that will come to the abusers of children even more than to those who commit murder. The point of Jesus' statements is not to suggest that murder is not a heinous crime. Rather, it's to declare how much Jesus loves children and these kinds of people, and how He loves them at a level we can't comprehend as humans. Although God is a god of love and grace, He is also a God of truth. And truth always brings consequences with it.

## Free to Follow

As I conclude this chapter, on the importance of right relationships, I'm reminded about our relationship with God and how much He loves us and desires for us to experience life to the fullest. When I was a kid living in Tucson, my parents gave my three brothers and I each a duckling for

Easter. We all thought they were a neat addition to our collection of pocket-knives, firecrackers, and snakes! We built a duck pen in our backyard to keep the ally cats away, as well as to protect them from wild baseballs.

One morning, after several months, my dad broke the sad news to all of us. "Boys, the ducks have to go bye-bye. They are crammed into a small pen, walk around all day in poop, and they're not happy living like this. This isn't how they should have to live the rest of their lives." He recommended that we each gather up our duck, take it down to a small lake at the local park, and set it free. I remember setting my duck free at the lake that morning. Slowly opening up my hands, I watched it burst forth and flutter away as it skipped off on top of the water. You could feel its enthusiasm, relief, and exuberant joy as it bolted forward into a brand new life. It was finally free and was now able to live as it was created to be!

In some ways, that's how God sees us, too: people whose lives are imprisoned by our sins, squelched in our potential, and living less than we were created to be. The good news of the Bible is why Jesus came. He came to set us free from sin. He came to give us a different kind of life, an abundant life. He invites us into the God-life, and this life begins and ends with forgiveness.

Whatever our backgrounds may be, God offers each of us the gift that will set us free—forgiveness. When we receive His forgiveness for our sins, something invisible, yet very real, catalyzes in our hearts and spirits. The Bible calls this being "born again" or being "converted." As we yield the leadership of our lives over to Jesus, and receive, by faith, His gift of forgiveness, we are free to pursue a new kind of life in Christ. The God-life is eternal life, and it's one that is filled with abundance, potential, grace, enthusiasm, peace, and wholeness. It's a life that allows us to be who we were created to be.

My prayer for us is that we would open our lives to God's grace, and receive from Him this lavish gift called forgiveness. As we have freely received forgiveness from God, let us freely give away forgiveness to others who have hurt us, betrayed us, left us, or talked about us. Not only is it the right thing to do, but receiving and giving forgiveness is a gift that will keep us free from our sins and other people's sins, and free us to follow God's plan, purpose, and design for our lives.

Matthew Chapter 19

# CHILDREN: THE HEART OF JESUS

*Then little children were brought to Jesus for him to place his hands on them and pray for them. But the disciples rebuked those who brought them. Jesus said, "Let the little children come to me, and do not hinder them, for the kingdom of heaven belongs to such as these." When he had placed his hands on them, he went on from there. (Matthew 19:13-15)*

## God's Original Design

This chapter begins with Jesus and His disciples preparing to head toward Jerusalem. Jesus' ministry to the masses is winding up. The triumphal entry into the great city is right around the corner. Jesus continues to teach about healthy relationships. He hones in on God's original design for marriage: one man, one woman, in a committed life-long relationship. Although He does explain some parameters of divorce from the Law of Moses, He ultimately leads His listeners to discover how God wants to guide people not just by laws (things that are required), but by His Spirit, and with grace, forgiveness, and restoration (things that are permitted). Therefore, Jesus adds to the first-century Jewish understanding of divorce, the principles of truth *and* grace.

## Three Types of Singleness

The disciples become confused and express their fear of the possibility of being in a lifelong unhappy marriage. They react by saying it might be better to not even get married. Jesus goes on to speak about celibacy (eunuchs) and how, in some cases, remaining single is a viable alternative to marriage. He explains three types of singleness:

1.  People who are born with severe physical limitations or birth defects. Some women and men are born with physical disabilities which won't allow them to have sexual relations. Therefore, they choose to remain single.

2.  People who are single because of others. In the ancient world it was common for slaves to be castrated so they would not be tempted to go after the women in the households where they served. Even today, some women and men are "emotionally castrated" by relationships that have been abusive. Something inside of them has been "severely traumatized." This "emotional castration" sometimes hinders them from ever getting married, or staying married (unless they are healed).

3.  People who remain single by of choice. Both Jesus and John the Baptist were men who chose this route. Because of their calling,

they chose to remain single in order to dedicate their entire lives to God's service.

## The Rich Young Ruler

Jesus then has a conversation with an up-and-coming young man who has a promising future (the rich young ruler). Jesus extends a personal invitation to him to become one of His disciples and to join His group of followers. The only catch was that this young man had to leave behind the things he loved most in life: his possessions and status. Like many today, this guy wanted to have his cake and eat it, too. He said "no" to Jesus because of his craving for possessions, his longing for a comfortable life, and his yearning for an esteemed reputation among his peers. These things were more important to him than moving forward into the God-life as a new and growing disciple. The story ends with the rich young ruler saying he wanted eternal life but both of his hands were still trapped inside the cookie jar. He had no intention of changing.

## Children: The Heart of Jesus

This chapter also highlights a beautiful encounter of Jesus with some small children. The scene begins with the disciples gathered around Jesus "doing ministry." Some small children appear and want to see Jesus in person. The disciples shoo them away, insinuating that Jesus is too busy to be bothered by a bunch of kids. Jesus immediately rebukes the disciples. He calls the children close to Him and blesses them. He teaches the disciples a great lesson about God's priorities, kids, and faith.

Back in the first century, life could be tough for a kid. Even today, in some countries and cultures, it's still scary to be a child. Did you know there are places in our world that limit how many children you can have? That there are societies around the globe that go out of their way to encourage abortions? Did you know that some parts of the world see no problem with discarding a physically disabled infant in the streets or into trash bins? Some societies over-value male babies to the point where some townspeople throw away their baby girls, or sell them into prostitution. Others abuse them, use them, or refuse them dignity, love, and opportunity. Devaluing and debasing children is still pervasive in many societies throughout the world.

## My Princess

My daughter, Megan, and I experienced a situation years ago that we both will never forget. The good news is that today we both laugh, even though it wasn't funny when it first happened. When Megan was a small child, we went up to a self-serve local moving company to rent a truck. Megan was standing next to me at the counter as the clerk was getting the paperwork ready so I could have the moving truck for the day. Out of the blue, the clerk looked at me, and then sneered at Megan, and quipped, "So I see you've brought your little rugrat out to help you move." Without hesitation I responded, "Oh, no. This little girl is not a rugrat. She's a princess." It would have been good if I had left it at that, but because I was ticked, I pushed back more, and said, "As a matter of fact, I'd like you to apologize to my princess for saying that, and if you would like to talk with her anymore, please refer to her as 'princess,' not 'rugrat.'"

Needless to say, it was awkward. Megan loved it, but I couldn't believe what I had just asked the clerk to do. I felt that how I would respond to the clerk would be forever etched into the heart of my young, impressionable daughter. Years later, Megan and I still giggle over that event. But one thing's for sure, Megan remembers that I didn't let some strange person try and define her identity and speak trash-talk over her while her father stood by idly. I'm glad I chose to speak up and bless her publicly.

## Children Matter to God

The old adage "kids should be seen and not heard" couldn't be further from the truth. Children are precious to God, and they should be precious to us, too. Not just our own children, but the children who are not our own, the children who are hard to love, and the children who live far away in other lands.

Loving children can be as simple as waving to the kids in your neighborhood as you drive by, smiling at them at the grocery store, serving them in your children's ministry (if you go to church), teaching children to read in a neighborhood school, or financially sponsoring them in a developing country.

Up on our refrigerator are pictures of our children and family, as well as some of our friends and their children. Also, up on our refrigerator is a picture of Chipo Mtizwa, from Zimbabwe. She's a child we've chosen to reach out to and help sponsor. I'm sure our finances help her live a better life, but she helps us just as much. When I see her face up on our refrigerator, I think of the millions of children who could benefit from just one adult stepping up to the plate and choosing to make a difference in their lives. Children matter because they matter to God.

My prayer for us is that we would value our relationships (children, marriage, friendships) the way that God has instructed in His word. Contend for healthy relationships. Allow both truth and grace to abound. Choose to love people the way God has modeled. Embrace the vulnerable, bless the child, and include the forgotten. When we do, we are exampling Jesus, and that's not only the good life, but it's the kind of life that accurately represents Jesus to a watching world.

Matthew Chapter 20

# RECEIVING AND STEWARDING
# GOD'S GRACE

*For the kingdom of heaven is like a landowner who went out early in the morning to hire men to work in his vineyard. So when those came who were hired first, they expected to receive more. But each one of them also received a denarius. When they received it, they began to grumble against the landowner. But he answered one of them, "Friend, I am not being unfair to you. Didn't you agree to work for a denarius? Take your pay and go. I want to give the man who was hired last the same as I gave you. Don't I have the right to do what I want with my own money? Or are you envious because I am generous?" So the last will be first, and the first will be last. (Matthew 20:1, 10-11, 13-16)*

## The Kingdom of Heaven

In the opening parable of the laborers in the vineyard, Jesus unpacks some of the attributes of how the kingdom of heaven operates in this life. The kingdom of heaven is not referring to a location (up in the sky some place). It's referring to Jesus becoming "king," and men and women choosing to live under His leadership and value system. Jesus was calling people to Himself, hoping that they would begin a genuine relationship with Him, as well as live out His teachings in their lives. The centerpiece of all reality, however you define it, is and always will be, Jesus.

God's desire to establish His kingdom is part of His long-awaited plan of bringing His saving grace to humanity through the person of Jesus Christ. The kingdom of heaven is actually ushered in through four stages: (1) Jesus' public ministry, (2) Jesus' death and Resurrection, (3) Jesus' sending of the Holy Spirit at Pentecost, and (4) Jesus' return to earth in the final consummation when both heaven and earth become one at the end of the age. Currently, we are somewhere between stages three and four.

## God's Grace

One of the defining characteristics of God's system of rulership is grace. Grace is to the Christian as water is to the fish. Because we live in a culture that teaches that people who get ahead in life are those who work hard and value a strong work ethic of sweat, effort, and high performance, many struggle when relating to a God who refuses to have a relationship with us based on performance. We relate to God by grace, through faith in Jesus. Grace is an unmerited favor we receive from Jesus that brings us close to our Creator. Grace is never earned, never deserved, never worked for; it's received. It's not about trying harder; it's about opening our hearts wider and trusting deeper in His gracious invitation.

The apostle Paul said, "For the wages of sin is death, but the gift of God is eternal life in Christ Jesus our Lord." (Romans 6:23) Paul also said, "For you have been saved by grace, through faith, not of works, lest any man should boast." (Ephesians 2:8-9)

Grace isn't contractual; it's a promise. Grace cannot be owned, packaged, or stored away. Grace is a gift from God. James, the Lord's brother, said, "Every good and perfect gift is from above, coming down from the Father of the heavenly lights, who does not change like shifting shadows." (James 1:17)

Because we receive grace, as well as all good gifts from our Creator, falling into envy, jealously, and unhealthy comparisons with others isn't part of the kingdom mindset. Jesus explains in the parable of the vineyard that each of us has our own assignments from God. These assignments require certain gifts, talents, callings, challenges, limitations, blessings, and responsibilities. Competing with each other rather than looking for ways to build each other up in our attempts to serve God, only brings us down and shows that we view God's kingdom more as a land of scarcity than as a field of abundance. A life teeming with grace aids us in serving God and serving others with a sense of privilege, gratitude, and healthy perspective.

## A Lesson From the Tarmac

Recently, I was at the Los Angeles airport where  my airplane was idling out on the tarmac. Our pilot was patiently waiting for permission from the control tower to take off. Finally, we received the go-ahead to move out on the final runway, and off we went. God often reminds me of the air traffic controller in the tower who sees from a radically different and larger perspective things that a pilot cannot see. Multiple blinking radar screens, far-away aircraft, incoming jets, circling turbo-props, shifting weather patterns, and in-and-out radio communications.

When we understand that God is good and that His sovereignty orchestrates women and men as He sees fit within His vineyard, it's easier to celebrate others who appear to advance beyond us in what we define as promotions, as well as look for ways to encourage others forward in the work of the gospel. When we trust our good and "heavenly controller," we take more joy in running our own races rather than always comparing ourselves and our kingdom assignments with other people.

## Experiencing Contentment

The psalmist was on to something profound when he said, "The boundary lines have fallen for me in pleasant places; surely I have a delightful inheritance." (Psalm 16:6) Learning to be content with our lot in life and seeing God's sovereign arrangement of many of our circumstances brings tranquility, peace, and rest into our lives. God is more generous than we can imagine, and often we are more insecure than we care to admit. But when we allow Jesus to become King, and when we receive His gift of grace into our hearts, righteousness, peace, and joy become normal expressions in our lives.

## Growing in Grace

My prayer for us is that we will grow in the grace of God. Grace is not only a gift to be received, but it's a gift to be stewarded well. God never gives us grace in order for us to continue in sin or neglect. Grace is given to lead us somewhere; that place is the cross. It's at the cross that we discover who Jesus really is and, at the same time, it's the place where we find our true identity. It's at the cross that we discover who Christ has called us to be. The most effective "doing" in life flows out of a true and Christ-ordained "being." May His grace help you "be" the real you, in order that you can "do" life from the wellspring of "being."

Matthew Chapter 21

# JESUS CHRIST: GOD'S CENTERPIECE

*Jesus said to them, "Have you never read in the Scriptures: 'The stone the builders rejected has become the capstone; the Lord has done this, and it is marvelous in our eyes'? "Therefore I tell you that the kingdom of God will be taken away from you and given to a people who will produce its fruit. He who falls on this stone will be broken to pieces, but he on whom it falls will be crushed." When the chief priests and the Pharisees heard Jesus' parables, they knew he was talking about them. They looked for a way to arrest him, but they were afraid of the crowd because the people held that he was a prophet. (Matthew 21:42-46)*

## Jesus: The Messiah Has Come

Jesus, along with His disciples, enters the city of Jerusalem. He heads for the Temple for a showdown with the Temple hierarchy. Along the way, crowds have lined the city streets to see Jesus. He enters the city with a spirit of humility, riding on a donkey. Shouts of praise and bursts of adoration fill the air. Jesus is publicly recognized as God's Messiah. This "triumphal entry," as it's called, is a fulfillment of the messianic scripture promises that declare Jesus as God's one and only Son, the Messiah. Matthew wants us to see that multiple prophetic promises of the Old Testament, predicted several hundred years prior, are now being fulfilled in the person of Jesus.

As foretold, Jesus (the Messiah) is thought to be the son of David (Israel's beloved warrior-king). Men and women alike hoped to be set free from the political oppression and constant economic exploitation that surrounded them on a daily basis. People assumed Jesus would be like King David and that He would lead them out from under these difficult circumstances. The crowds waved palm branches to Him like they would to royalty. Townspeople threw their cloaks in the road like a red-carpet entrance in honor of His messianic nobility (Zechariah 9:9, Isaiah 62:11, 2 Kings 9:13, 1 King 1:33, 38, 44). Although Jesus did enter Jerusalem as a messianic king, He did not come as a king like David, or a king like Herod, or any other king in Rome for that matter. Jesus came to rule through serving and to reign through dying on a cross for the sins of the whole world.

## Entering the Temple

As Jesus enters the Temple He begins to set right the things that have gone astray from God's original design. Jesus turns the tables over as a prophetic metaphor for what's gone wrong. It's important to note that the Temple in itself wasn't the problem. In fact, it was instituted by God as a place for the Israelites to offer their sacrifices to worship God, and a place to facilitate the Old Covenant's way for them to remain in good standing with God. But throughout the years, the Temple leaders had morphed into an exclusive, religious vigilante-like group of self-serving, self-seeking, self-justifying, and self-promoting officials. These Temple elites were willing to further their personal and religious agendas through any and every means possible—even violence. Jesus came to right every wrong, and He starts with the Temple elite.

## Jesus is God's Centerpiece

While in the Temple Jesus confronts these leaders' religious corruption head on. Something that was once instituted by God centuries earlier is now a religious system in opposition to God's will and His ways. Jesus tells the parable of the two sons and the parable of the tenants to forecast God's soon-coming judgment upon the entire religious system. Jesus declares that He is the rightful Son of God, and that His ways are God's ways. To choose Jesus is to choose God; to oppose Him is to oppose the Father. As always, people are invited to change their minds, and to begin to follow Him.

Jesus concludes His encounter with the Temple officials by linking more prophetic promises and scriptures from the Old Testament to Himself (Daniel 2). He declares He is the chief cornerstone, the centerpiece of God. He affirms that God will bring judgment upon the world's system of rulership (including the Temple) and, in its place, God will establish a new system of rulership called the Kingdom of God (see Matthew 20). This new Kingdom and way of living will come through the rejection and suffering of God's messianic servant, through the triumph of the cross, and the ultimate victory found in the resurrection of Jesus.

I'm reminded again of how important it is to always allow Jesus to be the centerpiece of our lives, families, and religious organizations. In this chapter, the Temple leaders are depicted at their worst, but I bet their demise was most probably a gradual process. Even well-intentioned people can drift from what was once a "Jesus-focused mission and message" to one that becomes diluted and subtly morphs into a "me-centered mission and message" cloaked in religiosity. It can happen to the best of us.

## Drifting Out To Sea

As a boy, I remember swimming offshore many times in Rocky Point, Mexico, with my brothers. During high tide, we would take inflatable rafts out about 100 yards in the ocean hoping to catch some big waves, and then ride the breakers back to the shore. Riptides could appear out of nowhere, and you would never know what hit you. There are no signs or warnings signals because the reverse under-currents are below the waterline.

One time I was pulled down the coastline about a half-mile due to a stealth undertow. I had no idea what was happening until I tried to paddle back to shore and couldn't get in. I was scared to death because no matter how fast I paddled I kept drifting further out to sea. From the shoreline my dad tried to rescue me by running along the coastline yelling instructions on how to get back in. I finally figured out that due to the powerful and relentless force of the riptide, I had to counter it by paddling back to the shoreline in a 45-degree angle rather than trying to attack it by coming straight in. The good news is that I made it back to shore that day! I also learned that when you are rafting in the ocean it's important to always keep your eye on the shoreline and assess ahead of time if you are drifting out to sea before it turns into something serious!

The same is true with our faith. Jesus tells us in the book of Revelation chapter two "how get back to shore" in our love for Jesus when we sense our hearts are beginning to drift. He tells us to do the things that we used to do in the beginning when we first experienced His love. His advice is timeless and can save us from experiencing a "spiritual riptide."

## A Defining Moment

As a young church planter almost two decades ago, about a year or so after our church was started, I sensed we were beginning to drift off-course of our mission just a bit. Our church was beginning to be a church "for us" rather than "for those outside our walls." We were slowly becoming more "me-focused" than "others-focused." The drift was subtle, but nevertheless real. The only people who were coming to our church were transferring Christians from other churches. No one was finding Christ in our services for the first time. I sensed the Holy Spirit redirecting our church mission to be more intentional and strategic in reaching out to people who were far from God. To love God was to love people, and it would require some changes.

I vividly remember a group of people telling me that they didn't like the new direction of our church. In fact, they actually told me that because of their affluence and influence that they would leave the church, and there would be others that would leave with them if indeed I did choose to move forward in this recalibrated mission of presenting Jesus this way. Then they looked right at me and said, "Without us, this church will fail. You need us and you need our money." I told them that we were going forward with or without them, and that Grace Chapel would be a church not just for us, but for others who did not yet know Christ. I told them that if this church was built only on them, if it was built only on me, or anyone else for that matter, then I hoped it would fail.

No church should be built upon anyone or anything other than Jesus. He is our centerpiece. He's the focal point. He is everything, and He's the only thing. I told them that I believed this church was, in fact, built upon Jesus and that the Holy Spirit was guiding us forward into something better. I told them that we had drifted just a bit from God's best and that we were simply re-dialing in our hearts again in simplicity and authenticity. I told them that we would miss them but that Grace Chapel would survive without them.

## Jesus Is the Foundation

It was a sad goodbye, but a defining moment in my life, and in the life of our church. Knowing that Jesus Himself said, "He would build His church and the gates of Hell would not overcome it" was a source of great strength to me over the next few years. (Matthew 16:18) We did lose many people during that season. Although they loved God, they did not want to embrace the "loving people" aspect of our mission. What was supposed to be only a small recalibration turned into a full-blown re-start of our church from the ground up. It was hard but it was the right thing because it was the God-thing. God calls us to be both fruitful and faithful.

It doesn't matter if it's a church, a family, or your own life, as we can all drift off of true north and lose our way. Life can get busy, pressures can mount, problems can surround us, and ways of doing things can solidify and become religious routine. Before we know it, we can lose our edge, drift from our passion, or wane in our vision. It's in those moments, like the Temple leaders, that we too can pursue our own agendas for self-preservation, and before we know it we are fighting against the very thing we first fell in love with.

My prayer for us is that we keep our eyes fastened on the author and perfecter of our faith, Jesus. May God help us to not only love Jesus but to love people and love the things Jesus is passionate about. God, give us grace so that we may possess the determination and discipline to be in accountable relationships with others who will tell us the truth when they see our hearts begin to drift. Thank You for Your word that equips us, trains us, corrects us, and encourages us in Your ways. May we be surrounded by an inner circle of men and women who love God and love us, in that order, so that God's best will always be lived out in and through our lives.

Matthew Chapter 22

# TRUTHS AND MYTHS ABOUT THE AFTERLIFE

*Jesus spoke to them again in parables, saying: "The kingdom of heaven is like a king who prepared a wedding banquet for his son. He sent his servants to those who had been invited to the banquet to tell them to come, but they refused to come. But when the king came in to see the guests, he noticed a man there who was not wearing wedding clothes. 'Friend,' he asked, 'how did you get in here without wedding clothes?' The man was speechless. Then the king told the attendants, 'Tie him hand and foot, and throw him outside, into the darkness, where there will be weeping and gnashing of teeth.' For many are invited, but few are chosen." (Matthew 22:1-3, 11-14)*

## The Parable of the Wedding Feast

Jesus continues His conversation with the Temple officials. Using the parable of the wedding feast, Jesus foretells God's soon-coming judgment on the delinquent religious clergy of His time. He declares that God has rejected the old guard and is unveiling a new plan of salvation through grace in Jesus. The gospel will be open to anyone and everyone, rather than just a specific people and nation. This chapter also explains truths surrounding the Resurrection, and the great commandment to love God with all you've got (and your neighbor, too).

## God's Invitation

Jesus explains that God's invitation of good news is extended to people in two parts. First, there is the "hearing" or sensing of God's call in our hearts and minds. Second, there is the "receiving" or responding to that invitation. In the parable of the wedding feast, Jesus uses rich imagery and colorful vocabulary right out of a modern-day wedding to explain spiritual truths found in the gospel message.

We are "clothed in righteousness" and made acceptable before God because of Jesus' death, burial, and resurrection. We are made right and beautiful before God not because of what we've done, or because of who we are, but because of who Jesus is, and because of what He's done on our behalf. In ourselves, we are not righteous (right before God), but because of what Jesus did on the cross for us, we are made whole and justified (made right) before the Father. When God sees the Christian, He sees Jesus and what Jesus did for him.

Hearing the gospel invitation is important, but acting on it is what causes the spiritual catalyzation within our hearts. It's a new rejiggered heart that brings us close to God. We must both hear and respond to the gospel message. It's not truth that sets us free; it's the truth that we apply into our lives that sets us free. This is what the apostle Paul was getting at when he said:

> That if you confess with your mouth, "Jesus is Lord," and believe in your heart that God raised him from the dead, you will be saved. For it is with your heart that you believe and are justi-

fied, and it is with your mouth that you confess and are saved. As the Scripture says, "Anyone who trusts in him will never be put to shame." For there is no difference between Jew and Gentile—the same Lord is Lord of all and richly blesses all who call on him, for, "Everyone who calls on the name of the Lord will be saved." (Romans 10:9-13)

Part of responding to Jesus and His message is to refuse to be the leaders of our own destinies and to instead trust Christ and His teachings to guide us. We receive forgiveness and cleansing from sin because of Jesus' crucifixion on Calvary's cross and His resurrection from the dead.

## Heaven and Hell

As the chapter continues, Jesus talks about the reality of heaven and hell. This portion of scripture is sobering. Jesus graphically depicts what happens to those who attempt to go around the gospel message of the cross, pursuing other avenues, in hopes to make themselves right with God (and get to heaven). In the postmodern culture in which we live, valuing tolerance and relativism are prevailing core values. Therefore, making statements about absolute truth, or suggesting that the biblical worldview is the correct lens in which to frame conversations about reality, spiritual matters, and the afterlife is frowned on. I realize that talking about the certainty of hell is not a way to make friends and influence people (although talking about heaven is). Jesus' goal was always to love people right where they were, but also to tell them the truth, even if they didn't like what He had to say.

For me, the people who have helped me most in life are the ones that have really loved me but who also were willing to tell me the truth about myself, a situation, a life principle, etc., even if I didn't really want to hear it. There are lots of people who love me, and lots of people who tell me the truth, but just a handful who love me and will tell me the truth. I consider those people true gifts from God.

## God's Gift to Us

The Bible teaches that God has given Jesus Christ as a gift to us. He loves us enough to die for us, and He tells us the truth about life, death, and the afterlife. Jesus is the Bridge, the Doorway, God's ultimate sacrifice, and the stairway to heaven. He is the Lamb of God who has taken away the sins of the world. He's God's one and only Son, the Christ, the anointed one, the Messiah. Jesus declared that He was the Bread of life, the Light of the world, the Truth, the Way, the Life, the Resurrection, and the great Shepherd. The Old Testament gives us a picture of Jesus through the water from the rock, manna in the desert, the pillar of fire by night, and the cloud by day. Genesis asserts that He was a co-agent of creation from the beginning. The book of Colossians affirms Jesus as the centerpiece of the universe and the one who holds everything together. John proposes that Jesus is the Word that became flesh and lived among us. The book of Revelation tells us that Jesus is the Alpha and Omega, the First and the Last. Therefore, no man comes to the Father or gets to heaven without first going through Jesus.

## Right or Wrong?

Someone once asked me, "Chris, isn't it true that in the end those who are going to be in heaven are those people who were right? And those who are going to end up in hell are those who were wrong?" I said, "No, not at all." I explained that the Bible teaches that everyone has sinned and fallen short of God's best (glory). No one is perfect, except for Jesus. He's the only one who lived a sinless and perfect life. I told my friend that those who will be in heaven are those who were wrong, but admitted it. Those who will end up in hell were wrong too, but refused to admit it.

Make no mistake: Jesus sends no one to hell. Hell was never created for people. It was created for the devil. People were created for heaven. But when we choose to reject Jesus, we reject God's bridge and doorway to heaven. Hell is the place where people go who are wrong and didn't want to admit it and seek Jesus' forgiveness. It's a place that is far removed from heaven. Hell is where God isn't; it's a place or dimension of His absence. In essence, when a person goes to hell, they are really getting what they've always wanted: a life that has nothing to do with God or Jesus. Why would God make someone live for eternity with Him in heaven if while alive, here on earth, they want nothing to do with any vestige of Him? He wouldn't. God allows us to choose our eternity and where we will spend it. Heaven vs. hell is our choice, not God's. God doesn't force anything on anyone. He gives us what we want: either a life with God and Jesus, or a life without them. The choice is always ours.

## Good is Relative

Other friends have asked me, "Chris, what about the people who are good? You know, people who do kind things for others, for animals, or for the environment, but who don't profess to be Christians or believe in God. Is God going to send these good people to hell and let other bad people who say they believe in God go heaven?"

"Good" is a postmodern concept; it's relative. When we say "good" in this context, we often mean "wonderful humanitarian." Yes, they are "good" in comparison to other human beings. But what we fail to account for is that no one is good in comparison to a perfect and holy God. The Bible is a book of truth, and the truth of the matter is that we are not compared to other humans, but to God. Even if our behavior has been "good" from a human perspective, there's no human who is perfect, no person who's never told a lie at least once in their life, and no person who never thought inappropriately or lustfully at least once in their life. The point is that no one is perfect, and God requires perfection to enter into His presence. That's why Jesus came. He's the only one who is perfect and has lived a sinless life. That's why Jesus is able to offer His life as a sin offering for us. His sacrifice on the cross makes us right and clothes us with perfection before a just and holy God.

## The Goal Vs. the Destination

Let me also say that the goal of Christianity is not to go to heaven. That's the destination. Yes, when Christians die they go to heaven, but the goal of Christianity is spiritual transformation into Christ-likeness for the sake of others. The goal of Christianity is to be the people of God, and to become healing and redeeming agents in the earth. That's why it's so important that Christians pursue spiritual formation and Christ-likeness. Otherwise, we will lose our voice of relevance within our culture and end up being just a bunch of talking heads fixated on heaven and hell while the earth is crying out for help, hope, and healing.

## Hear and Receive

We are destined for heaven and not hell when we hear and receive the gospel message. Saying yes to Jesus is the most eternal decision we will ever make. The second-most important decision will be the attitude in which we choose to follow Jesus. Let me encourage us to all be Christ's hands and feet in the world in which we live. My prayer for us is that we would be a gracious voice of persuasion for the things in life that really matter. Let's make Jesus' name famous to a culture whose views on God range from a feeble and elderly grandparent to that of Thor, the Norse god of thunder who hurls lightening bolts down on people in anger. Let's contend for both truth and love to be the identifying marks upon our lives as we accurately portray Jesus to a watching and skeptical world.

Matthew Chapter 23

# LOVING GOD IS LOVING OTHERS

*Then Jesus said to the crowds and to his disciples: "The teachers of the law and the Pharisees sit in Moses' seat. So you must obey them and do everything they tell you. But do not do what they do, for they do not practice what they preach. They tie up heavy loads and put them on men's shoulders, but they themselves are not willing to lift a finger to move them. Everything they do is done for men to see." (Matthew 23:1-5)*

## Blind Guides

In this chapter, Jesus warns the multitudes not to follow the Pharisees and the Teachers of the Law. Jesus delivers a series of prophetic pronouncements of God's judgment upon Israel's wayward leaders. In the language of Old Testament prophecy, Jesus explains why these leaders, and the city of Jerusalem, will suffer ruination in the future.

## Living a Congruent Life

Throughout Matthew's gospel, it's made clear that God's law (Torah) was good and God-ordained. God's laws were to be honored and obeyed. That's never where the angst was with Jesus when He conversed with the Pharisees, scribes, teachers, and Israel's other legal experts of the day. Rather, Jesus was going after the big issues, such as loving God, loving your neighbor, and keeping the law while at the same time showing justice and mercy to all. Most of the religious leaders of Jesus' day were great at instructing others in how they should live their lives, yet these leaders themselves had no intention of living that way, or in helping shoulder the burdens of their fellow countrymen and neighbors. The religious officials of the day were great at loading people up with guilt, shame, and legalism. Jesus came to make people's burdens lighter. He invited women and men into a genuine relationship with Him, one that puts the soul at rest (Matthew 11:28-30).

Although not every Pharisee in Jesus' day was corrupt, many were. Jesus' biggest beef with them was their desire to lead Israel astray from God's plan, and to distract the crowds away from God's promise, the Messiah. These self-preserving political and religious officials were leading the common people of Israel astray in such a crucial moment of history. Therefore, Jesus speaks clearly, truthfully, and boldly in hopes of catapulting them onto the right path.

Even today, Jesus cares about people in the same way. He's concerned with political, economic, activist, and religious ideologies (messages) and leaders (messengers) that camouflage themselves and their message as good, when in fact they lead people away from God's best, and away from God's promise, Jesus.

## Living Out the God-life

The gospel of Jesus is a promise of a new kind of life, fueled by His Spirit, and a new system of values (Beatitudes). The kingdom of God is about living this new God-life in such a way that Jesus is king of our daily decisions and life goals. We define both our problems and opportunities through the lens of His Lordship.

As we read God's Word on a consistent basis, we will better understand who He is, and thereby better understand what values are most important to Him, and how we should live our lives. This new orientation and goal realignment produces a strong foundation of confidence in our lives, a deeper love for people and the things God loves, and a far-reaching hope that colors our future with optimism, peace, and joy. As we allow God to work in us, the natural byproduct is a life that becomes a force for good and a force for God in the world in which we live.

## Why Jesus Came

Jesus concludes this chapter by declaring that the world has abandoned God in pursuit of worshipping idols, pursuing personal agendas, and engaging in destructive and counterproductive behaviors. The consequences of sin (falling short of God's best) are devastating. They've brought alienation, isolation, and ruination to mankind, and to the relationship with the Creator. The good news of the gospel is that Jesus was sent to earth to redeem the people of the world (Israel and beyond). He has come to save the world and bring it back into a right relationship with God through His crucifixion and Resurrection. With this final demonstrative act of love, Jesus will take upon Himself the full penalty for sin. He will soon become God's sacrifice on behalf of people everywhere. Through Jesus' act of love on Calvary's cross and the shedding of His innocent blood, He will redeem mankind, and bring them back into a place where God's pleasure and purpose will shine through them (those who receive His gift).

## Obeying God Vs. Agreeing with God

As I reflect on this passage of scripture, I'm challenged to assess the condition and depth of my own spiritual life again. Jesus shares some tough words with His audience in this chapter. But many times, hard words produce soft hearts, and soft words produce hard hearts. How about you? Is your spiritual life your highest priority? Are you living a life of integrity? Is your outside person congruent with who you are on the inside? Are you willing to obey the "hard words" that come your way when God is speaking into your life? Sometimes we obey God only if we agree with Him, or if it's something that we already want to do. I've learned there is a difference between agreeing with God and obeying God. God wants us to be "obedience-oriented" rather than "result-oriented." How about you? Do you obey God or just agree with Him? Are you complying with what the Holy Spirit is saying to you about your future?

God promises to guide us into all truth (and keep us in the truth), but we must obey and not just agree with Him. If we want Bible blessings, then we have to do life the Bible way (obedience). The more we become like Jesus, the more we find our true selves. The more we become like Jesus in our values, morals, and perspectives, the more there is a likeness of Christ formed deep within us.

## Botrytis Christians

A few years ago, one of the plum trees in my backyard received too much water during a rainy spring and summer. Because of the downward slant of my yard, pools of standing water gathered around the tree well for long periods of time. This water rot caused a discoloration on the leaves of my tree. I found out later that this was a fungus called *botrytis*. My tree was designed to take in only a certain amount of water. Too much water causes disease and damage. But because there was not a natural process for the water to flow out from my tree and yard, my tree began to die from a good thing.

The same can be true of us as well. There is a little Pharisee that is waiting to be watered within all of us. We stay healthy when we love God, but the out-flow of our love must make its way into the lives of others. It's wonderful to teach what we know, but we reproduce who we are. If we are not careful, we too can become "botrytis Christians," where we become waterlogged and only focus on ourselves and God. Don't misunderstand me, as those are good things (loving God and ourselves), but it's as we share our lives and our love with others that the gospel gains credibility within our culture, and we stay healthy in the process. It's as we love our neighbors, help right the wrongs of injustice, and partner with God in being a healing and redeeming force within our communities, churches, and workplaces, that the gospel is lived out in the midst of a watching world.

My prayer for us is that we would not succumb to unintentionally morphing into "botrytis Christians" that miss God's best because we misappropriate too much of a good thing. The world doesn't care how much we know about God until they know how much we care about them. The Pharisees knew a lot, but loved little. They taught from their heads, but had no heart for others. God's love didn't flow through them. It gathered only in their "tree wells," and ended up inflicting them with "spiritual botrytis." Let's love God with all we've got, but let's demonstrate our love for Him by loving others and investing in the lives of those who have questions, needs, burdens, and pains. Freely we have received. Freely we must give away.

Matthew Chapter 24

# JESUS' PROMISES:
# ALWAYS RIGHT ON TIME

*Therefore keep watch, because you do not know on what day your Lord will come. But understand this: If the owner of the house had known at what time of night the thief was coming, he would have kept watch and would not have let his house be broken into. So you also must be ready, because the Son of Man will come at an hour when you do not expect him. (Matthew 24:42-44)*

## Jesus' Last Big Talk

In this chapter, Jesus shares His fifth and final discourse with His disciples. While sitting on the Mount of Olives, He uses symbolic and prophetic language to describe a series of events that will occur in both the near and distant future. Using the analogy of birth pains, Jesus describes the new life God desires to bring forth into a living reality. People then understood well that the birth process was filled with promise, hope, and possibility, along with anxiety, discomfort, and potential dangers.

## New Life

I remember well the day my son, Luke, was born. Being that he was our first child, my wife, Mary, and I were filled with questions, excitement, and anxiety. We spent many nights talking and planning for the birth process. We took a birthing class, read some books, and talked with experienced friends. We also spent many days dreaming about what kind of man Luke would grow up to be. (Luke is a wonderful and amazing man today). Suddenly, when we least expected it, Mary's water broke, and labor pains arrived in the middle of the night. In a matter of minutes, we were out the door, in the car, and on the way to the hospital. Luke's birth was thrilling and dangerous. After many hours of labor, Mary was rushed in for an emergency C-section. It got dicey those last few hours; it went from good, to bad, to worse, but then it ended in indescribable joy. God's promise to us was right on time. Our lives were never the same. A new life for all of us came bursting forth and ushered in a new reality.

## Jesus' Prophetic Predictions

Jesus goes on to talk about suffering, revolutions, wars, famines, earthquakes, false prophets, persecutions, God's judgment, the fall of Jerusalem, the destruction of the Temple, preaching of the gospel, His return, and the importance of remaining spiritually sharp to the end. Jesus describes a time of great trial and testing. Many will fall by the wayside and tire. Some will lose focus. God's grace and endurance will be needed in order to stand firm.

Jesus predicts what is going to happen to Him, and what is going to happen throughout the world after His death and Resurrection. He foretells that the city of Jerusalem and the Temple will be destroyed within a generation. Jesus teaches His disciples that the Temple (a place of God's power and promise) will no longer be relevant. Jesus teaches that He Himself would be the wellspring of God's grace, truth, power, and promise.

### Three Interpretations of Jesus' Predictions

Most people hold one of three main interpretations in regard to when, where, and how the events that Jesus describes in this chapter will be fulfilled.

1. Jesus is forecasting the destruction of the Temple. The Temple was symbolic of all that was wrong with Israel during this era. Jesus came to forge a new way to God. He is describing the events right before and after the Temple's demise. He's warning the disciples of what's immediately ahead so that they (and the church) can prepare spiritually, emotionally, and physically for a century of intense suffering and persecution, as well as the worldwide preaching of the gospel. Jerusalem and the Temple were destroyed in approximately AD 70. Jesus is also telling the disciples how He will ascend into heaven and be seated at God's right hand.

2. Jesus is predicating events in the far, far distant future (2,000 years or more), and describes how the final judgment and His second coming will unfold in the last days (not during the first century).

3. A blend of both of these perspectives: Jesus was describing events surrounding the destruction of Jerusalem, the Temple, and His crucifixion, resurrection, and ascension to heaven, but that He is also describing bits and pieces of future events of God's judgment and His second coming that have been unfolding over the centuries with more still to come in the future.

## Lessons to Apply

No matter what biblical interpretations we hold, or what timetables we're convinced exist within this chapter, there are lessons to apply in every culture and in every age. Today, as Christian disciples, we are called to be both fruitful and faithful within the culture in which we live. Following Jesus isn't always easy, and it sometimes will require sacrifice, endurance, faith, and courage. At times, we must press forward and upward as we make a conscious choice to live out the God-life when there is a pressure to conform to a value system and/or societal philosophy that opposes Christ and His teachings. We must be willing to experience suffering for the sake of spiritual growth. Many of us will be called to live out our lives in difficult circumstances.

Even today, people around the globe are being persecuted for their love of Jesus, some are even being martyred. Certain aspects of our culture want to anesthetize us into spiritual apathy, spiritual disengagement, or spiritual unification that centers around love, rather than on the person of Jesus, who is love. But make no mistake about it—Jesus warns and challenges us to stay alert and pursue an honest relationship with Him.

## Stay Alert

As the chapter finishes Jesus uses the analogy of a thief breaking into a house to make His point about staying alert. I remember coming home from a family campout and discovering that our home had been ransacked. Unbeknownst to us, a thief (or thieves) pried open a side window, and gained entrance into our home. As we went from room to room to see what was missing, we noticed overturned furniture, dresser drawers emptied and on the floor, food spread throughout the house, hundreds of burned matches scattered everywhere, and sadly, lots of missing possessions and heirlooms. As a family, we all talked about what we could have done to prevent this, and how we could live differently to prevent something like this from happening again.

Jesus encourages us to stay attentive, to keep our eyes fixed on Him, and to be filled with His Spirit. We're exhorted to live a circumspect life. So, how do we do that? Pray. Read the scriptures. Stay connected in a local

Christ-centered church. Keep short accounts with God. Practice self-examination. Put accountable relationships around you. Worship. Give. Serve. Stand up against injustice. Obey God, and don't just agree with Him.

## Jesus' Promises Come True

My prayer for us is that we, like the Christians of the first century, will follow Jesus with passion, conviction, and courage. Like the ancients we are called to trust Jesus and His ways for our families and our futures. The birth pangs Jesus talked about 20 centuries ago are just as real for us in our generation. Yes, Jesus was vindicated through His resurrection, and one day soon, He will be exonerated again when every promise He made will come true. In the meantime, watch and pray. Be alert. Stay spiritually fit. The day is coming, when in God's perfect timing, the world will be made right once and for all, and God's new life will become fully grown. A day will soon blossom when every eye will see Him, every knee will bow before Him and everyone will call Him Lord.

Matthew Chapter 25

# TIMELY MESSAGE, TIMELESS APPLICATION

*At that time the kingdom of heaven will be like ten virgins who took their lamps and went out to meet the bridegroom. Five of them were foolish and five were wise. The foolish ones took their lamps but did not take any oil with them. The wise, however, took oil in jars along with their lamps. Therefore keep watch, because you do not know the day or the hour. (Matthew 25:1-4, 13)*

## Timeless Truths

Jesus concludes His final discourse with His new followers by explaining three stories: (1) the parable of the ten virgins, (2) the parable of the talents, and (3) the parable of the sheep and goats in the final judgment. In the first story, Jesus uses the language of wisdom literature that's found in the book of Proverbs. By contrasting the decisions and actions of two groups of girls at a wedding ceremony, Jesus urges His listeners to choose the path of wisdom rather than a trail of foolishness. In this parable, as well as all the parables in the gospels, Jesus has the uncanny ability to not only speak into the future (in this example, the second coming and the final judgment), but to also speak right into the immediate context of His day. So, Jesus addresses His listeners with a timely and prophetic message, as well as addressing the countless generations that will follow with His timeless truths and immutable principles (like only God can).

## Jesus is God

In this story, Jesus is also declaring that He in fact is the Messiah, God's one and only son, and that the Israelite people's decision to follow Him or not, will have immediate and long-term consequences attached to it. Therefore, both in Jesus' day, and in ours, it's paramount that we too stay spiritually alert, and make our decision to follow Him. Our futures depend on the decisions we make today. Therefore, we're encouraged to remain focused on God's new work. Don't get hoodwinked. Prepare for challenges. Make the wise choices. Plan for the future. Keep your heart set on following after Jesus, and know that one day the Master will return.

## Parable of the Talents

As the chapter continues, Jesus tells the parable of the talents. Through it we learn that each of the guys in the story respond differently to God's generosity in their life. Some make wise use of the money they were given to invest on behalf of their master, and some did not. Two were loyal, and one was not.

## Grace and Consequences

God has entrusted each of us with unique talents, opportunities, challenges, time, personalities, finances, and callings. How we steward these expressions of His grace in our lives matters. He loves it when we respond to His generosity through obedience and trusting Him. He delights when we are willing to apply what we know and learn from Him along the way. And yes, in the end, we will give an account to God for how we've lived our lives, and how (or how not) we've stewarded the gifts He's given us.

At the same time, God is not up in the heavens somewhere looking down on people waiting to scrutinize their every move. Yes, stewardship matters to Him, but God also deals with us patiently and kindly. He is our loving Creator and heavenly Father who looks at us as His beloved children. Remember, God's the one that so loved the world that He gave His one and only Son to come and die for us. He is the one that sent Jesus to the earth so we could experience His love, mercy, forgiveness, and grace, and thereby be the people we desire to be, so we can live the kind of lives that are pleasing to God.

Again, Jesus is speaking to the Israelite people and leaders of His day. He uses this story to remind the people that God had originally given them great gifts, responsibilities, and opportunities with which to example and lead throughout the centuries. God had always intended to bless them as "the people of God" so that as a nation they would be a blessing to the whole world on behalf of their Creator. Jesus uses this story to illustrate how they had buried God's promises in the sand. Jesus declares God's judgment and consequences, but invites His listeners to experience a change of heart and follow Him forward into the new God-life that is unfolding.

## The Coming of Justice

The last parable in this chapter uses the analogy of sheep and goats being separated at what appears to be the final judgment. This story depicts a heavenly scene that explains how important justice is to God, and how, in the end, He will right every wrong. Yes, bad things do happen to good people, but one day God will settle every account of injustice. Not only will God deal with sin and evil, but establishing justice also means bringing things back to the way God had originally created them. Justice will not only prevail one day, but it will be the new normal. God's sovereign rule will be the new reality found on earth. In the meantime, we are to pray for God's will to be done on earth (justice) as it's being done in heaven. We are called to be part of God's answer to the world's epidemic of injustice by standing in the gap and being part of the change that God desires to see across the globe.

## Be Wise, Not Unwise

Although Jesus was using this story to speak directly to the people of His day, it also has great implications to us as 21st century Christ-followers. As I reflect on this chapter, I'm reminded of the words of the apostle Paul who said, "Be very careful, then, how you live—not as unwise but as wise." (Ephesians 5:15) If there was ever a time to live with intentionality and wisdom, it's now.

I remember as kids we used to go camping and fishing in a sleepy Mexican town called Puerto Peñasco. It was located four hours from Tucson, off Baja California. The shoreline was bordered with magnificent coral reefs that attracted all kinds of marine life. Fishing for kabria (rock bass) was the best. I often wondered when pulling one out of the saltwater why they never tasted salty, even though they lived in the ocean. In fact, everyone I knew put salt on them before they ate them!

The same is true for us too. God puts us in the midst of a culture that is tweaked and in need of great redemption. The times in which we live sometimes aren't the easiest when it comes to living life God's way. Even so, God places His Spirit in us, and enables us to be wise, even though we are in the midst of an unwise generation if we choose to walk with Him. We can be His agents of wisdom and grace to others; the choice is ours. Yes, the Bible teaches that wisdom is given to us if we ask, but it's also cultivated through the choices we make, developed through the people we choose to hang out with, expanded by the kind of books we read, fostered by the experiences we learn from, and deepened as we invest time in learning and applying what the Bible teaches.

## Understanding Wisdom

Wisdom is seeing things from God's perspective, not from our own. Wisdom is more than possessing raw knowledge or understanding. Knowledge is acquaintance with facts. Understanding is discerning how the knowledge fits together. Wisdom is putting knowledge and understanding to work by applying what we know and understand and making prudent decisions.

Wisdom can be likened to a chess player who thinks three, four, or five moves ahead. The chess master studies his options and analyzes possible future moves his opponent might make. Then, once he sees what he believes is his best series of moves, he rewinds the tape in his head to where he's currently at in the game, and makes his move. The better the chess player, the further ahead he calculates strategic scenarios in his head. The same is true in life. When we are able to see the far-reaching consequences of our actions, through a biblical lens of how a situation or a decision will most probably turn out, and then like the master chess player, rewind the video tape of life to the present, push play, and make our best decision, that's wisdom at its finest. That's what the ancient writer was getting at when he said, "A wise man sees the evil (or the consequences) and hides himself (or makes the change today). Whereas a foolish man just simply proceeds and pays the penalty." (Proverbs 27:12)

We live in a culture where the line between what's right and wrong is often blurred, but understanding the difference between what is right and wrong is really just the first step toward attaining wisdom. My prayer for us is that we would seek after wisdom with all of our heart. Let's become students of God's word. Let's practice applying what we already know and understand. Let's learn to see what Jesus is doing in the world. Let's make an intentional decision to graduate beyond living in a mindset of just what's right and what's wrong, but rather seek to understand the difference between what is wise and what is unwise, what is permissible and what is best. Wisdom is that non-negotiable quality that's so prized and so needed as we move forward into the new millennium.

Matthew Chapter 26

# CALL ME CRAZY,
# BUT LOVE MADE ME DO IT

*While Jesus was in Bethany in the home of a man known as Simon the Leper, a woman came to him with an alabaster jar of very expensive perfume, which she poured on his head as he was reclining at the table. When the disciples saw this, they were indignant. "Why this waste?" they asked. "This perfume could have been sold at a high price and the money given to the poor." Aware of this, Jesus said to them, "Why are you bothering this woman? She has done a beautiful thing to me. The poor you will always have with you, but you will not always have me. When she poured this perfume on my body, she did it to prepare me for burial. I tell you the truth, wherever this gospel is preached throughout the world, what she has done will also be told, in memory of her." (Matthew 26:6-13)*

## Final Events

This chapter lists the events of Christ's final hours. There are 10 scenes that take place.

- The plot to murder Jesus
- Jesus anointed at Simon's house
- Judas' betrayal of Jesus
- Passover with the disciples
- The Lord's Supper
- Peter's denial, as predicated by Jesus
- Prayer at Gethsemane
- Betrayal and arrest of Jesus
- Jesus before Caiaphas and the council
- Peter's denial of Jesus

The religious leaders concoct a plan to kill Jesus. He has challenged their power, confronted their injustice, and in their minds stolen the hearts of the people from them. These jealous officials reject Him as Israel's promised Messiah and have only sabotage in mind for Him.

Jesus is invited to the house of Simon the leper. Out of nowhere, a woman approaches Jesus and anoints Him with some expensive perfume as a way to honor Him. The disciples become indignant because they think it's a waste of money. Jesus explains that this woman has anointed Him for burial with her lavish gift and heartfelt love.

## Passover

Next, Judas, known today as the most infamous betrayer of all time, cuts a deal with the religious hierarchy to betray Jesus and hand Him over at an opportune moment. The Passover begins. Jesus and the 12 celebrate a 1,000-year-old-plus ceremony commemorating God's deliverance of Israel from Egypt. Each year, the Jewish people remembered how God rescued their ancestors from slavery, and how God miraculously parted the Red Sea in order to lead them forward into a new life of promise and freedom. As Jesus retold God's redemptive epic story of deliverance, He began to change the storyline. As He held up the bread and wine, Jesus brought the focus directly onto Himself. He declared to the disciples that now Israel's (and for that matter, all people's) new life, freedom, forgiveness, rescue, and redemption would come from Him, through His spilled blood and broken body on the cross. That moment must have blown the disciples away, with both fear and love, especially since Jesus invited them to participate in this "new supper" and identify with Him by taking the bread and the wine.

## Garden of Gethsemane

After dinner Jesus heads to the garden of Gethsemane, with His disciples, to pray. He's burdened with and scared of what's ahead for Him. Jesus asks His Father, if possible, to take away the cross and His death. In the end, Jesus submits to God's will for His life. He prays, "Not my will, but Your's be done." He calls out to His friends for support in His moment of crisis. Jesus finds them disengaged and asleep.

I've always thought it was amazing how Jesus, the son of God, needed friends to stand with Him in His moment of trial. I think it's fair to say that if Jesus needed friends to stand with Him, then so do we. The familiar image of the stoic Marlboro Man, all alone except for his dog, floating down the Yukon River, isn't a biblical image at all. It's really quite a sad one; it's one that represents loneliness and isolation.

As the story goes, the disciples weren't sensitive to Jesus' needs. Their "others-awareness" was not there, as they were preoccupied with themselves. This account has always challenged me to strive to be a spiritually and emotionally sensitive friend to others. I don't always succeed, but it's my goal. I've learned you never know when someone might be going through his or her own "Gethsemane" of sorts. Be it a cancer diagnosis, loss of a loved one, deep depression, spiritual confusion, wayward kids, mounting financial pressure, painful loneliness, or betrayal from a spouse, "Gethsemanes" will visit all of us—eventually.

## Identifying with the Pain of Others

It's such a gift to have (and to be) the kind of friend that walks alongside others when they find themselves in dark valleys. It was Dietrich Bonhoeffer who believed that freedom of religion didn't mean the ability to hold church services, or to preach the gospel whenever and wherever, but to identify with the suffering and pain of others, and the freedom to stand by the victims of injustice. I've watched people go through "Gethsemane seasons" in their lives. I've been through a couple myself. You really only have two choices: (1) go it alone, or (2) go through it with others by your side.

The fact is that pain is a part of life. But going through pain all alone was never God's intention. Yes, we have the Holy Spirit. But we grow best and endure longer when we are in committed relationships with others. That's one reason I appreciate the local church so much. It's not perfect, but it does provide a place for people to gather and connect in healthy and caring relationships. It's a kind of "family" that stands with people going through hard times who will pray with them as they forge their way forward in their own "Gethsemane." It's a place to be known, to be loved, to be encouraged, and to be inspired to keep on keeping on in our attempts to love and follow Jesus and His plan for our lives. May God help us be this kind of friend to others.

As the chapter continues Jesus is arrested and brought before Caiaphas and the council. These insecure and selfish agenda-driven leaders feared that God's new way that was being introduced through Jesus and His teachings, would ultimately diminish their popularity and overtake their status as Temple elites. Even though these men knew Jesus had healed the blind, fed the poor, preached God's word, performed countless miracles, and even raised the dead, demonstrating that He was Israel's true Messiah, just like their scriptures foretold, they would rather murder an innocent man than change their hearts and ways to align with the new thing God was doing in the earth.

Peter's denial of Jesus, and the torrent of tears that follow, close out this chapter. I think most all of us can identify with Peter in that we've all denied Jesus, or have been embarrassed of Him at least once in our lives. It's a horrible feeling to be a "secret agent man," and cave into peer pressure, or the need to gain approval from others and abandon Jesus in the process. But, as we will soon see, God does some of His finest work in and through the life of Peter, and He promises to do that same powerful work in us through His grace.

## Love Made Me Do It

Jesus has provided such a wonderful life for us. It's a life of great quality and unending quantity. He came to rescue, to recover, and to redeem that which was lost. This new life is offered as a grace gift to each of us. When we stop and think about all of what Jesus endured (betrayal, pain, shame, loneliness, torture, and death), how can we respond to Him except with love? Some called the woman who anointed Jesus at the dinner crazy that night, but I bet if you'd asked her she would have said, "Call me crazy if you want, but love made me do it." Ask the poor widow who dropped in her last two pennies into the offering the same question, "Why'd you do it?" I bet she would answer: "When you are all alone in the middle of the night and the only certainty in this world that you have is your faith in God, sometimes you just have to do something to tell Him that you love Him. Call me crazy, but love made me do it."

I remember just a few years back when the community of Grace Chapel had a once-in-a-lifetime opportunity to purchase a Gold's Gym located in the middle of Boise, Idaho, and turn it into a church facility. Just ask them what happens when you catch a vision of all Jesus has done for us, how He died in our place, how impacting the new life He offers is, and how He has deputized us to be His ambassadors of good news to the Boise area and beyond. If you asked them that question, I bet they would say, "How can we not give Him our all, our lives, our sacrifice, our loving service, and even our finances after all He's done for us? Call us crazy, but love made us do it." It was in the fall of 2006 that men, women, teenagers, children, and a few foundations raised close to $500,000 in cash to put toward purchasing a wonderful facility that is dedicated to worshipping and honoring God, teaching His word, training disciples and leaders (young and old), reaching out to those who are far from God, feeding the under-resourced, serving our community, building healthy relationships, and furthering His work throughout our region.

My prayer for us is that Jesus' great love for us would again penetrate our hearts and minds. May God help us see anew Jesus hanging on the cross for each of us and the responsibilities that accompany such a lavish gift. May God help us hear Jesus' whisper in our hearts and spirits: "Why did I die for you? Call Me crazy, but love made me do it."

Matthew Chapter 27

# GRACE TO THE SEEKER

*At that moment the curtain of the temple was torn in two from top to bottom. The earth shook and the rocks split. The tombs broke open and the bodies of many holy people who had died were raised to life. They came out of the tombs, and after Jesus' resurrection they went into the holy city and appeared to many people. When the centurion and those with him who were guarding Jesus saw the earthquake and all that had happened, they were terrified, and exclaimed, "Surely he was the Son of God!" (Matthew 27:51-54)*

## Jesus' Trial, Crucifixion, and Death

As this chapter begins, Jesus is delivered into the hands of Pilate, the governor of Judea, who was under the command of the Roman emperor, Tiberius. Judas experiences a change of mind (not of heart) and attempts to return the money he received for betraying Jesus. Rather than repenting, he hangs himself.

Meanwhile, the Jewish council is bent on crucifying Jesus. Because they cannot impose a death penalty for blasphemy (which is what they found Jesus guilty of in their own trial), they turn Jesus over to be tried by the Romans as a political insurrectionist. The Israelite officials accuse Jesus of being a false king, which labeled Him as a radical revolutionary, and thereby, a direct threat to Caesar's throne. Jesus refuses to defend Himself. Pilate interrogates Jesus and finds no guilt in Him. Pilate's wife is warned in a dream about Jesus' innocence, and she pleads with her husband to set Him free. Pilate caves under the peer pressure of the masses. In his feeble attempts to intervene on behalf of Jesus, he instead frees a notorious criminal by the name of Barabbas. Jesus undergoes a brutal beating, is mocked and tortured, and is sent to the cross for execution.

While suffering on the cross, Jesus forgives His executioners, cries out to God in prayer, and eventually gives up His spirit to His Father. Jesus dies. Darkness covers the land. Earthquakes erupt. Rocks shift. Tombs are opened. Dead Christians rise. The Temple curtain is ripped in two (symbolic of how the Temple's system to forgive sins is now a thing of the past). Sins are forgiven. Soldiers are converted. It's finished. Over. Done. Israel's true king, the Messiah, our Savior, has died in our place.

Later that evening, Jesus is taken off the cross and is buried in a tomb. A huge stone is rolled in front of the cave. Some of Jesus' followers watch from a distance. Roman guards are posted in front to protect against anyone from taking Jesus' body.

## The Son of God

As I share with you the highlights of this chapter, I'm reminded of the short yet profound statement that the Roman centurion made when speaking of Jesus while He was on the cross. The centurion exclaimed, "Surely he was the Son of God!" (Matthew 27:54) One of the greatest joys in life is to watch and hear people express for the very first time their understanding of who Christ is, and who Christ is to them personally. Saying yes to Jesus and trusting our life to Him is the most important and eternal decision we will ever make. Each person must experience on their own the reality of who Jesus is.

## Finding Christ

As we read the gospels, we see that some people discovered who Jesus really was early on in His ministry, while others, like the centurion, found Him at the end of His ministry. Others met Jesus at a well, on a road, near a lake, at a teaching service, on a mountain, in a synagogue, secretly at night, at a neighbor's house, in the city square, in the courtroom, in a prison cell, at a food bank, near a swimming pool, at a festival, at a construction site, at their work, at the health department, at the I.R.S., or at a park with children playing. I've met some people who meet Jesus at the top of their game. I've met others who found Him in the dregs of life. It doesn't matter if we're down and out or if we're up and out. Each of us must experience who Jesus is in our own way and at our own time. We must each come to the place where, by God's grace, we see and acknowledge that Jesus really is God's Son, and that He's asked us to believe in and to follow Him.

But the great news of the Bible is that the Holy Spirit actually helps us find God. God doesn't leave it all up to us to find Him on our own. The truth of the matter is that God is seeking us. Like an awe-struck young man in pursuit of the woman he loves, God is in hot pursuit of us. He loves us and seeks us out in all kinds of ways. Jesus said, "For the Son of Man came to seek and to save what was lost." (Luke 19:10)

## Pursued By Jesus

There are many stories of people's journey to faith. In her book *Traveling Mercies*, Anne Lamott describes how Jesus pursued her in a season of her life that was littered with pain, despair, and confusion:

I didn't go to the flea market the week of my abortion. I stayed home, and smoked dope and got drunk. I discovered that I was bleeding heavily. Several hours later, the blood stopped flowing, and I got in bed, shaky and sad. After a while, as I lay there, I became aware of someone with me, hunkered down in the corner. The feeling was so strong that I actually turned on the light for a moment to make sure no one was there—of course, there wasn't. But after a while, in the dark again, I knew beyond any doubt that it was Jesus. I felt Him as surely as I feel my dog lying nearby as I write this. I thought about my life and my brilliant, hilarious, and progressive friends. I thought about what everyone would think of me if I became a Christian, and it seemed an utterly impossible thing that simply could not be allowed to happen. I turned to the wall and said out loud, "I would rather die." I felt Him just sitting there on His haunches in the corner of my sleeping loft, watching me with patience and love, and I squinched my eyes shut, but that didn't help. Finally I fell asleep, and in the morning, He was gone. But then everywhere I went, I had the feeling that a little cat was following me, wanting me to reach down and pick it up, wanting me to open the door and let it in. But I knew what would happen: You let a cat in one time, give it a little milk, and then it stays forever. So I tried to keep one step ahead of it, slamming my houseboat door when I entered or left.

And one week later, when I went back to church, and this time I stayed for the sermon, which I just thought was so ridiculous, like someone trying to convince me of the existence of extraterrestrials, the last song was so deep and raw and pure that I could not escape. It was as if the people were singing in between the notes, weeping and joyful at the same time, and I felt like their voices or something was rocking me in its bosom, holding me like a scared kid, and I opened up to that feeling—and it washed over me. I began to cry and left before the benediction, and I raced home and felt the little cat running along at my heels, and I walked down the dock past dozens of potted flowers, under a sky as blue as one of God's own dreams, and I opened the door to my houseboat, and I stood there a minute, and then I hung my head and said, "I quit."

I took a long, deep breath and said out loud, "All right. You can come in." So this was my beautiful moment of conversion.

And like that cat, Jesus pursues each of us as well. He's following us. He's searching for us. He's standing at the entrance of our hearts and whispering. Jesus said, "I stand at the door and knock. If anyone hears my voice and opens the door, I will come in and eat with him." (Revelation 3:20) He's waiting for us to respond to His invitation.

## Grace to the Seeker

My prayer for us is that wherever we find ourselves in our journey to know God, that we would discover who Jesus really is—God's one and only Son. May we pursue Jesus as He is already in pursuit of us. Jeremiah, the Old Testament prophet said, "You will seek me and find me when you seek me with all your heart." (Jeremiah 29:13) May the Holy Spirit help us to see the evidence of God's presence that is all around us, rather than His absence. May God find us as we seek Him. He promises to accept us just like we are, with all of our foibles, imperfections, and sins. Give us eyes to see anew how You have been following each of us in the most amazing of ways. Let us hear and see Your workings in our lives, and allow that awareness to stir our hearts in such a way that we invite You into our lives by saying yes.

## Matthew Chapter 28

# SIGNED, SEALED, SOLD OUT

*Then the eleven disciples went to Galilee, to the mountain where Jesus had told them to go. When they saw him, they worshiped him; but some doubted. Then Jesus came to them and said, "All authority in heaven and on earth has been given to me. Therefore go and make disciples of all nations, baptizing them in the name of the Father and of the Son and of the Holy Spirit, and teaching them to obey everything I have commanded you. And surely I am with you always, to the very end of the age." (Matthew 28:16-20)*

## Final Moments

This is the final chapter in Matthew's gospel. It begins with details surrounding Jesus' resurrection from the dead. Earthquakes make the ground tremble. Angels appear. Stones shift. Guards quiver. Terror and joy fill the hearts of the nearby women. Jesus steps forward and instructs the women to carry news to His disciples that He's alive, and that He's heading to Galilee to meet them.

## Redemption Has Come

This climatic chapter celebrates the fact that Jesus is not only raised from the dead, but that God's great redemptive plan from the beginning of time has now been completed. Salvation has come. Sin has been forgiven. Death has been defeated. The devil has lost. Forgiveness and grace is offered to all. God's Kingdom has come. History has forever changed.

New life has burst forth over the landscape of humanity once and for all. God's new way of living and being has been ushered in with titanic measure. The tide has finally come in. Yes, Jesus is vindicated as the true Messiah, the Christ, God's one and only son. But God's redemptive story and promise to recover, rescue, and restore humanity's brokenness and alienation has become a living reality as well. "Old things" have passed away and "new things" have arrived. No longer is the way to God through upholding the laws of the Torah, the Temple, and it's leadership. Rather, a new way of "being human" and accessing God has emerged. It's now the law of faith and of grace that is provided through the death, burial, and resurrection of Jesus Christ, our risen Lord.

As the chapter unfolds, pessimism, rumors, and disbelief surface. Worldviews and dearly held belief systems are challenged (just like they are today with the Resurrection). Some scoff, but many believe. God's plan to rescue humanity and His promise to right every wrong has taken a huge leap forward toward being accomplished. (It will be fully accomplished when Jesus returns to earth, and when heaven and earth are made one).

## God's Great Summons

The chapter ends with the great commission. Christians everywhere are summoned to go out into the world and share God's great story of redemption. Jesus promises to be with us and to help us in His work. We're asked to make new disciples (which means leading people to faith in Christ and then teaching them how to obey His teachings in their daily lives). We are also challenged, as followers of Jesus, to baptize these new converts and disciples in water (which is symbolic of Jesus' death on the cross and the new life that is in Him through the Resurrection).

## Baptism - God's Spiritual Tattoo

Many of my friends have different kinds of tattoos. For most, their tattoos tell a story of some kind. For some, it signifies something they cherish. For others, it's about something they experienced in their lives or something that has value to them. Tattoos are a kind of "branding." Baptism is like that too. Baptism is the way a person is "marked out" as a Christ-follower. Water baptism is the way Jesus has asked us to identify publicly with Him and with His story that takes root invisibly within our hearts. It's the way "His name" is sealed upon us. It says we belong to Him.

## Branded By His Love

As I conclude this final chapter, I can't help but reflect on what just happened three days ago (as I write this). I, along with a large group of people, witnessed firsthand one of the most powerful water baptisms I've ever seen. While down at the Boise River, several people walked out into the river with me, and publicly identified themselves as whole-hearted followers of Jesus. They took the "brand" of water baptism upon themselves. They tattooed upon their spirits "Christ-follower."

Words can't describe what it was like to see a young Bhutanese woman step out from her past life of Hinduism and publicly identify with Jesus as her Lord and Savior. Her father, now a new Christian himself, was a Brahman priest in the Hindu religion back home in Nepal. Now, their whole family has come to Christ.

I can't fully express how moving it was to see a young married couple celebrate their one-year anniversary by choosing to make a public statement about their lives in Christ as disciples. Standing in the Boise River in knee-high water, they were baptized. Tears filled their eyes as they went under the water.

Another young woman had just accepted Christ two hours earlier in a Sunday service. She stood on the shore and boldly declared, "I don't want to wait. I'm identifying with Jesus today." God's brand was set upon her spirit.

Finally, a young man rolled his wheelchair to the edge of the riverbank while four men lifted him out of his chair, and carried him into the water. While he was being held up by two of the men standing in the water, he boldly said to the crowd, "Two years ago today, I was in a major car accident. It left me paralyzed. Today, I'm making a public statement about my future in God. I choose to identify with Jesus and the good plans that He has for my life as a follower of Jesus." The men carefully lowered him into the river and then up. Trust me, there was not a dry eye among the crowd.

## Created For His Purpose

My prayer is that each of us would meet the resurrected Jesus personally, just like the women at the tomb, and just like the disciples in Galilee. Part of being a follower of Jesus is having a relationship with Him through the Spirit. As we seek Him, God promises to reveal Jesus to us through the Holy Spirit. As we love Jesus and learn from Him, we'll grow in Him. May we be unafraid to be "branded" by His calling, and "marked out" for His purpose for our lives. One of the great epiphanies in life is discovering that we don't exist for our own purposes, but rather that we were created and exist for God's purposes. God promises to do wonderful things in and through our lives when we trust Jesus as our Lord and Savior. May God's very best be a reality in your life as you pursue Him wholeheartedly.

**Mark Chapter 1**

# GO PUBLIC WITH YOUR LOVE FOR GOD

*John appeared, baptizing in the wilderness and proclaiming a baptism of repentance for the forgiveness of sins. And all the country of Judea and all Jerusalem were going out to him and were being baptized by him in the river Jordan, confessing their sins. "I have baptized you with water, but he will baptize you with the Holy Spirit." (Mark 1:4-5, 8)*

## The Good News of the Gospel

The gospel of Mark is the shortest of the four gospels. Many theologians think it was the first gospel to be composed and that it may have been used as a resource for the other three. Written by John Mark, the gospel of Mark is a summarized documentary that focuses on concise vignettes, events, conversations, and speeches that form a colorful mosaic of the life, ministry, and mission of Jesus Christ. It speaks clearly about God, about Jesus, and about our response to God's invitation to believe in Jesus and follow Him. The events in the gospel of Mark take place primarily in the region of Palestine. This book begins with Jesus' baptism by John and ends with the crucifixion and resurrection of Jesus three years later.

Chapter one begins with the announcement of the gospel (which means "good news"). The good news is both declared by Jesus and "is" Jesus: the fulfillment of God's promises to mankind. God has sent the Messiah (which means "the anointed One"), the Son of God, Jesus, into the world, to save the world, by extending the forgiveness of sins to human beings.

## John the Baptist

Mark introduces us to John the Baptist as the forerunner of Jesus Christ. John calls upon people to wake up and smell the coffee! He sounds the siren and proclaims a stirring message of repentance followed by the act of water baptism. Repentance means doing a U-turn from going in the wrong direction and beginning to move in the right direction (which is God's path and plan). Repentance means embracing God's reality for your life.

As a response of genuine repentance to God, John tells the people that they must be water baptized. The people of Israel knew well the story of their exodus out of Egypt and their deliverance from the Pharaoh's evil grip. They remember well how they went through the waters of the Red Sea and through the desert wilderness in pursuit of God's promised land. John used water baptism as a visual image, or live drama, to illustrate their need to again flee Egypt (to leave behind their life of sin and rebellion toward God), move through the waters (be baptized and wash away their sins), and move toward the promises of God (following anew after God and His ways).

## Water Baptism

To Christians, water baptism is the public declaration of our identification with Jesus and His death, burial, and resurrection. When we get baptized, we're saying publicly that we have "died" to ourselves and have decided to "follow" Jesus. As a marriage ceremony and the exchange of wedding rings is an outward expression of an inward love and statement of commitment for a husband and wife, so too water baptism is an outward sign of an inward love for Jesus. Scripture indicates the prerequisite for water baptism is that a person has trusted their life to Jesus Christ, by faith, and wants to yield the leadership of their life to Him in an honest and ongoing relationship (Acts 2:32, 2:41, 8:12, 8:36, 9:18,10:48, 16:15, 19:15, and Romans 6:3).

## Choosing a New Path

I remember well the day I gave my heart to Jesus Christ and chose to repent and  "leave Egypt." While previously living in San Diego in the early 1980s, I had chosen a life path that I thought was the way to find happiness, solve my problems, define who I was, who I thought God was, and what place God would have in my life, if any. My life was fueled with drugs, excessive partying, and crazy living in the hope that I would find the answers to my questions, or at least haze over my problems, confusion, and pain until I did. I look back now and know that I was searching for the meaning of life and what my purpose in life was all about. In a very real way I was "lost," in that I was in the dark as to how to find the real answers to what I was seeking, for which I probably couldn't even completely articulate or identify.

With God's grace, my decision to do a "U-turn" was the single greatest decision I ever made in my life. Choosing to go a different direction (God's plan) not only changed the trajectory of my life, but saved it. On July 3, 1983, I not only chose to become a follower of Jesus, but I was water baptized the same day. I chose to trust Jesus with my life earlier that morning, in a church in Texas, and came back that evening to be water baptized. I figured there was no need to wait. I wanted to "pass through the water" and make a public statement of the old life I was leaving behind and the new life and path I was pursuing in Jesus.

## Jesus' Ministry

As the chapter continues, John baptizes Jesus in the Jordan River. God the Father affirms His love for God the Son, Jesus. The Holy Spirit descends on Jesus. Jesus' baptism ushers in a tangible, heavenly presence at the place of the baptism. It was a supernatural phenomenon that caught everyone's attention at that moment. It was like a small part of heaven intersected our earthly reality. For a snapshot in time, God's kingdom became discernible, apparent, and tangible right before the eyes of man.

Jesus is then led into the wilderness, by the Holy Spirit, to be tempted by the devil. He returns to begin His ministry. He chooses the 12 apostles and invites them to be "fishers of men." Jesus demonstrates His deity and compassion for people by launching a supernatural ministry of healing the sick, restoring lepers to health, casting out demons, and preaching the good news of the gospel. Crowds begin to come out of the woodwork to see Him.

I'm reminded again that following Jesus and pursuing His plans for our lives is the most eternal decision we can ever make. In this chapter, John calls the masses to follow, Jesus calls the 12 to follow, and the disciples call their friends to follow.

## Heaven's Hope-filled Invitation

Heaven's invitation goes out even today. The good news of the gospel is a message of repentance, grace, forgiveness, and relationship with God. God is still calling out to people and wanting to do something supernatural and significant in their lives. He asks people to trust Him.

My prayer for us is that we will embrace the good news of the gospel. When we capture a glimpse of how good God really is, trusting Him becomes a whole lot easier. I've found, in my own life, that when I'm hesitant to trust God it's because deep down I'm not confident in His goodness.

God's goodness is the foundation for trusting Him. My hope is that we will grow in our understanding of His goodness.

As a Christ-follower, I've found that one of the secrets to moving forward in my relationship with God is asking for His help to let go of the things of Egypt (my old ways) that want to hold me back and hold me captive. God gives grace to us all along the way.

Finally, if you are one who has believed in the good news of the gospel and you've asked Jesus' forgiveness for your sins, I encourage you to embrace God's plan and direction for your life. Go public with your faith and with your love for Jesus. Get water baptized. John the Baptist did. The disciples did. Jesus did. Millions of other Christ-followers have, too. Don't be a secret agent for God. Accept the call to follow. Walk in it. Be outwardly identified with it. Let go, let God, and watch what He will do in and through your life.

Mark Chapter 2

# FRIENDSHIP:
# THE FAITH OF ETERNAL FRIENDS

*And when he returned to Capernaum after some days, it was re-
ported that he was at home. And many were gathered together, so that
there was no more room, not even at the door. And he was preaching
the word to them. And they came, bringing to him a paralytic carried
by four men. And when they could not get near him because of the
crowd, they removed the roof above him, and when they had made
an opening, they let down the bed on which the paralytic lay. And
when Jesus saw their faith, he said to the paralytic, "Son, your sins are
forgiven." (Mark 2:1-5)*

## A New Value System

Jesus returns from Galilee to His home in Capernaum. Gathered inside a modest house, Jesus teaches a large group of people the importance of trusting God. The home is packed to capacity with eager listeners; anyone else wishing to hear must listen from the outside.

As Jesus was teaching, four friends arrived carrying their paralytic buddy. Desperate to see Jesus, the four friends lower their disabled friend down through an opening in the roof, right into the middle of the room. Jesus sees the genuine faith of this guy's four friends and heals the man based on that faith. Jesus then forgives the man's sins. Controversy breaks out over Jesus stating that He has the divine authority to forgive sins, just like God. The man gets up from the stretcher and walks out completely whole—a new man with a new future. The crowd gasps in amazement and glorifies God because of what they have seen with their own eyes.

## Friend of Sinners

Jesus goes on to call Levi (Matthew), a tax collector, to follow Him. Folks who are part of the religious majority of the day diss on Jesus and criticize Him for hanging out with people like Levi. In those days, tax collecting was considered a low-life job. Scum. Even today, people in our society are often unfairly judged by the jobs they have, the political ideologies they possess (or don't possess), and the lifestyle choices they embrace or find themselves trapped in.

Jesus upsets many people because He chooses to befriend men and women who are often on the fringes of society. They are the folks in the subcultures of our society. Jesus' response to His critics is plain and simple. He says He's like a doctor who's come for the sick, the outcast, and the disenfranchised. He's come to bring health to those who are physically sick and those who are sick in heart. It's amazing that the people who were most unlike Jesus liked Him the most. They enjoyed listening to Him and hanging out with Him.

Conversations about sterile religious rituals, regulations, and rules take place. Jesus explains that the new things He's teaching and the new values He's modeling don't fit into the old, stiff, religious paradigms of yesteryear.

He was encouraging the old guard and the well-meaning religious gate-keepers to be willing to grow, change, adapt, accept, love, and embrace new ways of kingdom-thinking and living. He's inviting them to join in with what God was doing rather than oppose it. The chapter ends with Jesus reiterating His deity: the fact that He is the Son of Man (a title used for God's one and only Son, the Savior, the anointed Messiah).

## The Gift of Friendship

This is such an inspiring chapter. I'm moved, whenever I read it to see the collective faith of four friends in the first story. Jesus commented on it because it touched Him, too. When I get to heaven I want to meet these four brave guys. I really want to meet the paralytic though, because he must have been a very special friend to have warranted so much love and loyalty that his four friends would be willing to rip apart a rooftop so he could encounter Jesus.

I've conducted many funerals for people in my life. During those memorial services, many endearing remarks are made about the person who is being remembered and celebrated. When recollecting the life of the person who has died, I never hear people hone in on all of the particulars that person had accomplished, how many deals they closed, how much money they made, or what kind of clothes and possessions they had. Do you know what they always talk about? They talk about their relationships and friendships.

Someone once told me to choose the kind of friends you want and then become that kind of person. That's good advice. I've also learned about friendship from times when I've not been a good friend.

## A Tucson Tragedy

I remember one friend that I had in high school. We used to be partying pals. We played guitars for hours, shared bongs of pot, and drove around late at night in his fast, tricked-out old car that was fueled by nitrous oxide. After high school, we went our separate ways. In my early 20s, I became a Christ-follower and was living in Texas. I had heard through the grape vine that my friend had become a spiritual-seeker and was talking about Jesus with folks. Rumor had it, he even went to church a few times. I went to Tucson that summer but never called him. I got too busy with my own life and the things I wanted to do while I was there. I thought several times about calling him to see if I could encourage him in his pursuit of faith, but I didn't call.

Back in Texas, six months later, I was sent a short newspaper clipping from the *Arizona Daily Star* describing how my friend had been kidnapped, robbed, hog-tied, taken out to the outskirts of the Tucson desert, and murdered execution-style with several bullets to the back of the head. I felt sick. Horrified. Haunted. I felt like a failure. In my heart, I was the epitome of a selfish pig. I learned that day what being an eternal friend was and wasn't. And I wasn't.

## Good Friends Tell the Truth

For those of you who are reading this devotional and are not followers of Jesus, I really hope you would consider becoming a Christian. I hope you know that I'm not interested in religion for religion's sake. Jesus is not religion. He is real. Eternity is real. Our decisions have real consequences. I hope you will seriously consider trusting your life to Christ. I want to be an eternal friend to you. I don't want to be like I was with my friend from Tucson, where I didn't tell you how I really feel and what I really think about life, death, Jesus, and eternity. I want to be a good friend to you; good friends tell the truth.

## The Faith of My Friends

I've also learned about friendship through my friends. Just a few years back, I had a small group of folks who were praying for me, encouraging me, believing in God for me, and even helping me out financially (as they could). I wasn't paralyzed, but I was in a paralyzing financial situation. A long story short, I worked with no salary at Grace Chapel, for one year, to help the church through a tough time. That season's now over and I'm happy about that. I know that God is my provider, but I believe the faith of my friends made all the difference in the world. My friends exampled the kind of faith like those four guys in the story. They were ripping off rooftops on my behalf.

We make a living by what we make. We make a life by what we give. I'm grateful to my friends who shared part of their lives, prayers, words of encouragement, and even their finances to help me in one of the most difficult times of my life. They are not only great friends, they're eternal friends because they helped bring me closer to Jesus and were committed to God's best in my life.

## Friendship with Jesus

My prayer for us is that we will first become friends with Jesus Christ. He's the greatest friend of all. He's a friend that will accept you just as you are and help you change into the person you desire to be. He wants to help you. He will never leave you. He forgives our sins and loves to do miracles in and through our lives. I also pray that we will be eternal friends for others that might be going through tough times and are in need of a miracle or two. Let's be the kind of friends that will help them encounter Jesus, and if necessary, do what we can to be part of the miracle in their lives.

Mark Chapter 3

# BREAKING FREE FROM FAMILY EXPECTATIONS TO FOLLOW JESUS

*And his mother and his brothers came, and standing outside they sent to him and called him. And a crowd was sitting around him, and they said to him, "Your mother and your brothers are outside, seeking you." And he answered them, "Who are my mother and my brothers?" And looking about at those who sat around him, he said, "Here are my mother and my brothers! For whoever does the will of God, he is my brother and sister and mother." (Mark 3:31-35)*

## Jesus Cures the Sick

The first several chapters of Mark's gospel show Jesus' divine command over the natural elements of the universe, sickness, disease, and demonic powers. Jesus' ministry team is galvanized as He moves forward teaching and preaching the good news of the gospel. Jesus incites controversy by healing a man with a withered hand on the Sabbath. He demonstrates the value of loving God and loving people as the highest of all religious priorities and values to uphold. Jesus challenges the status quo to love people and to do justice above staunch legalism and tradition.

Crowds gathered around Jesus primarily with the hope of being healed. As in many parts of the world today, the first century was filled with suffering, pain, disease, and primitive medical care. Doctors and medical technicians were ill-trained at best, and non-existent at worst. Life expectancy at that time was approximately 40 years of age (due mainly to the high infant mortality rate). Most families had someone in their extended circle of relationships that was afflicted with some kind of medical malady and were in dire straits because of it. With the word spreading fast through the countryside that Jesus was healing anyone and everyone, people did whatever it took for them or for their loved ones to come out and see Jesus with the hope of being cured.

## Power Over Evil Forces

Jesus' healing power was supernatural and "otherworldly." His healing power was operating at a different level and authority than just the natural medical realm. Jesus' spiritual power was not only healing sickness and disease, but it was confronting evil forces at work in people. People were becoming "set free from evil" to follow God and His plans for their lives. These evil spirits (or demons) would influence and harass folks in ways that were degrading to their humanity and counter to the way God originally created them as human beings. Jesus was turning the spiritual realm upside down. The Bible describes several occasions that when these demonic spirits even saw Jesus, they would "surrender and secede," and call out His name as the "Son of God "(which means the Messiah, God's anointed one, Israel's true king).

## Misunderstanding the Messiah

Many people were insecure and confused as to the "what" and "how" of Jesus' healing ministry. And so, even today when we don't understand something, they found it easier just to be against it. Others explained away these supernatural encounters by accusing Jesus of being in cahoots with Satan. Jesus warned them to be careful about calling God the devil. (Jesus suggests that's a sin you don't want to commit!) Still others, including His family, thought Jesus had gone off His rocker. Yet some believed that Jesus was the Messiah because they were in fact recipients of His healing touch and they had experienced genuine life change. Jesus retreats into the hills with His disciples to rest, debrief, and rally together as He forms this new "messianic movement" away from the eyes of the religious critics and naysayers.

## Family Redefined

In the midst of all of this, Jesus' family tracks Him down in order to do a type of "family intervention." They think He has lost it and has gone off the deep end. From the family's perspective, all of the rumors about Jesus are dishonoring their family name and reputation in their village. His brothers and mother were probably being asked nonstop about the things Jesus said and did. So they confronted Him.

On a cursory reading of this story, we can miss the emotional severity of this particular event. In the Western world, families are much more transient and mobile than they were in the first century, or for that matter, still are in many places of the world today. In the United States, people move from state to state all the time to take new jobs, go to school, or just for the heck of it. But in the first century, it was not uncommon for children to not only settle down permanently in the same town as their parents and grandparents, but also to live in the same house and work in the same business all their lives. So in a real sense, Jesus was upsetting the family apple-cart in regard to their expectations.

Jesus tells His brothers and mother that His mission and purpose in life is different than what they would like. He tells them that His priorities are to fulfill God's calling, which involves breaking out of the tight mold and expectations that His family has for Him. He explains to them that

His new "brotherhood" and "family" involve people who are pursuing a similar direction with their lives. This new direction includes adding new relationships and reprioritizing old ones. Jesus also explains there are even situations when we must sever some relationships altogether. Sometimes when we pursue an all-out allegiance to Jesus, relational division occurs. Jesus is once-and-for-all coming out from under the control of His family and friends to pursue God—no holds barred. His family finds this troubling.

## Leaving San Diego

I remember that when I first became a Christ-follower, many of my friends in San Diego (where I was living at the time) had lots of questions and concerns about me. I know my local drug supplier was concerned, as were some of my late-night partying pals. They thought I had lost my mind. Some thought I had become part of a cult or bizarre religious commune (it was really just a small church). My friends didn't understand what was happening inside me or the changes that were taking place. They didn't know what being a follower of Jesus entailed. I don't fault them, but I wanted to be a Christ-follower and live a new kind of life. So I chose to move away from San Diego and from the collection of friends that I had. Many of my friends were good people, but they didn't want to go in the same direction with their lives as I now wanted to go.

Initially my decision to follow Jesus brought about division and a severing of many of my close relationships. Jesus said this could happen. It did for me. It was painful and, in the beginning, lonely. But now, looking back in the rear-view mirror of life, that was one of the best decisions I ever made. Because of it the trajectory of my life was eternally altered. I'm convinced that if I hadn't changed my current set of friends I would not be a Christ-follower today.

## A New Beginning in Texas

I moved to Tyler, Texas, where I began my new life of following Jesus. I moved to Tyler because of a pastor named Bill Fowler who extended his friendship to me and told me he would help disciple me as a new Christian; and because of a church called Tyler Christian Fellowship (TCF).

TCF was, and still is, a vibrant and loving faith community of men and women who love God and love people.

Let me say that not everybody needs to make the break and sever their "San Diego" like I did. That was what God was leading me to do. I'm glad I did, and I'd do it again in a heartbeat. But everyone does need to be a part of a vibrant and loving faith community. Everyone needs to be surrounded by relationships that encourage you to follow Jesus and His assignment for your life. Everyone needs friendships that want God's best for your life and for your future. Everyone needs to be connected with friends and a faith family (local church) that cheers you forward when you fall down in your attempts to serve Jesus. Everyone needs to be surrounded with people that will pray for you and help you stay accountable in the things of faith and in the things that really matter. We need community. We need a spiritual family. We need other people who love God and love us, and in that order. It's too easy to just wax cold or freeze over in our faith. In the wrong environments, it's easy to pull away from Jesus or fall back into the destructive relationships and lifestyle habits that hold us back from God's purpose for our lives.

## Go for God

My prayer for us is that we will go forward with Jesus no matter what it costs. Even though following Jesus is sometimes difficult, and sometimes the people we love don't understand what's happening inside of us, let me encourage you to go with God. Don't punt; throw deep. Put healthy relationships around you. Be part of a local church, and be assured that God always gives us grace for each step of our journey.

My prayer is also for those of us who feel controlled by "family blood" or "friendship blood" more than we do the "blood of Jesus." Remember that we are His workmanship. We are called by God to love and serve Him because we belong first to Him. He made us in His image and likeness, and He has redeemed us by shedding His very own blood on Calvary's cross. Let go and let God. Don't be afraid to let go of the relationships that bring you down and stifle God's call on your life. Seek out and connect in relationships that will encourage you in being all that God created you to be. You'll never regret it. Just wait. Just watch. You'll see.

Mark Chapter 4

# PROCESS GROWTH:
# THE MYSTERY OF SPIRITUAL TRANSFORMATION

*And he said, "The kingdom of God is as if a man should scatter seed on the ground. He sleeps and rises night and day, and the seed sprouts and grows; he knows not how. The earth produces by itself, first the blade, then the ear, then the full grain in the ear. But when the grain is ripe, at once he puts in the sickle, because the harvest has come." (Mark 4: 26-29)*

## Jesus: The Great Storyteller

Crowds swell. Jesus teaches beside the seashore. He unpacks the parable of the Sower (which discusses four levels of spiritual growth that bring about four levels of fruitfulness). Some of the townsmen get the meaning and some don't. Although fascinated with Jesus, they are puzzled about why His particular method of storytelling sometimes camouflages the interpretation at the first hearing. The answer is straightforward. It was intentional for several reasons.

## A New Message

First, Jesus' radical message of "God's new kingdom" emerging upon the Israelite landscape was dangerous. To many, it was considered high treason and political insurrection. If Roman officials were in earshot, Jesus could be executed on the spot.

Second, the ordinary folks hearing Jesus talk about "God's good news" often misunderstood His motives and the implications of His message. Their collective understanding of the "Messiah's role" was of one who would lead and overthrow the oppressive political and military forces ruling Israel at the time. Jesus' message was completely different than they were expecting to hear. This would have frustrated most and infuriated many once they realized what Jesus was actually proclaiming.

Third, because Jesus is using organic, natural language and images to explain spiritual truths and principles, a person must first believe in God and trust Him in order to truly make sense of the parable's full meaning (John 3). There is more to the parables than just a "natural" understanding. Spiritual mystery is packed inside as well.

Jesus goes on to teach a few more parables. He elaborates on the obvious purpose of an everyday household oil lamp: illumination in the midst of darkness. Jesus reiterates that what He's teaching now privately to groups of people will soon be broadcast publicly to everyone everywhere.

## Broadcast the Right Message

I remember one time I broadcast publicly something that was supposed to be kept private. It was at our very first Sunday service at Grace

Chapel. The church began on October 31, 1993, at a local hotel in Boise, Idaho. When we advertised our "Kick-off Sunday," we (me) failed to notice that our grand opening was on Halloween, and it was the same Sunday that Daylight Saving took effect. (As you can tell, we had a few planning issues to work through!) As the service was about to begin, I dashed one last time into the bathroom. I was nervous to speak. Within a few minutes I was out of the bathroom and up front to open the service with no time to spare. After my morning talk, somebody came up to me and humorously informed me that when I was in the bathroom, before the service began, I had my wireless lapel microphone turned on and that I was broadcasting loud and clear throughout the whole congregation. At that point, I'm sure I winced. I didn't want to know, but I asked, "Could you hear me?" The guest paused and kindly responded, "Yes, loud and clear," with a twinkle in his eye and a grin on his face. Talk about being embarrassed. Immediately, I started replaying in my mind everything I said and did while I was in the bathroom. I was running the scenarios though my mind... things I might have said...sounds they might have heard...you get what I'm saying!

The purpose of a microphone is to broadcast what the speaker is saying (obviously not from the bathroom). The purpose of the gospel is not to keep it private, but to broadcast it publicly. As Christ-followers, we are to share the good news of the gospel with our friends, work associates, family members, school buddies, neighbors, and even with groups of people we don't know well. Jesus' teachings spiritually illuminate and bring focus to life with an amazing clarity.

## The Process of Spiritual Growth

Throughout this chapter, Jesus refers to spiritual growth as a "process" rather than an "event." He uses images of soil, seeds, plants, and fruitfulness to convey His insights.

Spiritual growth is more than a single silver-bullet principle. Rather, it's several things coming together, over time, that interact with each other in such a way that they produce something healthy and alive. Just like plants need a combination of vitamins, nutrients, good soil conditions, temperature, geographic location, and water to come together in the right quantities in order to produce a healthy and growing plant, so too a human heart needs the right elements and components to come together in the right doses if a person is to be the kind of disciple that is healthy, alive, and blossoming.

## Growth Under the Radar

I'm learning that one of the many elements contained in the process of spiritual growth is patience. Many times spiritual growth is happening under the surface of the soil of our hearts. If we're not careful we can become impatient with God's timing and unintentionally misdiagnose the growth process in ourselves and in others.

Growing up, I learned a simple, yet valuable lesson that illustrates what I'm talking about. One summer, in Tucson, my brothers and I got interested in gardening (which was strange, because we usually liked things that got us in trouble). We lived in a subdivision with a backyard that was surrounded by a six-foot high cement wall. We didn't want to share a family garden but, as competitive brothers, wanted our own individual gardens. In his attempt to be equitable, my dad gave each brother a 4x4 foot section in one of the four corners of the backyard where we could plant some vegetable seeds like corn and zucchini. Twice each day, we would water our little seed patch in our corner of the backyard. Being brothers, I'm sure there was some competition among us as to who had the greenest thumb and who had a possible future in farming.

Long story short, I got impatient and couldn't take the mystery any longer. I was dying to know if my seed had "germinated" or not. A whole week had gone by and nothing! Somehow I had convinced myself that my little seed should have broken through the surface by now! "Something's gone wrong," I thought. After not being able to persuade my younger brothers to dig up their seeds, I dug up mine, and wouldn't you know it, they were germinating and growing just fine. But they were growing under the surface of the topsoil. I thought growth only happened above the surface. I then tried to replant my seedling back into the ground, but failed—it died a few days later. On the other hand, my brother Matt, had patience and refused to dig up his seed. In the end, he had several nice stalks of sweet corn that summer, and I had none.

I did learn a lesson about spiritual growth (and no, I still don't have a green thumb): Just because you can't see something growing on the surface doesn't mean that the something isn't growing beneath the surface of the soil. God often does some of His best work out from under our natural eyesight. He is often working in us before external changes are evident.

## Process Growth

Spiritual growth is a process. Too often, we get a little impatient and want to see and measure change (at least I do). Some of you might be wondering about your own spiritual progress or the spiritual growth of someone you love. I'm learning that we need to be slow to make a judgment whether God is or is not working just because we can't always see it or quantify it. Yes, we should pray and do the things we know that are part of the growth process, but maybe what's happening is that it just hasn't "broken the surface yet." It might be quietly sprouting, evolving, and maturing out from under our natural eyesight. God loves to work in us through a process. Not only does the natural world work that way, but so too does the spiritual world.

It's been said that the main difference between God and us is that God doesn't think He's us! It's good for me to remind myself that God's ways are not my ways. His timing is not my timing. Why? Because I'm not God! (And neither are you!)

## Patience in the Process

Let me encourage you to be patient with yourself and with others in the process of spiritual growth. God's grace works through different processes. Everyone grows at different rates and for different reasons. Different seasons of life produce different rates of growth. In the end, we will grow and reap a harvest if we don't give up or dig up what God is doing. We plant, other's water, and God gives the growth (1 Corinthians 3:6). My prayer for us is that we will discern what part of the growth process is ours, what part is God's, and then rest and trust in Him.

Mark Chapter 5

# JESUS CHRIST:
# LORD OF LIFE, CONQUEROR OVER DEATH

*They came to the house of the ruler of the synagogue, and Je-
sus saw a commotion, people weeping and wailing loudly. And when
he had entered, he said to them, "Why are you making a commotion
and weeping? The child is not dead but sleeping." And they laughed
at him. But he put them all outside and took the child's father and
mother and those who were with him and went in where the child
was. Taking her by the hand he said to her, "Talitha Koum," which
means, "Little girl, I say to you, arise." And immediately the girl got
up and began walking (for she was twelve years of age), and they were
immediately overcome with amazement. (Mark 5:38-42)*

## The God-Man: Jesus Christ

Jesus demonstrates His power over the devil, sickness, and death. This chapter describes three supernatural events in Jesus' ministry that point to His authority as God's one and only Son, the Messiah: (1) the healing of a man tormented by demons, (2) the healing of a woman's physical body, and (3) the raising of Jarius' daughter from the dead.

In this chapter, Mark's gospel gives firsthand accounts of these spectacular and supernatural encounters that point to Jesus' deity as the Son of God. Jesus is able to perform the very same works as the God in heaven. In the first story Jesus heals a man that is tormented and harassed by demons. The man runs toward Jesus, falls at Jesus' feet, and addresses Him by name. Jesus looks at the man and asks the demon his name. The demon replies, "Legion." (A legion consisted of up to 6,000 Roman soldiers in a full military battalion, indicating that there were multiple demons harassing this man.) Jesus performs an exorcism, casts the demons out, and directs them to go into a nearby herd of 2,000 pigs. The pigs freak-out and all 2,000 run off a cliff and fall to their death. Shock and awe fill the countryside. The man is now grateful, in his right mind, and at peace in his soul. He's totally healed. Jesus sends the guy back to his village to tell everyone the good news of the gospel and what God had done for him.

## The Spiritual Reality of Evil

I remember first reading this story and coming away puzzled as to why Jesus would send a demon into a bunch of innocent animals to harm them. What did they do to deserve that? Sure, I could see casting a demon out of a human being, but cast it out into outer space or something like that; why into an animal?

Let me offer a few comments. First, just because there are weird people with bizarre ideas and theology about demons, spiritual forces, and the devil, don't discount that these things are real. They still happen today. The devil still harasses, oppresses, and torments people from the inside out and outside in. Jesus is still the answer!

About the pigs: How you answer that depends on whether you think the owner of the pigs was Jewish or Roman. The Bible doesn't say. If he was

Jewish, any Israelite knew that pigs were forbidden by God to eat or herd because they were unclean. They literally weren't kosher.

## An Invitation to the Devil

In short, a Jew had no business working with pigs. It was disobedient to God. As you read the scriptures, you'll notice that the demon asked to go into the pigs and Jesus permitted it. Jesus allowed the demon to enter the area of willful and sinful disobedience. The principle is this: The devil has permission to harass us and oppress us through the doorways of sinful, willful, and intentional disobedience to God's will.

For example, if I have pornography, illegal drugs, books on witchcraft, and stolen property in my home, then in a real way, I'm inviting the devil into my home to cause havoc in my life. In a sense I've given him authority in my life when I harbor "his property" in my home.

I remember that this was a real issue I had to address as a young Christian. After coming to Christ, I still had a few *Playboy* magazines hidden in my house, some marijuana tucked away for a rainy day, and some stolen property that I had picked up when I lived in Southern California. Once I understood this principle I threw away my magazines, flushed my weed down the toilet, and returned the stolen property to the rightful owner in San Diego.

This isn't the answer to demonic oppression every time, but it sure is a good starting place to begin the assessment process. If you feel attacked and harassed by the devil, my first suggestion is to make sure you don't have any of his stuff in your home. We invite the devil to come close when we coddle and cradle his stuff in our lives. This is what the Ephesian church got so pumped up about. Once they received Jesus, they took all the idols and books on witchcraft and burned them publicly in a huge bonfire in the city center for all to see. That's radical repentance in response to a radical faith in Jesus (Acts 19:19). These new believers took Jesus seriously and didn't want the devil to have any foothold in their new lives as Christians. They weren't superstitious, but were very serious and sharp about spiritual things.

In the second story, Jesus heals a woman with an ongoing physical ailment. She can't find any relief through her doctors. The woman reaches out and touches Jesus' outer garment as He's passing through an enormous crowd. Jesus stops and heals the woman. Once again, another God encounter takes place.

## A Funeral to Remember

Finally, Jesus shows up at a funeral of a young girl. Mourners are everywhere. The room is filled with wailing, crying, and grief. The family and close friends watch as Jesus prays for the girl and tells her to get up! Some laugh and jeer. Suddenly, color begins to reenter her face, her eyes open, she sits up, and then gets up to walk around in the room. To prove she is not a ghost, or some holograph-like hallucination, someone gets her something to eat. She starts chomping away on solid food right in front of everyone. Stunning wonder and awe fills the room.

I don't know about you, but sometimes when you read accounts like this in the Bible, you might be tempted to think, "I wonder if the girl was really dead in the first place. Maybe she was in a deep coma and everyone misdiagnosed her condition. Accidents do happen. After all, this was the first century, and although the people might have been well-meaning, they didn't have the sophisticated medical technology that we have today that can accurately identify if in fact a person really is dead or just in a coma."

## Seeing Death as a Teenager

As I reflect on the story, I vividly remember the many encounters I had with dead people while working in a hospital in Tucson, Arizona, when I was about 18. I worked in the Transportation Department. One of my job responsibilities was to transport patients throughout the hospital as needed (surgery, radiology, admissions, discharge, E.R. and sometimes the morgue). It was a very eerie and uncomfortable part of the job (at least to me) whenever we had to transport a body to the morgue.

This was the protocol at that time: When someone died, in their room or in surgery, two transportation employees would move the body down to the morgue. After covering the body with a sheet, we would use the employee elevator that was out of sight from the rest of the hospital guests and visiting family members. Our job was to hide the body from plain sight as we transported it to the morgue. Once in the morgue, we would take the body and put it into a horizontal refrigerator. The refrigerator could hold three bodies. The first few times that I had to do this a thought would enter my mind that I might be putting a live person (one who was in a coma) into the refrigerator.

Being in a room alone with a dead body, having to look at it, touch it, move it, and then lift it into a refrigerator is a very sobering experience. When someone has been dead for a few hours, there's absolutely no way of misdiagnosing it. The look, the feel, the smell, the presence—it's unmistakable. I can still picture in my mind the stiffness and coolness of those bodies as we were lifting them off of the stretchers and onto the large metal trays that held them in the refrigerator. I didn't need a medical degree or a heart monitor to confirm whether the person I was moving was dead or not. Death is unmistakable.

This is exactly the situation that Jesus walked into. It was undeniable what had happened. Everyone really knew! When you see death eye-to-eye and on a semi-regular basis, you don't forget it. Many Eastern cultures don't hide death like we do in the West. We use "employee elevators" all the time in our regular lives to shield us from the inevitable reality we will all face. Again, this was the scene for Jesus. Death was obvious and right out in the open. It must have been indescribable for the family and friends to see the dead body of their loved one resuscitated right in front of their eyes. Amazing!

## Life Over Death

My prayer for us is that we would take a moment to step back and reflect on the greatness of God; to allow the magnitude of who Jesus really is sink deeply into our hearts and souls. He's bigger than death, stronger than sickness, and the conqueror of evil. He still heals. Jesus still sets people free from the clutches of oppression and harassment from the enemy of our faith. He still can raise people from the dead, but one day, all will rise out of their graves at the final judgment and the resurrection of the dead. Every eye will see Him and every tongue will declare He is Lord over heaven, earth, life, and death.

## Mark Chapter 6

# COURAGE:
# STAND AGAINST THE SWAY OF THE CROWD

*And the king said to the girl, "Ask me for whatever you wish, and I will give it to you." And he vowed to her, "Whatever you ask me, I will give you, up to half of my kingdom." And she came in immediately with haste to the king and asked, saying, "I want you to give me at once the head of John the Baptist on a platter." And the king was exceedingly sorry, but because of his oaths and his guests he did not want to break his word to her. And immediately the king sent an executioner with orders to bring John's head. He went and beheaded him in the prison and brought his head on a platter and gave it to the girl, and the girl gave it to her mother. (Mark 6:22-27)*

## Jesus on the Move

Jesus is rejected by His family members and by the people of His hometown in Nazareth. They failed to recognize God's hand on Him and His ministry. Consequently, Jesus performs only a few miracles among them due to their criticism, skepticism, and disbelief. Belittling questions and whispered rumors surface within the small community concerning Jesus' supposed illegitimate birth (the virgin birth). People become jealous of Him and thereby take offense at Him.

Jesus continues to teach and train His 12 disciples. They gain hands-on experience in praying for the sick by anointing them with oil and casting out evil spirits by Jesus' authority. God responds miraculously as the disciples put action to their faith in God's words.

## Jesus' Identity

Speculations surface among the general public as to Jesus' identity. Some think Jesus performs miracles because He is a prophet. Others think He's the Old Testament prophet Elijah back in the flesh. Still other townsmen think Jesus is the resurrected spirit of the recently murdered John the Baptist. Just like today, lots of people have many different definitions of who they think Jesus is (and some of the definitions are wacko), rather than who Jesus says He is.

John the Baptist is beheaded in prison at the request of Herod's stripper during a party. John was earlier imprisoned for preaching the gospel and for calling the political authority (Herod) on the carpet for an immoral and incestuous relationship in which he was involved.

## Seeking the Crowd's Approval

Herod gave in to the peer pressure of the crowd. Even though he was mad at John for calling him out, he knew deep in his heart that John was right. Herod violated his conscience because of the pull of the crowd. Herod cared more about the crowd's approval than he did God's approval. Herod didn't want to look bad in front of others. He wanted the approval of his friends.

## Approval Addicts

For many years I too had some Herod-like characteristics. As kids our motto was, "It's not whether you win or lose. It's if you can look cool whether you win or lose!" Even into young adulthood, I cared very much what people thought about me (and of course, at the time, I didn't realize that about myself). Looking back I can see that it was driven by a deep fear of rejection. I gave in often to peer pressure. In short, I was an "approval addict." I've learned that behaviors of an "approval addict" come in lots of different colors:

- The workaholic who still reacts to the words of his parents: "You'll never amount to anything."
- A man who won't ever speak what's really on his mind.
- A fickle, chameleon-like person who can never stand up definitively for anything.
- A teenager who gives in to having sex even though they know better.
- A Christian who is afraid to speak out about their faith with friends at work.

These are just a few examples of how the fear of rejection and the addiction for approval manifests itself in our lives. I'm sure you could add some more examples.

Herod was a jerk, not for struggling with peer pressure, but for murdering John the Baptist. Each of us is susceptible to peer pressure. It happens to teenagers and to CEOs of large companies. It's part of being human. God wants to help us grow and heal so that we don't cave in to the sway of the crowd in those tumultuous moments that can unintentionally destroy our lives, our futures, and the lives of others in the process.

## Overcoming Negative Social Pressure

Here's a few suggestions to consider that I believe will help us in the face of full-on peer pressure. Let God occupy the highest place and priority in your life. Someone once said, "If you will fear God, you'll fear nothing else. If you fear man, you'll fear everything else."

Let people occupy their appropriate place (which is not above God). We're kidding ourselves if we think we can get everyone to like us. How could we ever accomplish that when even God can't get everyone to like Him, and He's God? When other people's opinions of us become more important than God's opinion of us, we're setting ourselves up for trouble and disappointment.

I'm not saying that we don't have feelings and that we are to somehow become so stoic and hard-hearted that we aren't affected by other people's comments and opinions of us. What I am saying is that we are not to be directed by their opinions. Rather, we're to be directed by what God says.

## Accepting God's Approval

That's why the Bible is good news and why Jesus came. He didn't come to bring another religion. Jesus came to give us an opportunity to be found. He accepts us, approves of us, and forgives us based on His merits, not ours. We are valuable to God.

My prayer for us is that we will trust our lives to Christ. Because of Jesus, we've secured God's approval once and for all. We don't have to earn His acceptance or jockey for His love. It's unconditionally extended as a gift because of the cross. The Bible says that God is our light and our salvation. Whom shall we fear? (Psalm 27:1)

My hope is that we will not look to other people to meet needs that only God can meet. Let me encourage you to concentrate on God's approval because that's what really matters in life. With Jesus' grace and truth we can experience strength and emotional fortitude in the face of peer pressure. Put God in first place and put others in the right place. Then watch how a new confidence will begin to emerge in and through your life.

Mark Chapter 7

# TRUTH, TRADITION, AND THE SUPERNATURAL WORLD

*But immediately a woman whose little daughter had an unclean spirit heard of him (Jesus) and came and fell down at his feet. Now the woman was a Gentile, a Syrophoenician by birth. And she begged him to cast the demon out of her daughter. And he said to her, "Let the children be fed first, for it is not right to take the children's bread and throw it to the dogs." But she answered him, "Yes, Lord; yet even the dogs under the table eat the children's crumbs." And he said to her, "For this statement you may go your way; the demon has left your daughter." And she went home and found the child lying in bed and the demon gone. (Mark 7:25-30)*

## The Messiah Has Come

Jesus has been healing the sick and casting out demons nonstop for several chapters. He now shifts gears and enters in to what appears to be a debate with the Pharisees over issues of Jewish practice and moral purity. Jesus explains that God wants to turn the tightly legislated rules of religious and human tradition upside-down in favor of God's message of good news (grace, repentance, forgiveness, and acceptance for everyone). It's not that the old ways were all wrong, it's that they had served their purpose. The old ways are over because Jesus the Messiah (the Christ) has come!

God is now doing something new on earth. Jesus is blowing holes into the protective iron doors of religious tradition that keep people at arm's length from God. He's draining the water from the moats of religious institutionalism that forces people to work through an ecclesiastical system and hierarchy in order to enter into a genuine relationship with God. Jesus is preaching good news and explaining that the time has come for all people to be able to draw close to God and access Him based on what Jesus will accomplish on the cross, rather than what a particular system of rules or rituals prescribe.

## It Begins and Ends with Jesus

Jesus teaches that spiritual motivations inside our heart influence our outward actions and behaviors. Like the age-old question that asks, "Which came first: the chicken or the egg?" Jesus explains that the heart is a source. If we fix the spiritual motivations inside the heart, then we can fix external actions and outward behaviors. We start the "adjusting process" inside by giving our hearts over to Jesus, by believing in Him, and by recalibrating our thinking to align with His. Jesus is the cure for a troubled and problem-filled heart. This is what the writer in Proverbs was getting at when he said, "Watch over your heart with all diligence for out of it flows all the issues of life." (Proverbs 4:23)

## Tradition Vs. Scripture

Even today, questions remain over who speaks for God. How much weight should be given to "tradition" versus "scripture" in Christian circles? Catholics place a high value on human customs and traditions. Protestants place a high value on God's Word. The Reformers of the 16th-century Reformation movement led the church out from under the off-balanced view and practice of the preeminence of human tradition as the highest divine voice that speaks as the authority for Christianity. Divine revelation through scripture should trump the traditions of human beings and their customs. In some ways this is what Jesus was telling the staunch religious guard of His day.

## People in Need

As the chapter unfolds, Jesus moves on and encounters more folks in His wake who possess great pain in their lives and that are in need of His touch and compassion. He heals the sick and disabled and restores a young girl who is harassed with an unclean spirit. Astonishment fills the air.

Before I comment on the scripture in this devotional, let me first say something about unclean spirits and demons. I think you've noticed that as we have been reading through the gospels that Jesus encounters unclean spirits quite frequently in His ministry. He sets people free by casting them out. It's as if it's all normal and part of a good day's work of ministry!

I'm not an expert on evil spirits or exorcisms, although I have prayed for many people who have been afflicted by them. I've encountered the realm of the demonic throughout my journey as a Christian. I don't con-sider myself preoccupied with the realm of evil. My focus is on Jesus and it always will be. It's been my observation that people who become preoccu-pied with demons develop spiritual dysfunctions and become a bit weird. Even so, the demonic realm is very real, then and now.

## Fascination with the Supernatural

I was first exposed to the demonic realm when I was in high school and before I was a follower of Jesus. I remember a few times in high school when some of my buddies and I would take hallucinogens, go out into a graveyard a few miles from my house in the middle of the night, and walk around reading headstones while trying to scare each other. We conducted what we thought was a séance in hopes of experiencing a "supernatural thrill." We were all young teens fascinated with the supernatural world, were a bit troubled, and addicted to adrenaline rushes.

I also remember, soon after coming to Christ in the 1980s that I once went to pray for a friend in need. I took my new wife, Mary, because I didn't want to go alone. As we entered this person's house, we found the person sitting in a corner with all of the lights in the house turned off. All of her furniture and possessions throughout the whole house was turned upside down (couch, end tables, lamps, picture frames, chairs, drapes, etc.).

You could have cut the ominous dark presence with a knife it was so thick. Fearful, and not really knowing what to do, I wondered how I had gotten my wife and I into this situation. I offered to pray for the release of the emotional and spiritual torment this young woman said she was encountering daily. I was scared. We prayed.

## What About Today?

I'm telling you this not to offer you a step-by-step checklist of what to do or what not to do or what works or what doesn't work. I'm simply sharing these experiences because I want us to see that the realm of the supernatural and the invisible world of "unclean spirits" is very real. Just because we don't see these situations as much in our culture and day-to-day lives as they did in Jesus' day and age, it doesn't mean they aren't real, or present.

## Jesus Rules Over the Supernatural World

I do know that Jesus is Lord over the spiritual and supernatural world. He still sets people free. He hears us when we pray. I know that even when I began my journey as a Christ-follower at 23 years old, I had some "spiritual rebooting" that needed to take place (and that's putting it mildly). Jesus heals us from the outside in and from the inside out. I'm not saying that every negative experience, sickness, or malady is related to the realm of the demonic. I'm just saying that some are. I can also tell you that over the years I have prayed on behalf of people that did get better—some suddenly, and some through a process.

I like the advice that James, the brother of Jesus, gives: "Submit yourselves therefore to God. Resist the devil, and he will flee from you. Draw near to God, and he will draw near to you." (James 4:7-8)

## Prayer of Surrender

My prayer for us is that we would make a decision to submit our lives to God, to yield ourselves to the Holy Spirit, and to fully embrace the teachings of Jesus with all aspects of our lives. When we are cognizant of the devil's harassment in our lives, we can resist his temptations through God's grace. Above all, we draw near to God through the person of Jesus Christ through faith, repentance, prayer, reading the scriptures, reflection, confession, giving, connecting with others in a local church, service, fasting, and worship. When we do, God's freedom becomes not just another promise but a living reality.

"If you hold to my teaching, you are really my disciples. Then you will know the truth, and the truth will set you free. If the Son sets you free, you will be free indeed." (John 8:31-32, 36)

# Mark Chapter 8

# THE JESUS TRILEMMA: LIAR, LUNATIC, OR LORD

*And Jesus went on with his disciples to the villages around Caesarea Philippi. And on the way he asked his disciples, "Who do people say that I am?" And they told him, "John the Baptist; and others say, Elijah; and others, one of the prophets." And he asked them, "But who do you say that I am?" Peter answered him, "You are the Christ." (Mark 8: 27-29)*

## Jesus: Fully God, Fully Human

This chapter begins with Jesus miraculously feeding a crowd of 4,000 people. Providing bread to people that struggle daily to make ends meet is a big deal and more than we might realize if we come from a society where food is not a daily worry. Jesus is not only the bread of life, but He's more than enough.

Jesus moves onward and soon winds up in a conversation with a group of Pharisees. They challenge Him to prove His divinity, even though they have no intention of submitting their hearts and ways to His leadership. Jesus refuses to bite their bait and moves on.

The disciples gather around Jesus for more instruction and mentoring. Jesus merges imagery from both the feeding of the 4,000 and His prior conversation with the Pharisees to explain the growing tension that's percolating in the air. Jesus' opponents sense that His agenda is bigger than just feeding and healing people. They are beginning to understand that it's a radical and revolutionary movement with undertones that threaten their power and prominence within the current religious system of their day. Jesus' vision for "God's kingdom" to be on earth as it is in heaven is one that will overturn the religious status quo. Jesus' accusers know it and want nothing to do with Him or of His inclusive God-birthed vision for humanity. In fact, they want to kill Him in order to stop Him dead in His tracks.

## Who Do Folks Say That I Am?

Jesus goes on to spectacularly heal a blind man at Bethsaida. He moves on and enters some small villages near Caesarea. Along the way, He has a conversation with His disciples regarding His identity. He asks them, "Who do people say that I am?" They respond with "John the Baptist," "Elijah," or one of the other heroic prophets. (There were lots of opinions floating around concerning Jesus.)

## Jesus' Renaissance Makeover

I think it's interesting to note that Jesus was compared to other strong, masculine, tenacious, courageous, justice-seeking, and repentance-preaching prophets. None of the popular first century notions circulating about Jesus were that He was soft, gentle, and effeminate (like He is portrayed today). Those images of Jesus weren't introduced until centuries later through various Renaissance artists who gave Him a silky white robe, blue eyes, and flowing blond hair. The Jews of Jesus' day never would have dreamed of using such images to describe the soon-coming Messiah.

Today if you would ask people in our society that question, "Who do you think Jesus is?" They would say things like:

- A good man
- A compassionate teacher
- An enlightened man, like the Buddha
- A prophet or guru
- A loving philosopher
- A caring religious leader
- A really nice guy who talked about love

Of course, sitcoms like *South Park*, movies like *The Da Vinci Code*, and various celebrities, rockers, rappers, talk show hosts, and other social activists all put their twisted spin on Jesus as well. But never mind what everyone else says about Jesus. Let me ask you, who do you say that He is?

## Liar, Lunatic, Or Lord

In today's culture people's definition of Jesus could be slotted into one of three categories: (1) liar, (2) lunatic, or (3) Lord. First, some people feel Jesus is a liar because He said He was God but really wasn't. He intentionally misled people and abused them intellectually by deceiving them with false promises and notions about Himself. He might have been a good man, but he lied. My question to the folks who embrace this image of Jesus would be: How can a person be good and be a liar? If he's a liar, then he's evil. So are we saying that Jesus is evil?

Second, some would say that Jesus was insane or a lunatic. He didn't lie to people intentionally because He really did think He was the Messiah, God's one and only Son, the second person in the Trinity, but in fact, He wasn't. He was delusional and/or mentally ill. Jesus only thought He was God. My question to folks who think this is: How can a lunatic be so instrumental in changing human history and radically affecting billions of people? Why would your closest friends (the disciples) be martyred for a concocted lie or an insane friend with a bizarre idea? They wouldn't. So are we saying that Jesus was insane?

Third, some would say that Jesus is, in fact, who He said He was: Lord. These folks believe that Jesus is the Savior of the world because they are sinners who need to be forgiven. These "forgiven sinners" (which are what Christians are) desire to not only believe in Jesus as Lord, but to follow Jesus and trust their lives to His leadership. So is He Lord and God?

What many people don't realize about Jesus is that He has to be one of these three categories: liar, lunatic, or Lord. It's not a trick question. There are no other options. Jesus never gave us the categories that popular culture offers to us (the bulleted list). As a society, we've made up those titles because we like them. People in the First century wouldn't have chosen those.

## Who Does Jesus Say He Is?

When trying to understand who someone is as a person, I think it's important to ask the person himself. Who do they think they are? What does Jesus actually say about Himself? Who does He say He is? The Bible clearly says that Jesus emphatically claimed that He was Lord. God. Messiah. Christ. Redeemer. Savior. Son of God.

As a kid, I did believe there was a God, or some higher power, out in the universe somewhere. I thought God existed in some far, far away place in the galaxy. I had heard about Jesus and believed that He was a religious teacher way back when, and probably really did heal a few individuals with some kind of ESP or a mental gymnastic trick. But I had never read the Bible or really ever talked with anyone who had. I knew lots of people who attended church, but no one who could show me, in the scriptures, the things that Jesus said about Himself. Everyone I talked with was like me: well-intentioned, but ill-informed.

## The Invitation of a Lifetime

Then one day in San Diego, when I began to hear what Jesus actually did say about Himself, I wanted to blow it off and not wrestle with it. It made me uncomfortable. (Part of it was that I liked living the kind of life that I was living and didn't want to change or have anything rain on my party.) Once I really did think about it (liar, lunatic, or Lord) someone helped me see in the scriptures that Jesus really did say that He was God. And it was clear that He (by His Spirit) was inviting me (and everyone for that matter) into a real relationship with Him.

Jesus didn't want to be a historical religious figure, or a distant god in some other solar system, or some image of a god that was a celestial kill-joy, just waiting to squash me or get down on me. Jesus was God. He was inviting me into a dynamic, alive, supernatural, peace-filled relationship that was authentic and genuine. Eventually I said yes to His offer and it has changed my life.

One of the things I've discovered along my spiritual journey is that for new understanding, learning, and growth to take place within me, sometimes it doesn't require "adding" something new (idea, concept, truth, skill) into the mix. Rather, it requires "discarding" something or unlearning a concept that I've been embracing as right or true. Often the greatest hindrance to discovery is the old paradigms and structures of thinking that invisibly trap and limit us.

## Choose Who You Will Believe

Let me encourage you again to consider, reflect, and see for yourself what the scriptures say about Jesus, and to have the courage and humility to unlearn well-intentioned yet misguided assumptions about Jesus, if you have them. Great spiritual discovery is right within your reach if you will seek, ask, learn, and unlearn.

My prayer for us is that we would honestly evaluate who we say Jesus is. It really doesn't matter what anyone else says, but what we think and the conclusion we arrive at. Let me encourage you to think deeply and honestly. The decision we make about Jesus is the most important and eternal decision we'll ever make.

Mark Chapter 9

# THE PARADOX OF TRUE DISCIPLESHIP

*They went on from there and passed through Galilee. And he did not want anyone to know, for he was teaching his disciples, saying to them, "The Son of Man is going to be delivered into the hands of men, and they will kill him. And when he is killed, after three days he will rise." But they did not understand the saying, and were afraid to ask him. (Mark 9:30-32)*

## Supernatural Transformation

This chapter begins with Jesus and three of His closest disciples (Peter, James, and John) ascending to the top of a mountain. While there, Jesus' body suddenly undergoes a supernatural transformation that radiates a brilliant white light from His physical body. The three hear heavenly voices conversing with Jesus. Other Old Testament prophets appear. The disciples' eyes are opened to the divinity of Jesus in a new way. They experience an epiphany regarding the Messiah's assignment to fulfill God's great plan on earth. They leave changed and are charged not to tell anyone.

## A Night on the Mountaintop

A while back I visited Kitt Peak National Astronomy Observatory located just outside of Tucson with my father and youngest daughter Allison. We spent an evening star-gazing and learning about our solar system from the observatory staff. The highlight that evening was peering through a high-powered telescope that magnified and illuminated the planet Saturn. Seeing it so clearly was breathtaking and hypnotic. Because of the sun's reflection, you noticed details and definition that you normally wouldn't see with just your eyes.

As we left the observatory that night, I looked back up into the sky to search for Saturn one last time. I found it, but this time it was nothing but a tiny dot in the sky with no astronomical pizzazz. But, because of what I'd encountered a few hours earlier through the telescope, I didn't (and still don't) look at Saturn the same. I projected the illuminating majesty that I had just seen a bit earlier on this tiny little dot in the night sky. Now when I look at Saturn, I see both a dot and majesty at the same time.

This is what must have happened to the disciples. They never saw Jesus the same after that encounter on the mountaintop. Yes, they saw Jesus' humanity, but they also got a glimpse of His divinity and God's glorious plan for mankind.

## Fresh Courage

As the chapter continues, the four rejoin the other disciples who are surrounded by a crowd of people and a company of religious elites. Jesus dramatically heals a boy tormented by an evil spirit. He continues to teach and mentor the 12 about servanthood, humility, sacrifice, and commitment.

Southern Arizona is home to several underground caves for those who like spelunking. When I was eight years old, my dad, brothers, and I went deep into Onyx Cave, which was a dark and damp world filled with stalagmites, stalactites, and bat droppings. I remember one adventure where after about an hour of hiking we hit a solid wall in the back of the cave. We could go no further. It was either turn back or find a new route deeper into the belly of the cave. They fastened ropes around me, gave me a flashlight, and lowered me about 15 feet into a dark, deep, and dreary cavern. My dad asked me to be a "scout" and to search for a passageway forward. It was both thrilling and terrifying.

As Jesus converses with His disciples, He ups the ante too, and tells them that they are going to need fresh courage if they are to take new ground and move forward as His followers. He tells them that, as the Messiah, He must go up to Jerusalem, die on a cross, be buried, and on the third day, rise from the dead. This is a defining moment in the lives of the disciples, as following Jesus hadn't been that hard up to that point. But from here on out, being a true disciple would become more challenging, and it would cost more. This is a time of reassessment and recommitment for the disciples. Jesus tells them that going to the next level will entail not just embracing a Christianity that is filled with blessings, but a Christianity that also endures challenges and even, at times, sacrifice and suffering.

## Following Jesus Full-On

Jesus finishes up the chapter with a challenge to serve God wholeheartedly. He warns the disciples about the danger of sin and uses outrageous hyperbole to make His point (plucking out eyes, cutting off hands). He alerts His followers to the very real danger that accompanies being a Christ-follower.

Following Jesus is not a game or some ethereal philosophy. It's a very real battle. There are evil forces that are in opposition to Christ and His followers. So be alert. Stay sharp. Pray. If necessary, be willing to struggle and suffer for the sake of spiritual growth. Endure. Stand strong. Yes, being a disciple is joyful, but it's also sacrificial and at times, difficult. But at all times, God's grace is sufficient.

We live in a culture that says Christianity exists to make us happy (because most of the time it does), and that its purpose is to provide us a life of blessing, comfort, and convenience. We're led to believe that our personal fulfillment and satisfaction is the end goal of Christianity. Many people attend churches for what they can get, not for what they can contribute. Many Christians have been hoodwinked and mesmerized by a subtle consumer mindset that is counter to the call of a true disciple. Too often, churches have become "listening centers" rather than "launching pads" for discipleship.

Jesus understands natural human tendencies, then and now. So He rallies the disciples together, and reminds them that Christianity is about a cross, and the cross is where people go to die, that death brings about new life, and new life changes the world. As we choose to lose our lives for Christ, we in fact, find our lives anew. It's one of the great paradoxes of discipleship and one of the great joys of following Jesus.

My prayer is that you and I will grow deep and strong in our faith. Let me encourage you if you are new to Christianity to move from being a convert to that of becoming a mature fruitful disciple who will go out into the world and reach others for Christ.

Mark Chapter 10

# MARRIAGE AND DIVORCE: WHAT DOES JESUS SAY?

*And Pharisees came up and in order to test him asked, "Is it lawful for a man to divorce his wife?" He answered them, "What did Moses command you?" They said, "Moses allowed a man to write a certificate of divorce and to send her away." And Jesus said to them, "Because of your hardness of heart he wrote you this commandment. But from the beginning of creation, 'God made them male and female.' Therefore a man shall leave his father and mother and hold fast to his wife, and the two shall become one flesh.' So they are no longer two but one flesh. What therefore God has joined together, let not man separate." (Mark 10:2-9)*

## Pressing Toward the Finish

Jesus prepares to make His final journey toward Jerusalem where the cross awaits Him. Once again, He's teaching scads of people spiritual truths and life principles from God's point of view. Surrounded by cynicism and fierce opposition, Jesus introduces a "kingdom value system" that is foreign to most men and women. The chapter continues with Jesus having a conversation with the 12 regarding the dangers of greed, the importance of financial contentment, the value of biblical stewardship, the need for true humility, and the reality of eternal life for those who believe in Him. Jesus explains that His death on the cross, for the sins of mankind, is imminent. He foretells His sadistic brutalization, horrific execution, and miraculous resurrection from the dead that is to come. The chapter ends with Jesus, God's one and only Son, filled with compassion, healing a blind man named Bartimaeus near the town of Jericho.

## Jesus and Divorce

Early in the chapter, Jesus addresses the topic of divorce. His opponents are trying to trap Him into saying something politically incorrect that could land Him in jail, or have Him beheaded like John the Baptist. The Pharisees were well aware that Herodias had recently divorced Philip so she could marry King Herod. (Remember: John the Baptist was executed for speaking out about their immoral relationship together—friends with benefits—and the inappropriate divorce they rigged.) Jesus evades their deceptive tricks and chooses to address the topic the way He wants to.

## One Man, One Woman

Rather than discussing the particulars regarding divorce, Jesus calls His listeners back to the book of Genesis and explains the Creator's original design and intention for marriage: one man, one woman, in a committed, life-long relationship. He explains that the two become one new entity.

Jesus' statement reminds me of the illustration of taking a glass of water sprinkled with blue food coloring and another glass of water laced with pink food coloring, and then pouring both glasses of colored water into a new glass at the same time. Together they produce purple water: the color of royalty. In essence, the two unique colors form a brand new color, which makes a brand new whole. This is a picture of marriage.

There are also other passages of scripture where Jesus addresses some specifics regarding marriage and divorce. The apostle Paul addresses marriage, divorce, and remarriage in detail in 1 Corinthians 7. As well, Malachi 3:16 talks about divorce, violence, and abuse. There are unfortunate and special circumstances that do occur where both Jesus, the apostle Paul, and others state that divorce is permitted (adultery, abuse, and abandonment). Jesus exhorts His listeners that all efforts should be made to keep the marriage covenant strong, healthy, and intact. The Christian worldview sees marriage as a covenant with God more than just a civil contract.

## Fusing Together

Once, when I was younger, I remember accepting a dare from a friend to put a freezing cold popsicle on my tongue. When I did, it instantly adhered to it. Running warm water from the kitchen sink saved me that day. I hate to admit it, but another time I stuck my tongue onto the side of a metal ice cube tray. (Don't ask me why.) The difference, this time, was that my tongue didn't pry loose with warm water. It was fused to the cold metal tray. I panicked. Long story short, I ended up ripping my tongue away real fast from the ice cube tray in hopes of freeing it. It worked, but in the process I left a layer of my skin on the freezing cold metal ice cube holder. I think this is what Jesus was getting at when he said, "What God puts together let no man separate."

When two people come together as one, in marriage, there is a real fusing and adhering that takes place. Marriage brings two people together in such a way that it isn't supposed to separate easily. They are still individuals, with their own identities, but they are one entity. The Bible says it's a mystery how it happens. Nevertheless, it does happen. In a sense, divorce is a "ripping away" of the very core of two people. Each person tears away but keeps a piece of the other person. It's incredibly painful. That's one of the reasons why even unmarried couples that are having sex with each other also experience such a deep wounding and a painful ripping inside themselves when they break up. Sex is like the glue that cements relationships together. God has designed it to work that way.

There's a famous test called the Holmes Stress Scale. It measures how much stress a human being can endure before experiencing a complete physical or emotional breakdown. The test says that if a person ever gets a score of 300, they are destined to experience a severe breakdown. Both the death of a spouse and the divorce from a spouse equal 100 points on that scale.

### Kids And Divorce

I think kids feel the "ripping," too. I know I did. My parents divorced when I was 14 and something ripped inside of me. It was devastating to witness how much pain my mom and dad went through while I was trying to deal with my own pain. I'm not trying to blame my parents' divorce for some of the stupid and crazy decisions that I made as a young person, (those were my choices), but their divorce did contribute to some emotional complications and sensitivities that my other siblings and I developed––some even into early adulthood.

### Grace Extended

My point isn't to induce guilt or shame in those that have experienced divorce. Jesus never speaks to us in words of condemnation, only in words of invitation. He always invites us to experience grace, healing, and wholeness. He weaves together our mistakes, others' mistakes that are forced on us, and pain, along with God's grace, forgiveness, and healing in such a way, that makes something beautiful in and through our lives. God is a good God and His plans for us are always good.

### Think Twice

The reason I mention my story is to challenge those of you who might be considering divorce right now to please think twice. If you find yourself in a difficult relational situation, please don't bail without seeking biblical counsel. Find some friends that love God and love you and in that order. Let these friends come alongside of you and pray with you and talk with you. Don't isolate yourself. Be courageous and endure some heartache, frustration, and pain while you work out your marriage. Find a pastor or a Christian counselor that you can talk with and that will pray with you and coach you. There's a false theology out there that says "God wants you to be happy above all things, and that He would never want you to be unhappy." That theology is not in the Bible. Problems are part of life. It actually says that, even in good marriages, you will have trouble because human beings are imperfect and they sin. Don't give up without exhausting all of the options and resources that can help you. If you must go through a divorce, you will be glad that you at least did everything humanly possible to try and work it out first.

## A Prayer to God

My prayer today is for those of us who find ourselves in the throes of marriage woes. May God give you wisdom, grace, and healing in your relationship. I pray that you will not give up. Let God help you and intervene on your behalf. My prayer is also for those of you who have experienced a divorce when it was the last thing you ever wanted. My hope is that you will receive Jesus' invitation to come close to Him and experience His promise of healing, hope, and wholeness.

Mark Chapter 11

# MOVING BEYOND
# A TAME AND DOMESTICATED JESUS

*And many spread their cloaks on the road, and others spread leafy branches that they had cut from the fields. And those who went before and those who followed were shouting, "Hosanna! Blessed is he who comes in the name of the Lord! Blessed is the coming kingdom of our father David! Hosanna in the highest!" And he entered Jerusalem and went into the temple. (Mark 11:8-11)*

## The Passover

The festival of Passover is near. Jerusalem's population begins to dramatically swell. Passion Week now begins (the time period between Palm Sunday and Jesus' Resurrection). Jesus enters Jerusalem with His cadre of 12 disciples. He's given an exuberant and royal greeting fit for a king. The red carpet is rolled out. People spread their cloaks on the dusty streets for Jesus to ride a young colt over. Shouts of praise and prayer fill the air. People salute. Women cry. Palm branches wave like banners. The crowd shouts, "Hosanna! Blessed is He who comes in the name of the Lord." The Messiah of Israel is here! People call out for God's son to save them and for every wrong to be made right.

## Entering the Temple

The next day, Jesus enters the Temple and pronounces judgment on it. Israel's religious elite are guilty of more than just "commercializing" their faith. They're trying to make a quick buck off of the out-of-towners who are desperate to buy animals to be sacrificed, on their behalf, so they can be forgiven for their sins (Mosaic Law). Jesus speaks out and condemns a more grievous and systemic issue that is under the radar of most people.

Israel was to be the light of the world to those in darkness. God told Abraham that He wanted to bless them so that they could be a blessing to the whole world. But instead of being a blessing, Israel's temple (symbolic of the current religious system), had become a burden on the people and a source of injustice to many. The religious establishment condemned and alienated outsiders rather than including and making provisions for them. Extreme religious zeal was nothing more than camouflage for political and nationalistic agendas (just like today with many of our extreme fringe movements). Instead of loving God, and loving people, the leaders loved their agenda. Rather than being a welcoming community and a bridge to the lost, the marginalized, and the outcast, Israel's elite had become a wall of exclusion with a system of inequity and privilege to the few.

Jesus blasts them out of the water. He overturns the tables in the Temple as an illustrative prophetic drama of God's pending judgment that looms if they do not repent and embrace this new God-life and value system. The chief priests hate Jesus for it and now will do anything they can to get rid of Him. This prophetic act signs Jesus' own death warrant.

This chapter highlights Jesus' role and authority as "king." He has come as God's divine agent to bring deep change within a religious system, a country, a people, the world, and even the cosmos. God's promise of new life is breaking on the shores of humanity. Nothing can stop it now.

Jesus has come to be the ransom for all of mankind. Sin is being dealt its own deathblow by the cross. Jesus' sacrifice makes it possible for people everywhere to get right with God and come close to worship Him. Jesus is the Messiah. For this moment in time, the worshiping crowd gets it right. The only problem is that they misunderstood what Jesus was really trying to accomplish in His earthly mission. Misunderstanding still happens today.

## Royal Entrance

As I reflect on this passage of scripture, I ask myself a similar question: Why do I think Jesus came? What is the point of His royal entrance into the world in the 21st century and my life? If you're like some folks, it's only to save us from hell so that we can go to heaven.

Others are like the religious leaders of Jesus' day in that they use religion as a covering to fuel political agendas and desires. We categorize certain current events as "Christian" issues, but sometimes they are driven more from political webcasts and talk shows than from the Bible or a deep conviction to live out God's new life in its totality.

## A Domesticated Jesus

Still others have settled for a domesticated Jesus. He's a nice, sweet, tame addition to already full and comfortable lives. They add Jesus to their lives rather than allow Him to rule and reign in and over them. It's like we want just a "little dab" of Jesus to make us nice people and somewhat spiritual. This is the "Suburban Christian Consumer Syndrome" that is so prolific today. All three of these maladies were happening back then just like they are today; same heart, different package.

When Jesus gains royal entrance into our lives, everything changes. I remember when I first became a follower of Jesus. He was everything and the only thing to me that mattered. Some friends back home got word about my new conversion and expressed that they were worried about me. They had heard I'd gone off the deep end. They told me that they were happy that I was no longer a wild, out-of-control partier, but they also warned me to not get too radical about this "Jesus thing." "You don't want to become an overboard religious fanatic. Don't get off-balance with this new Jesus kick you're on," they said.

I know my friends meant well. They cared about me, but they also cared that our relationship might have to change if I got serious with Jesus and they didn't. Their answer was simple: Just embrace the idea of a tame, housebroken, domesticated Jesus. Sure, go to church on Sunday and even wear a cross around your neck if you want to, but don't embrace the life-altering, value-changing, justice-focused Jesus. Believe in a god, but not that Jesus is the God of the universe who calls you to prioritize Him above everything and everyone. Talk about Jesus, but don't let Him affect your goals, your finances, your time, your relationships, your sexuality, or your decision-making. That would be too radical!

## Becoming a Radical Christ-Follower

My prayer is that we would again become radical followers of Jesus; that we would be men and women who love Him above anything. I know I'm guilty at times of domesticating Jesus and using him for my own agenda. How about you?

Let our lives be as the cloaks spread on the road that day before the soon and coming King. Let's lay down our agenda for His. Let our goals, our property, and our lives be at His service.

God forgive us for the times we trivialize our commitment to You. Forgive us for the times we say it's about You, but it's really about our agenda and us wanting our own way. Come anew into our lives, king Jesus! Turn over the tables within our hearts, like You did in the Temple, so that we might see You clearly and thereby follow whole-heartedly. Save us Jesus, and use us to help You right every wrong!

Mark Chapter 12

# OUR MISSION IN THE MARKETPLACE

*"Is it lawful to pay taxes to Caesar, or not? Should we pay them, or should we not?" But, knowing their hypocrisy, he said to them, "Why put me to the test? Bring me a denarius and let me look at it." And they brought one. And he said to them, "Whose likeness and inscription is this?" They said to him, "Caesar's." Jesus said to them, "Render to Caesar the things that are Caesar's, and to God the things that are God's." And they marveled at him. (Mark 12:14-17)*

## Messenger with a Message

Jesus continues to speak in parables to the religious elite. He begins this chapter with a story about some tenants, a vineyard, and a landlord. The parable ends in calamity. The message from the storyline is clear: God wants the people of Israel to be in an obedient and fruitful relationship with Him. Instead, Israel rejects God and forsakes His ways. God sends messengers (Old Testament prophets) time and again calling Israel back into an obedient relationship with Him. Each time, they reject the message and murder the messenger. In a last-ditch effort to communicate His heart and intentions, God sends not just an ambassador on His behalf, but His very own son. They reject Him, too. As the parable concludes, instead of listening and obeying, or at least showing respect to God's heir, they kill the Son (Jesus). The religious elite want their way and agenda more than anything else. It's either they change, or Jesus dies. They choose death on a cross for Jesus.

To reject Jesus the Son is to reject God the Father. God's original plan was to use Israel and their leaders as the fountainhead and channel for His blessings to the world. God will now move beyond Israel as the only source of influencers to shift the leadership office to Jesus' disciples as well as to the greater community of gentiles (non-Jews). His plan is to impact the world with the Messiah's message. God is serious and committed to fulfilling His plans throughout the earth.

## Collecting Taxes

Jesus' enemies hate Him for the way He talks and would kill Him on the spot if it were not for His popularity with the throngs of people. So instead they try and trap Him with a trick question regarding the subject of paying taxes. They ask Jesus if the Israelites should pay taxes to Caesar. They figure if Jesus says yes, the Jewish people would rise up against Him. He would lose their support because they believed paying taxes was an infringement on their autonomy as a people, and Rome had no right to exact taxes from them. If, on the other hand, Jesus says no, then the Pharisees would go right to Pilate and press for His arrest on charges of treason against Rome.

## Becoming a Voice of Persuasion

Jesus responds like He normally does: brilliantly. He tells them to give to Caesar what's his, and give to God what's His. He refuses to play into the carefully crafted snare. Many today have used this verse about paying taxes as support for the separation of church and state, or separation of church and politics, but that's not what Jesus is really suggesting. As a matter of fact, that interpretation did not even surface until the 1700s. Jesus never intended this phrase to indicate that we are not permitted as Christ-followers to address various social, political, and economic policies and agendas.

Christianity is concerned with the whole person; therefore, it is concerned with the whole of society as well. Everything under heaven and everything on earth is of concern to God. As followers of Jesus, we are called to not just give our verbal critiques of policy, but to be about the business of righting every wrong and living out God's new life within us by applying His system of values within our communities and cities. We are to be a force for good and a force for God in the world.

I'm reminded again how God desires for us to live an integrated life. Often we are tempted to compartmentalize portions of our lives, but in fact, we are to be "whole" people. Jesus desires to be Lord over Sunday as well as Lord over Monday through Saturday.

## Integrating Faith and Values

Some of my friends used to tell me that it was impossible to integrate their Christian faith and values into the workplace. What took place on Sunday didn't work on Monday. They told me that you would get your butt kicked in the business world if you didn't swim with the sharks and, at times, act like one yourself. "There's no place for love and turning the other cheek out in the marketplace," they said. "They'll laugh at you and will take advantage of you every time." Although I disagree, I totally understand that perspective. In fact, it was part of my business mantra as a 20-year-old in my "B.C. days" (before knowing Christ).

## Selling Books Door-to-Door

During the summer of 1983, I joined a sales company that sold books and encyclopedias door-to-door. My team consisted of eight young college-age students from many different cities throughout the southwestern United States. The owner of the company told us that we could make approximately $20,000 over the summer if we worked hard and did what we were taught in our one-week intensive sales school. It was an offer I couldn't refuse. I can't speak for everyone else, but I learned somewhere along the line that part of closing sales was going to have to include telling some white lies to customers and doing whatever it took to reach my weekly sales quota. I was convinced, that to reach my goals, I had to be a fast-talking hustler.

My team was sent to East Texas, which is just west of the Louisiana border. Showing up in Crockett, Texas, I found it to be a different world than living on the beach in San Diego, where I had just come from. My goal was to do whatever I needed to do in order to win, close sales, and make lots of money. The only problem in my "success formula" was that I had become a Christ-follower in the middle of the summer. I started feeling conflicted (which was actually God speaking to my conscience through the Holy Spirit) whenever I would make false promises or start making things up to customers in order to get the sale.

Long story short, I ended up resigning rather than getting some coaching on how to sell and close deals with integrity rather than deceit. This new paradigm shift was overwhelming to me. I didn't know how to reach my business goals while embodying a new set of values. At least to me, on the surface, there was conflict and inconsistency.

## 10 Success Principles

Integrity at any cost was new to me. In the beginning, it was easier if I could just block out "Sunday" in my mind when Monday came along. God has designed us in such a way that our conscience is really our friend rather than our foe that needs to be silenced or ignored. I didn't know what to do, but I knew that I couldn't keep doing what I was doing. Looking back through the rear-view mirror of life, I see some success principles that could have served me well if I had understood them like I do today.

Here are 10 timeless truths:

1. **"Lazy hands make a man poor, but diligent hands bring wealth." (Proverbs 10:4)** Learning to work hard and execute daily diligence will triumph in the end. It beats using deceit in the race to win. Sometimes the answer is found in simply getting up earlier than others to start your day. In Old English, the word "diligence" meant getting the strategic place in the city center to display your wares. As kids, I loved going to the swap meets, and selling junk to people, and getting money for it. The secret to making lots of money was to get a booth to sell your stuff close to the food court. To get a stand by the food court meant you had to arrive at the swap meet early in the morning while it was still dark. That's what diligence is about. It's executing the discipline to get up earlier so you can place yourself in the place with the most potential to succeed. (The early bird catches the worm.)

2. **"Ill-gotten gain has no lasting value, but right living can save your life." (Proverbs 10:2)** Money and possessions that are obtained fraudulently aren't just illegal, but they also won't build healthy self-esteem or bring about inner peace. There's a special kind of value and worth you possess when you're right with God and you treat others well. In the end, right-living actually adds to your advantage, happiness, and sense of worth.

3. **"If the ax is dull and its edge unsharpened, more strength is needed but skill will bring success." (Ecclesiastes 10:10)** You can approach tasks and assignments with hard work and fortitude, and eventually you will "bring down the tree." A dull ax works, but inefficiently, and you'll expend a lot of effort and time at it. But if you develop skill and use wisdom you'll "cut down the tree" faster and with less effort. Wisdom has an advantage.

4. **"Food gained by fraud tastes sweet to a man, but he ends up with a mouth full of gravel." (Proverbs 20:17)** There's a pull, and an appeal, to get the things we really want in life fast, even

if we have to bend rules at times. But in the end, the "sweetness" of it will wear off and leave you unsatisfied and disappointed. We may smile in public, but we frown in the mirror when nobody is watching. It feels better to be able to smile at the man in the mirror.

5. **"One man gives freely, yet gains even more; another withholds unduly, but comes to poverty." (Proverbs 11:24)** This is a counter-intuitive financial principle of how God's economy works. People who are generous and giving end up having more. Stingy folks lose out because, in their attempt to hold on, they actually miss out on some of the richest rewards of life. This principle is at the very heart of why tithing, giving to the poor, and sharing with others produces increase in our lives.

6. **"A tyrannical ruler lacks judgment, but he who hates ill-gotten gain will enjoy a long life." (Proverbs 28:16)** Leaders lack judgment when they compromise values for short-term profits. Sometimes we win just by staying in the race longer than our competitors and building a stellar reputation. It's a modified principle of "The Tortoise and Hare." People love to do business with those who have a long track record of integrity and honesty. Long-standing ethical qualities, in a person or organization, produce trust. Trust is non-negotiable for success in today's world.

7. **"I am sending you out like sheep among wolves. Therefore be as shrewd as snakes and as innocent as doves." (Matthew 10:16)** Jesus never intended for Christ-followers to lack discernment, good judgment, rational thinking, and smart decision-making abilities. We can demonstrate both a gracious and generous spirit and possess a strategic and shrewd intelligence at the same time. As people we can be both/and rather than either/or.

8. **"I have seen something else under the sun: The race is not to the swift or the battle to the strong, nor does food come to the wise or wealth to the brilliant or favor to the learned; but time and chance happen to them all." (Ecclesiastes 9:11)**

The formula for success is not always leveraged on the side of the smartest, strongest, or the wealthiest. Rather, it's more about good timing and capitalizing on opportunity. Over a lifetime, we are all given huge quantities of time and unique opportunities along our journey. The secret is to recognize opportunities when they come and then move on them. Opportunities are like visitors; welcome them in when they come knocking because they might not return our way again.

9. **"Do you see a man skilled in his work? He will serve before kings; he will not serve before obscure men." (Proverbs 22:29)** Thank God for your strengths, passions, and gifts, but don't stop there. Heart is not enough. We must be willing to do the homework and the hard work to develop our gifts, talents, and skills. Malcolm Gladwell calls this "The 10,000 Hour Rule." Research states that most successful people have spent at least 10,000 hours practicing and sharpening their skills and career acumen. Go to school. Take lessons. Find a mentor. Read. Get engaged in the hands-on learning process. Practice. Practice. Practice. In the end, that, coupled with your passion and natural giftedness, and with God's grace, will more than likely leave you in a place you never imagined 10,000 hours earlier.

10. **"Unless the Lord builds the house, they labor in vain who build it; unless the Lord guards the city, the watchman keeps awake in vain. It is vain for you to rise up early, to retire late, to eat the bread of painful labors; for He gives to His beloved even in his sleep." (Psalm 127:1-2)** As Christ-followers, we believe that God is in control of our lives. He knows our needs. He cares. He provides, and at times He will ask us to trust Him in the process. Every time we trust Him we'll grow in our ability to lean more into Him. Practice makes perfect. To trust God means to trust His character. He is good and can only do good things for you. To trust God means to trust His values and the way He says life is supposed to work. Even if some of His values are counter-

intuitive, God knows best. Trusting God means going by what we know God says is right, not by how we feel. Every promise from God comes true. We must always remember that the truest things about our circumstances are what God says about them.

As you can see, it all comes down to an issue of faith. Which system of success do we really trust? Do we trust our old set of success principles, or do we trust God's principles? God desires for us to be successful in life. Part of true success is being able to look at ourselves in the mirror. From God's perspective, in order to be successful, we must be integrated. Our values must be in alignment with God's. Our inner values must be congruent with our outer behavior as well. One of the most confusing representations of Christianity today are people who believe in Jesus, say they are followers of Him, and yet possess a mean-spirited, selfish, non-Christ-like set of values and practices in the workplace.

## God Desires to Build Christ in Us

The good news is that God will help us accomplish this by forming Christ in us little by little. One of the jobs of the Holy Spirit is to shape and fashion our character into the likeness of our Savior, Jesus Christ.

My prayer for us is that we would be successful and influential in the workplace wherever our feet take us. May our Sunday morning reflections about Jesus carry over into our Monday morning business dealings. God, please help us to better integrate our life of faith with our mission in the marketplace. We know the world is watching. Help us reflect You accurately. Teach us. Mold us. Empower us. Let us make Your name famous in the marketplace.

Mark Chapter 13

# PLAN FOR 100 YEARS,
# BUT LIVE AS IF YOU HAD ONLY ONE

*And as he came out of the temple, one of his disciples said to him,
"Look, Teacher, what wonderful stones and what wonderful buildings!" And Jesus said to him, "Do you see these great buildings? There
will not be left here one stone upon another that will not be thrown
down." And as he sat on the Mount of Olives opposite the temple,
Peter and James and John and Andrew asked him privately, "Tell us,
when will these things be, and what will be the sign when all these
things are about to be accomplished?" And Jesus began to say to them,
"See that no one leads you astray. Many will come in my name, saying, 'I am he!' and they will lead many astray. And when you hear of
wars and rumors of wars, do not be alarmed. This must take place,
but the end is not yet. For nation will rise against nation, and kingdom against kingdom. There will be earthquakes in various places;
there will be famines. These are but the beginning of the birth pains."
(Mark 13:1-8)*

## Impending Challenges Ahead

This chapter begins with Jesus forecasting judgment on the land. He predicts the destruction of the Temple and challenges the disciples to be spiritually alert and prepared to suffer for being Christ-followers in the midst of a culture that is hostile toward Christianity. Jesus tells the disciples that God's plan is to bring about a new world and a new creation, but that there will be challenges along the way. He tells them to take heart. To be encouraged. To trust God in the midst of difficulty. Jesus' gospel message sets in motion, once and for all, God's plan to accomplish His purposes on the earth and within humanity.

There are different interpretations regarding this chapter where Jesus talks about the destruction of the Temple, the signs of the close of the age, the abomination of desolation, and the coming of the Son of Man. Some have suggested this chapter is about the end of world and they project its meaning and implications far into the future. Even today, lots of people are more consumed with end-times charts, graphs, and sensationalistic discussions of the Antichrist than they are about preaching the gospel, feeding the hungry, clothing the poor, and righting social wrongs and injustices. They argue, "If the world is going to end soon, why even try engaging society and helping humanity by being a force for good and for God?" If you ask me, that sounds a bit depressing and fatalistic.

## Gaining the Right Perspective

While living in Tyler, I visited with an older man who shared some of his life story with me concerning his infatuation with end-times theology when he was younger. He told me, "I don't even remember how it all started, but I ended up off-balance." This gray-haired gentleman began to unload his woes. He explained that because he thought the world was going to end real soon, he never saved money for his retirement, never bothered to develop his career by either going to school or being mentored by someone, or ever made any deep friendships. "Why would you go through all that effort if it's all for naught?" he told me. He went on to describe that he was known among his friends for all the things he stood against rather than what he stood for. But his eyes winced when he talked about his kids. He continued, "They only heard in our church and home about a God who was angry and who was anxious to come back and obliterate everything and everyone. It distorted their view of God." He continued, "But my biggest regret is what my theology did to my kids' future. I never dreamed with them about their future because I thought they would never have one."

## Balancing Juxtaposed Perspectives

He concluded by telling me that he was now trying to do the things that he should have been doing all along. He hoped the consequences of his shortcomings could be reversed and would hopefully serve as wise advice to me, a young Christ-follower. They did. And because of that story, I've adopted a mantra over the years that I try and live by: Plan like you are going to live for 100 years. Live like you're going to die in one year. Invest your life in the things that will outlive your life.

## Trials of the First Century Church

As the chapter continues, others think Jesus wasn't referring to events thousands of years into the future, but rather speaking to His disciples and their generation. Jesus was predicting the literal destruction of the Temple, which did happen in the year 70 (approximately 40 years from when Jesus was speaking). It was the Roman emperor Vespasian that orchestrated the destruction of the Temple and the city of Jerusalem, as well as the executions of thousands of Israelites. Jesus is giving them a heads-up.

At first glance, this passage can appear to be more historical in nature. But I would suggest that the first century church perceived it much differently than we do today. It wasn't historical to them. This passage of scripture wasn't about the end of the world. It was timely and relevant. It was a prophetic prediction that came true within many of their lifetimes. Jesus was warning the disciples, and the current generation, about what was fast coming upon them as a new culture counter to the status quo. Imagine what this first generation went through as a Christian community:

- They witnessed first-hand some of their own family members beaten, dismembered, tortured, sawed in two, and buried alive.

- Many people's small children were stripped naked and told to run into the surrounding fields while packs of dogs chased them for sport and ate them alive in front of their weeping mothers.
- Brothers and sisters were taken by force from families, submerged into molds of hot wax, and then set on fire as human candles to light up Rome's streets at night.
- Whole families were forced to fight gladiators and ward off wild animals in the public colosseum for entertainment.
- Children watched their parents burned alive in human barbeque pits.
- Whole neighborhoods of people underwent mass crucifixion as they lined city streets dangling from crosses.

To the first century church, Jesus' warnings in this chapter were their "end times" more than any of us could ever imagine. It would unfold right in front of them. Jesus knew He would soon be leaving the disciples. It would now be a small community of followers led by a small band of disciples that would have to carry out the gospel mission to the whole world. This was a daunting task, especially with the Messiah gone. Jesus is preparing them not just for His death, burial, and resurrection, but for the future persecution and immense challenges that awaited this new community.

## Relevance for Today

There are still others who believe this chapter in the Bible has warnings and alerts for all generations (both first century and today). Although Jesus was primarily concerned, in this passage, with the destruction of the Temple and the challenges of this newly-formed Christian community, there are lessons and implications for all people, in all cultures, in all eras of time. God's words have the ability to speak to yesterday, today, and tomorrow, all at the same time.

Yes, Jesus was addressing His contemporaries. And yes, Jesus is addressing us in our day and time as well. There are people being persecuted and tortured in other countries around the globe today. They need our prayers and support. Persecution isn't just a first century calamity. Our Christian brothers and sisters are encountering great hardships for the sake of Jesus.

Others of us face challenges in the political, social, educational, and cultural spheres. They are not as volatile and overt as some types of persecution, but they're just as toxic. The gospel is still being opposed on many levels and in many spheres.

Let me conclude by saying that we all still await the greatest day in history when Jesus Christ will return again to the earth to establish His rule and reign forever. That was a promise Jesus made, in Mark's gospel, that has not happened yet. We are looking to the future with anticipation and wonder. But let me encourage you that no matter what your perspective is, you must still plan, live, and invest!

The advice Jesus gave His disciples is good advice to us as well as we look our futures brightly in the face: Trust God, stand on the promises of His word, pray, be alert, abide in Him, love people, stand up for justice, and rejoice, because God is faithful and true.

## Mark Chapter 14

# JESUS: THE GOD MAN

*And they went to a place called Gethsemane. And he said to his disciples, "Sit here while I pray." And he took with him Peter and James and John, and began to be greatly distressed and troubled. And he said to them, "My soul is very sorrowful, even to death. Remain here and watch." And going a little farther, he fell on the ground and prayed that, if it were possible, the hour might pass from him. And he said, "Abba, Father, all things are possible for you. Remove this cup from me. Yet not what I will, but what you will." (Mark 14:32-36)*

## Final Days

Jesus' final few days are now upon Him. The last events of His life include: sharing a meal and teaching a group of people, celebrating the Passover with His disciples, instituting the Lord's Supper, experiencing sabotage and betrayal by Judas, praying at Gethsemane, undergoing false arrest and a secret trial, and enduring severe beatings, brutality, and torture. In the previous chapter, Jesus explained how the Temple would be destroyed and how the disciples are to remain alert and on-guard as their futures unfold. This chapter begins with the detailed narrative of how Jesus Himself will not only be betrayed but endure crucifixion on a cross for the sake of sinful humanity. Jesus knows that the end is now upon Him. His life is now numbered not by days but by hours and minutes. The Pharisees want to kill Him but need to do it in secret if they are to avoid riots. Planning begins.

## The Passover Meal

Jesus partakes of the traditional Jewish Passover meal with the 12 as a way to introduce the Lord's Supper. The Passover festival was a celebratory meal that commemorated God freeing the nation of Israel from the clutches of a non-God-honoring ancient empire: Egypt. The Lord's Supper was a new symbolic meal that celebrated and memorialized God, using Jesus, not to just bring freedom to a nation, but to bring freedom to the entire world through Jesus' sacrificial death, burial, and resurrection. In a very real way, this symbolic meal was acted out on the cross for all to see. The wine and the bread are symbolic of Jesus' very life on the cross: His shed blood and broken body.

Even today, when followers of Jesus partake of the Lord's Supper (communion), they too remember Jesus' crucifixion, burial, and resurrection, and how it applies to them. They celebrate the grace-initiated invitation of forgiveness and the new life of freedom that is available because of what Jesus did on the cross. The Lord's Supper is that "special meal" of bread and wine where, as the people of God, we take time to remember Him, honor Him, thank Him, trust Him, receive from Him, and follow Him anew as we live out a new life in God.

## The Lord's Supper

Regularly partaking of the Lord's Supper within a faith community, allows us constant opportunities to reflect, receive, recalibrate, and renew our love for God and for people. Engaging in the thoughtful act of communion with others allows us to not only keep the main thing the main thing, but it provides opportunity as Christ-followers to sense and enjoy the mysterious and spiritual presence of God, to be aligned in gospel mission, and to be empowered by the Holy Spirit to fulfill this assignment with passion and enthusiasm. The chapter continues with Jesus praying in the garden of Gethsemane. His true humanity is exposed like never before as He displays the emotions of fear, stress, and sorrow. Yes, Jesus was fully God and He was fully man.

## Pressing Past Fear

I remember working with my dad one time when I was 16. It was on a Saturday, 5:30 a.m. cold, and pitch black outside. My dad had just changed jobs from being a public comptroller to that of an entrepreneur. He had purchased a retail used appliance store. He would go out early, before the sun came up, buy appliances from people, restore them, and then resell them in his showroom. Early that morning, as we were en route to find appliances to purchase, my dad confided in me the stress, pressure, uncertainty, and fear he was feeling as a new business owner and about his ability to provide as a father. About 10 minutes into our conversation, he caught himself, and changed the subject back to something more positive. I had seen his humanity many times before that conversation but, for some reason, it greatly impacted me this time. I could feel his fear; I could have cut it with a knife. This was the first time I had ever witnessed anything like it.

## 10 to 1

As a kid, I had never seen my dad fearful. Once I watched him stand up fearlessly to 10 men, some of whom were armed. Our family was camping on an abandoned beach in Mexico. This gang of men had stalked us and surrounded us by surprise. They wanted to rob us and some of the men were also eyeing my mother. My dad sent us (Mom and five kids) to the car and told us to lock ourselves inside while he single-handedly packed up all of our camping equipment, loaded each item that he could into the trunk of the car, all the while clutching a pistol to the outside of his pant leg. I thought either my dad was going to be killed, my mom kidnapped and raped, or all of the above. But instead of going home, my dad just got in the car and we moved up the beach to another location and continued our camping trip. He wasn't about to go home. He never showed any fear during or after that event (at least that's what we thought).

## Jesus' Humanity Exposed

The disciples must have felt similar to how we felt in that Jesus had always been strong, confident, and clear-headed about what the Father was saying to Him. Jesus always knew what to do in every situation. He was never afraid and never unsure. But now they are seeing a side of Him that they'd never seen before. In this moment of indescribable agony for Jesus in the garden, the disciples must have felt paralyzed. When they heard Jesus cry out asking the Father three times to make another way than the cross, it must have made the disciples feel helpless and fearful.

The Bible clearly wants us to see not just Jesus' full divinity, but His full humanity as well. Jesus experienced suffering, pain, temptation, and emotional agony on a scale that is hard to imagine, yet He remained sinless, and is thereby qualified to be our Savior.

## Learning to Express Emotions

Jesus teaches us how to express our human emotions to God. God created us with emotions because we are human and because God loves humans. Learning to be fully alive is learning how to pour out our emotions honestly to God. Openly expressing our emotions to our heavenly Father is actually a sign of health and maturity. As we are able to express our feelings to God, we are then able to gain His perspective and His strength for our journey, even if His answer is "no" like it was for Jesus. If God told Jesus that the cross was the only way and was His will, then we shouldn't be surprised if, in our own lives, there will be times when God says "no" to us as well.

## Staying in Tune

My prayer for us is that we will not despise our humanity. Bring your heart, your life, and your emotions to God. Like tuned keys on a piano, I pray that we will be able to be in tune with each emotional rhythm from our hearts as we learn to bring the full range of our emotions in prayer before our Creator. Like the master piano tuner, God will tune, tighten, loosen, and sometimes even replace every string that needs tweaking so that our song will not just be in tune, but that it will bring harmony and beauty to the great symphony that God is composing throughout the world.

Mark Chapter 15

# REVISITING THE CROSS:
# A FIRST CENTURY ELECTRIC CHAIR

*And Pilate again said to them, "Then what shall I do with the man you call the King of the Jews?" And they cried out again, "Crucify him." And Pilate said to them, "Why, what evil has he done?" But they shouted all the more, "Crucify him." So Pilate, wishing to satisfy the crowd, released for them Barabbas, and having scourged Jesus, he delivered him to be crucified." (Mark 15:12-15)*

## Trial, Crucifixion and Burial

This chapter focuses on the trial, crucifixion, and burial of Jesus. It begins with Jesus being brought before Pontius Pilate, who is the local ruling Roman authority. The Jewish religious leaders have accused Jesus of being a false prophet and of blaspheming God because of the things He said and the actions He displayed at the Temple in the previous chapter. The chief priests hated Him and wanted to snuff Him out. Although the Roman authorities could care less about those particular "Jewish" matters, they were concerned with rumors and accusations of Jesus being the Messiah (the anointed one, the heaven-sent Redeemer of mankind). If true, that was a direct threat to Roman political hierarchy and to Caesar. It was a charge they would take seriously.

Therefore, Pilate seeks to question Jesus to see if, in fact, He really is a political ringleader, and the newly emerging "king of the Jews" who is supposedly responsible for spearheading an underground political insurrection that is in direct opposition to Roman rule. Pilate determines that the chief priests are just jealous of Jesus and that He is really not a threat to Rome at all. Pilate doesn't fear Jesus. He fears possible uprisings and riots from the Israelite community if he doesn't handle the situation in a way that pleases the crowd. The masses cry out for Pilate to crucify Him. Pilate concedes. Jesus is sentenced to death on a cross.

## The Cross: Then and Now

The cross means different things to different people. First century townsmen saw the cross much differently than we do today. For many today, the cross triggers images of beautiful Renaissance artwork, church regalia, structures on tops of buildings, and fine pieces of silver jewelry and necklaces at the local mall. Our culture has systematically removed the horror and shame that was originally associated with the cross in first century Roman society. To the people of that era, the cross was an instrument of torture, humiliation, and capital punishment. It was reserved for political offenses against Rome. If first century Christians were to wear the cross as jewelry, like we do today, it would be like us wearing a piece of jewelry molded to look like an electric chair or a gurney that prisoners die on during an execution by lethal injection. Just like we wouldn't even consider doing something like that today, they would never have considered wearing crosses around their necks.

(Let me be clear: I love crosses. I don't think it's wrong to wear one on your neck. I have one up on a wall in my home and we have one in our church. I'm just making the point that the cross has lost its meaning and significance in our culture, and even at times in our lives.)

The cross was an instrument of torture, horror, and death. Jesus, an innocent man, was stripped naked and nailed brutally to a cross. He was publicly humiliated, shamed, tortured, and then He died, not for a capital offense, but for the offenses that we have all committed against God by choosing to be "God" and leader of our own lives, and to live autonomously out from under His leadership and direction. The Bible calls that sin. Jesus' death on the cross allows us to be forgiven of our sins and thereby to be at peace with God. Because of Jesus' sacrifice, we can now be friends with God and enter into the authentic Christian experience of knowing God and being known by Him. The cross of Christ makes that possible.

As the chapter continues, we see Jesus crucified as King of the Jews. That title is written on a placard and fastened on top of His cross by Roman authorities. Jesus is placed between two political revolutionaries, probably not common thieves as we're sometimes taught. Common thieves might have had their hand cut off for stealing, but wouldn't have been crucified on a cross.

Jesus hangs on the cross, suffering. Haunting darkness manifests at midday. Jesus dies. Earthquakes erupt. The Israelite Temple curtain is ripped in two. God's purpose has been completed. Humanity's sin has been atoned. We can now all access God through Jesus rather than through religious ritual and hierarchy. It is finished. Done. The kingdom of God has arrived. A new age has come. The God-life is open to all. Eternity has been altered. Repercussions are felt in the cosmos. The world has been forever changed.

## Jesus Paid It All

My heart is filled with gratitude when I think of what Jesus has done for us. He bore our sins on the cross. He paid the full price to save us and make us whole. His blood was shed and His body broken for us. He extends mercy, forgiveness, and grace to all.

I'm reminded of a story I once heard of a merciful king who'd heard that his people had been violating the laws of his kingdom. They were bribing officers in order to get away with their crimes. So the king made an edict and posted it throughout his kingdom. It said: "Anyone caught violating the laws of the kingdom and bribing an officer will be whipped at the stake immediately." News spread throughout the land. The consequences were clear. Everyone understood. All seemed well throughout the kingdom for several weeks.

Then one day officers burst into the king's chamber and threw a young woman onto the floor in front of him. The king sat on his throne of judgment to hear the case brought before him. The woman was crying. Her hair was disheveled. Tears streamed down her face. The officers said, "This woman has been caught in the act of immorality." "Guilty!" they said. "She even tried to bribe us." Eyes downward, she nodded in agreement.

When the young woman lifted her head and looked at the king he recognized that she was his half-sister who, years earlier, had been banished from the royal family for an ongoing life of immorality. Because she wouldn't change, she was rejected and banished. The king hadn't seen his sister for years. His heart was moved. No, he thought, the law must be fulfilled, and even the king is bound by the law. The king nodded at the officers. They grabbed the woman and took her away where she was strapped to a wooden post and prepped to be whipped. Just as the officer's arm was cocked back and ready to punish her for breaking the law of the kingdom, the king rose from his throne and said, "Stop!" Confused, the officers obeyed. The king stepped off of his throne, took off his jewel-studded crown, and placed it off to the side. He took off his regal velvet robe and walked toward the woman who was tied to the stake. He said, "Untie her." They did. The king said, "Now tie me in her place." He took off his shirt and was tied to the post. He said, "The law must be kept. The consequences of her sin must be paid. I will take her place. Once the law has been fulfilled, her consequences have been met, and her sin has been dealt with, she will be free to go."

As the story ends, the woman watches her brother, the king, have his back shredded and ripped open on her behalf. Not only is the young woman forgiven, her heart is never the same. She would end up living a life of continual gratefulness for what the king had done for her that day. She would not be just appreciative, but she would live differently because of the great mercy she received.

## The Gift of Forgiveness

My prayer is that we would always see the magnitude of what Jesus has done for us on the cross. We are now accepted by a Holy God, forgiven as spiritual lawbreakers, and justified by grace through faith in Jesus because of His shed blood and broken body on that horrific instrument of death, the cross. Because God is loving, He sent Jesus to die in our place. In a very real way, the King of heaven and earth entered humanity, lived a sinless, perfect life, and went to the cross for our sins. He paid for our consequences that we owe before a Holy God. Jesus paid the full price for our spiritual law-breaking.

God's grace offers forgiveness and new life to each of us as a gift because the consequences for our sins have been met in Jesus. A new beginning awaits each of us. But first, we are asked to believe this promise and receive it by faith into our lives. We can not earn it and we do not deserve it; it's a gift from God. We are encouraged to turn toward God, receive the gift of grace called forgiveness, and begin to follow Jesus and His teachings.

I pray that as we see the cross of Christ everywhere throughout our culture, we will treasure it anew and remember each time that it is a symbol of our way back to God. Finally, may God's love penetrate our hearts in such a way that we too would live differently because of the great mercy that we received that afternoon on the hill of Golgotha.

Mark Chapter 16

# DECLARING AND LIVING
# THE WHOLE GOSPEL

*And he said to them, "Go into all the world and proclaim the gospel to the whole creation. Whoever believes and is baptized will be saved, but whoever does not believe will be condemned." So then the Lord Jesus, after he had spoken to them, was taken up into heaven and sat down at the right hand of God. And they went out and preached everywhere, while the Lord worked with them and confirmed the message by accompanying signs. (Mark 16:15-16, 19-20)*

## The Great Commission

This is the last chapter in the gospel of Mark. It begins with the resurrection of Jesus Christ and His appearing to Mary Magdalene and two disciples. Jesus' prediction concerning His resurrection does in fact come true. He rises from the dead three days after His brutal crucifixion on the cross.

This chapter concludes with Jesus instituting the great commission to go into the world and share the gospel (good news) with all of creation. It's interesting to note that the word "creation" is selected instead of the word "creatures." Using this word suggests that we broaden our thinking in how far reaching the gospel of Jesus really goes and how encompassing the new God-life extends into our world.

Of course, Mark is talking about human beings, but it appears he's suggesting there is more to it than that. How far reaching is the gospel? Are there limits? How pervasive and sweeping is this newly birthed kingdom's scope and jurisdiction? As spirit-filled Christ-followers, how expansive is our biblical responsibility of gospel stewardship? Does our assignment and responsibility as followers of Jesus reach beyond human relationships? Should our attitude about and relationship with our own creation change?

## Creation-Care

I think it's unfortunate that this discussion, and asking these types of questions, sometimes degenerates into political camps of liberal and conservative, Democrat and Republican, Green and Independent, or stripes and polka dot! Caring for God's creation is first a biblical issue, even though it's found its way into many conversations within the political arena.

In a culture where debates rage over the question of origins, it's important to remember that it was God (actually the Trinity) who was the creator of humanity and creation. "Creation," in a sense, is the first living sermon preached by God that gives us glimpses of His attributes and divine nature. The reason there is so much relational electricity surrounding the question of "origins" is because the answer to that question has huge implications in how we live our lives.

## Back to the Beginning

The book of Genesis says there is a beginning of history, which suggests there will be an end to it. History is linear, not circular. When I was in elementary school, I'd love assignments that required us to draw historical time lines of civilizations and famous events. I would use several sheets of poster board taped together that would cover the top of the dining room table. Working left to right, I would make vertical hash marks along the horizontal time line that went from "B.C." to "A.D." I remember always having a clear starting point, but never an ending point. My time-lines always concluded with an arrow pointing off to the right, suggesting that history (humanity and creation) would go on and on unchanged forever. The truth is, history does have an ending point (or should I say a "re-creating" point). Just as computers sometimes need to be "re-formatted," history will experience the same in God's providence (Revelation 19-22).

Genesis also asserts that creation not only originated from God, but that it also belongs to Him. The scriptures describe God as one who is continually involved in the details of His creation, including making the grass grow (Psalm104:14; Matthew 6:30), feeding the birds (Matthew 6:26), and feeding other creatures (Psalm 104:21, 25–30).

If creation belongs to God we have a responsibility to care for the things that God owns. God's first assignment was to care for the earth. Genesis 2:15 says, "The Lord God took the man and put him in the Garden of Eden to work it and take care of it." That's why, as Christ-followers, we should be leading the way in environmental concerns. Those who hold a Christian worldview have far better reasons philosophically for caring for the earth than those who believe the world is accidental, meaningless, and a result of random chance.

## It All Belongs to God

Psalm 24:1 says, "The earth is the Lord's, and everything in it, the world, and all who live in it." Because we are "stewards" or "managers" on behalf of God, the earth is not ours to abuse, plunder, or do with as we wish. In a very real sense, we are to take care of the planet out of our respect and love for God. Not only human beings, but animals, ecosystems, and the environment are all under the umbrella of "God's creation" and should be stewarded and cared for in a way that pleases and honors God. The gospel of Jesus impacts everything. As the human heart undergoes an authentic Christian experience of conversion and renewal, it not only responds differently to God and other human beings, but to God's creation as well. Followers of Jesus are called to care for their neighbor as well as God's creation.

So, in a very real way, "nature" or "the environment" and "human beings" all come under the canopy of God's creation. Maybe this is what this passage of scripture is trying to get at? Maybe it is trying to expand our understanding of God and His intentions for our lives? Christians are indeed called to "care" for not just other human beings, but for the whole of creation, large and small.

If God has indeed created the world and Jesus has redeemed all of "creation," and we are "commissioned" to carry forward that holistic message to the ends of the earth, than our response to Christ and our actions here on planet earth should align with His desires.

Listen to the words of the apostle Paul in the book of Colossians. He explains how Jesus Christ died to reconcile all of creation back to God, demonstrating how much God loves His creation in its entirety.

> "He is the image of the invisible God, the firstborn over all creation. For by him all things were created: things in heaven and on earth, visible and invisible, whether thrones or powers or rulers or authorities; all things were created by him and for him. He is before all things, and in him all things hold together. And he is the head of the body, the church; he is the beginning and the firstborn from among the dead, so that in everything he might have the supremacy. For God was pleased to have all his fullness dwell in him, and through him to reconcile to himself all things, whether things on earth or things in heaven, by making peace through his blood, shed on the cross." (Colossians 1:15-20)

## Creation-Care Isn't Political, It's Biblical

Going into the world to proclaim the gospel to the whole of creation is not a political issue, it's a biblical one. It's connected to the great commission. Caring for our creation is not just a hot button of public policy, but part of fulfilling the redeeming plan of our Creator.

Finally, to care for creation is also an indirect way to demonstrate our love for people. Yes, it's a biblical stewardship issue, but it's also a response of love. Creation-care is in some ways a Christian social justice issue because a lack of creation-care ultimately affects the poor. Water pollution, water scarcity, air pollution, and environmental degradation all have a unique negative domino effect on millions of under-resourced children, families, communities, and countries around the globe.

God made the world and all that's in it. He asks us to not only look after it, but to allow the redeeming message of Christ to impact it through how we live our lives. The gospel of Jesus becomes larger when we see it's redemptive scope is broader than just affecting "creatures" (human beings) but all of "creation."

## The Whole Gospel

Declaring the good news of the risen Savior to our family, friends, neighbors, and communities is both a privilege and a responsibility that Jesus Himself has asked us to engage in. My prayer for us is to see the great commission of Jesus in new ways in order that we might form new connections of application and thereby find new ways to obey, honor, and worship God. May God stretch our understanding of how we are to live out the message of Jesus in the midst of the 21st century. It's an eternal assignment, with broad responsibility, that has far reaching eternal rewards. May our minds expand, our hearts be illuminated, and our reach increase as we extend the whole gospel to all of God's creation. May we experience Christ in the deepest and fullest dimension, and in new avenues that bring glory to God. Ready, set, let's go!

Luke Chapter 1

# LOVE HAS COME: GOD'S GREAT REVERSAL

*And Mary said, "My soul magnifies the Lord, and my spirit rejoices in God my Savior, for he has looked on the humble estate of his servant. For behold, from now on all generations will call me blessed; for he who is mighty has done great things for me, and holy is his name. And his mercy is for those who fear him from generation to generation. He has shown strength with his arm; he has scattered the proud in the thoughts of their hearts; he has brought down the mighty their thrones and exalted those of humble estate; he has filled the hungry with good things, and the rich he has sent away empty. He has helped his servant Israel, in remembrance of his mercy, as he spoke to our fathers, to Abraham and to his offspring forever." (Luke 1:46-55)*

## Introduction to Luke

The gospel of Luke is the book with the most details surrounding the birth of Jesus. It describes how Jesus lived a perfect life as a man and therefore became the perfect sacrifice for our sins so that we could experience salvation. This gospel contains many parables which show Jesus' compassion for people and how, as Savior, He seeks and pursues those who are lost, discouraged, confused, and far from God.

The author of this gospel is Luke, a physician, researcher, and non-Jew who wanted his readers to know that Jesus was not only God, but a man. That's why Luke uses the phrase "Son of Man" when referring to Jesus. He traces the genealogy of Jesus all the way back to the first man, Adam. Luke begins his account by explaining that he was not an eyewitness to Jesus and therefore has conducted careful research and investigation in collecting all the facts in order to report the details accurately. Luke was a close friend and ministry partner of the apostle Paul which allowed him to interview firsthand the disciples who were eyewitnesses to Jesus. Luke also watched the birth and rise of the early church, which he wrote about in the Acts of the Apostles.

## John the Baptist

The first chapter describes the birth of John the Baptist and the purpose and thrust of his ministry as a forerunner to Jesus Christ. John's father, Zechariah, encounters his own miracle in the midst of John's birth. Fame surrounding John grows. Mary, the mother of Jesus, encounters the angel Gabriel who explains that she will supernaturally conceive and give birth to a son. She is told to name the baby "Jesus," and that He will be great and His kingdom will never end. Early in her pregnancy, Mary visits Elizabeth and shares the good news. Elizabeth, at this time, was still pregnant with John the Baptist. When Mary shares what the angel told her about Jesus, John the Baptist (at this time a six-month-old fetus) leaps inside his mother's womb, filled with the Holy Spirit.

## Mary's Song - "The Magnificat"

Mary then busts out a song of thanksgiving and praise to God for His faithfulness, sovereign power, and grandeur. Mary's song is often called

"Magnificat" (Latin for "magnifies"). Mary's song soon focuses in on Jesus and God's great plan of salvation for all of humanity.

As I reflect on this chapter and particularly on Mary's song, I'm reminded again of the amazing message that's loaded within. You don't have to play the album backward to unlock the mystery—it's out in the open for all to hear. Mary's song is not only one of the greatest Christmas carols ever written, it's a song of uprising, subversion, and justice. When you look closely at the lyrics, you'll notice there is a pattern to her song: It's about what God is *doing*.

Let me ask you that same question: What do you think God is doing? Mary says that He was bringing down rulers, lifting up the oppressed, dismissing the rich, filling the hungry, scattering the proud, and drawing close to the humble. God was reversing everything! Many scholars call this "the great reversal." Dallas Willard, world renowned theologian, speaks of it as "the law of inversion." Mary's saying, in so many words, that the world's system has it all wrong. What it defines as successful, powerful, and beautiful is counter to God's thinking. In fact, God's now going to turn everything right-side-up that has been despised, marginalized, and passed over.

## God's Great Reversal

Mary's lyrics are not the words that you'll find on any first century Hallmark card. Rather, these lyrics are penetrating, politically incorrect, and disturbing. So much so, that king Herod was disturbed enough to launch a full-on genocide to go after Jesus, and put down this "new king," and His future kingdom. Herod understood the message in the bottle.

God's plan of reversal had been set in motion. There was no turning back. The time came to declare God's new value system throughout the earth. A few chapters later, in the gospel of Luke, we'll see Jesus teaching on the "Beatitudes" and doing the very same thing: redefining success, beauty, wealth, happiness, security, ethics, and values.

What I think is so amazing about Jesus is how He chooses to wage war and fight the injustices of the world and of Herod. It's not by force but through love. Jesus' plan to defeat hate, combat violence, stand up against injustice, put down cruelty, overpower racism, and to overcome sin was laying down His life in love and suffering on the cross for me, you, Herod, the rich, the poor, everyone. Jesus' love is His power. That is what Mary's song was all about.

Yesterday, I heard a new song that has a similar theme about God's love and how it can cause a great reversal even in our day. It was from the Michael Gungor Band and the song was "White Man." Here's what it says:

> God is not a man. God is not a white man.
> God is not a man sitting on a cloud.
> God cannot be bought. God cannot be boxed in.
> God cannot be owned by religion.
>
> But God is love. God is love. And He loves everyone.
> God is love. God is love. And He loves everyone.
>
> God is not a man. God is not an old man.
> God does not belong to Republicans.
> God is not a flag, not even American.
> And God does not depend on a government.
>
> Atheists and charlatans and communists and lesbians,
> And even old Pat Robertson, God, He loves us all.
> Catholic or Protestant, terrorist or president,
> Everybody, everybody, love, love, love, love.
> Stop the hating. Please just stop the hating now, cause God is love.

## Turning Things Right-side Up

My prayer for us is that we would see the evidence of what God is doing and not His absence. God is at work in the world and in our lives. He is turning things right-side up by the power of His love and the ongoing work of the cross. As Christ-followers, we're called to stand up and declare the good news of Jesus and sing out loud the song of His love in the face of greed, racism, sterile religion, and injustice. There's an uprising happening. Songs are echoing throughout the land. God's Spirit is stirring. Let God use our voices and our lives to live out loud as we magnify Jesus in a land that is aching for authenticity, answers, and hope.

Luke Chapter 2

# HEAVEN'S GIFT:
# JESUS, SAVIOR, HOPE FOR ALL THE EARTH

*And in the same region there were shepherds out in the field keeping watch over their flock by night. And an angel of the Lord appeared to them, and the glory of the Lord shone around them, and they were filled with fear. And the angel said to them, "Fear not, for behold, I bring you good news of great joy that will be for all the people. For unto you is born this day in the city of David a Savior, who is Christ the Lord. And this will be a sign for you: you will find a baby wrapped in swaddling clothes and lying in a manger." And suddenly there was with the angel a multitude of the heavenly host praising God and saying, "Glory to God in the highest, and on earth peace among those with whom he is pleased!" (Luke 2:8-14)*

## The Birth of Jesus Christ

This chapter features the birth of Jesus Christ. There are three sections: (1) Jesus' birth, (2) His presentation in the Temple as a baby, and (3) Jesus as a young teen back at the Temple growing in His relationship with God. Before we move forward, let me give you a little context as to what was going on in the Roman culture at this time.

Jesus was born during the reign of Caesar Augustus, who was the adopted son of the late, great, Julius Caesar. Herod was the king over Palestine, which was the particular region where Jesus was born. As you may remember from high school history class, Julius Caesar was the one who unified the Roman Empire. He was revered and noted as the first great "Caesar." The year Julius Caesar died (44 B.C.), some people testified before the Roman senate that they had seen Julius Caesar in a comet traveling across the sky and ascending up into the heavens. The officials soon declared Julius Caesar a "god." Most historians ascribe this event as the beginning of emperor cult worship.

## Pax Romana

Because Caesar Augustus was Julius Caesar's adopted son, he became known as the "son of god." During his reign, there were remnants of Rome's past civil wars, and Caesar Augustus worked hard to bring the fractured Roman Empire together as one. He thereby instituted what was known as "Pax Romana," the peace of Rome. Because Augustus brought peace to the Roman Empire (which was regarded as the whole of the civilized world at that time), he was referred to as the "Savior of Rome." As this announcement went forth about him throughout the land, it was referred to as the "good news" of Rome. When you put it all together, it's quite striking: Caesar Augustus, God's son, had become the savior of Rome. He had brought peace to earth, which is good news to Rome and all its inhabitants!

This context is what Jesus was born into that night in Bethlehem. It was a dangerous pronouncement the angels were making, one that could get you killed if you went around talking about it. That might be why the shepherds were freaking out when the angels started heralding the message. Maybe it wasn't just the presence of the angels that brought fear to the shepherds, but their message of a peace on earth, other than Pax Romana, being declared loud and clear for all to hear! When the heavenly choir erupted about a new kind of savior being born (other than Caesar), the shepherds must have thought they would be crucified along a Roman road for a capital crime against the government if anyone heard and told. Proclamations and songs declaring a different Son of God, other than Caesar, weren't politically correct or covered under a free speech amendment. And they surely didn't think it was a Christmas carol like we do today.

## Prince of Peace

Peace attained outside Pax Romana was treason. But this is the message that was proclaimed to Mary, Joseph, Zechariah, and the shepherds. It was the message about Jesus: who He is and what He would do. It's a promise to us as well: Savior, peace, and good news!

I visit this portion of scripture every year at Christmas, and each time hope to see something new about the birth of Jesus (so I might be able to say something new). But I've discovered that some things don't always need a new perspective; they need to be experienced just like they are, but deeper. They need to be applied with both greater intentionality and intensity into our lives.

We still live in a world that offers "saviors," "promises of peace," and a barrage of advertisements of "good news" concerning people, places, and things. Our society is saturated with products, ideas, distractions, and philosophies that promise happiness and satisfaction. As a people we long to be rescued from our boredom, delivered from our anxiety, and fulfilled in our relationships.

## Our Savior

The good news about Jesus is that He is our Savior. He is our peace. He is good news. When Jesus endured the beating and suffering and went to the cross and died for us, a new reality was born. Sin and death were defeated. Jesus triumphed. Peace was available. Good news was not a distant hope. All of this is available to us today because of Jesus.

My prayer for us is that we will revisit, with a new heart, who Jesus is and what He has done for us. As our Savior, He offers us forgiveness and salvation. Because of Jesus, we can now experience peace with God through what Jesus has done for us on the cross, through the shedding of His blood. This is good news, and it's news we can share with others: Jesus, God's one and only Son, is our hope and Savior, peace on earth! This is a message beyond Christmas; it's a message for every day. A few years back, my wife, Mary, and I were so deeply inspired by this chapter in Luke that we wrote a song that we still sing in our church. The lyrics are listed below.

*"HEAVEN'S GIFT"*

*Jesus, Savior, hope for all the earth*
*Babe in a manger, born a lowly birth*
*Come our Redeemer come*
*With longing heart we sing*
*Heaven's gift our Majesty*
*Worship our great king*
*Worship our great king*

*Glory hallelujah, Glory hallelujah*
*Glory hallelujah, Jesus Christ is born*
*Jesus Christ is born!*

*Jesus, Savior, Name above all names*
*Light in the darkness, to our lives He came*
*Wonderful Counselor, Prince of Peace is He*
*Joy has come into our lives*
*Let His praises ring, Let His praises ring*

If you'd like to hear this song live, visit the website: www.WorshipAlive.com.

Luke Chapter 3

# GENEROSITY:
# THE FRUIT OF GENUINE REPENTANCE

*And the crowds asked him, "What then shall we do?" And he answered them, "Whoever has two tunics is to share with him who has none, and whoever has food is to do likewise." Tax collectors also came to be baptized and said to him, "Teacher, what shall we do?" And he said to them. "Collect no more than you are authorized to do." Soldiers also asked him, "And we, what shall we do?" And he said to them, "Do not extort money from anyone by threats or by false accusation, and be content with your wages." (Luke 3:10-14)*

## John the Baptist's Assignment

John the Baptist begins his prophetic ministry by announcing the coming of Jesus. John is the first prophet in over 450 years, since Malachi, to walk the landscape of Israel and proclaim God's word. John preaches with passion and power. The arrogant will be brought low, the poor raised up, and the crooked made straight. He tells men and women to get their lives right with God. He cuts through the spiritual apathy of the day and declares the way forward in the Lord. John explains that honest repentance always works its way into our behaviors and relationships.

Faith in Christ affects our ethics in the marketplace, how we make money, and how we spend it. John then baptizes the masses with a message of repentance. Although John's fiery sermons begin in the wilderness, they end up in the palace court confronting Herod (a ruler of Galilee) and Herodias, who were engaged in a sexual tryst. John boldly confronts them and their behavior. They hate him for it and throw him in prison.

Jesus then gets baptized and the Holy Spirit descends on Him. God the Father declares His love for Jesus before His ministry even begins, showing that God loves us for who we are and not for anything we do for Him. Remember, at this point Jesus had not yet performed any miracles or taught even one sermon. God publicly made known His pleasure, in regards to His relationship with Jesus first, and to the ministry second. That's true for us as well. Ministering to other people ought to be a by-product of our relationship with God. The chapter concludes with the genealogy of Jesus traced all the way back to Adam. Jesus is shown as both fully God and fully man.

## The Fruit of Genuine Repentance

I find it interesting how John responds to the crowd, the tax collectors, and the soldiers. After one of John's convicting messages, all three groups asked him what their "next step" should be after believing and receiving the message of repentance into their lives. John tells them that true repentance has fruit that follows. Genuine faith always has actions that accompany it. Faith is designed to work its way out through our relationships.

Many tax collectors were known in that day for being crooks. They collected Roman taxes and tariffs from the people. They would often enrich themselves, at the expense of others, by collecting more than they should and then skimming money off the top before turning the money over to authorities. They were told to knock it off and be honest in their business dealings. Soldiers were told to not abuse their power or use their position of authority to bribe people, and squeeze money out of them by strong-handed fear tactics. They were told to be content with their paychecks and deal honestly and uprightly with the people. One of the telltale signs of true repentance, in the life of a Christ-follower, is a life of generosity. We don't use our influence and affluence in the marketplace to take advantage of others; we use it to serve them.

## Cultivating a Life of Generosity

It's interesting to note that all three of the "next steps" that John suggested had to do with money and/or possessions. The crowd is challenged to be generous and to share with those in need. They were challenged to step up to the plate by sharing their money, food, and clothes with those who needed a helping hand. Taxes collectors were to make a living in the marketplace with integrity and honesty. Soldiers were to learn how to live within their means and not lust for cash, kickbacks, or favors.

My prayer for us is that we would honestly evaluate the way we make money, spend money, save money, and give money. There is more of a correlation between money and faith than we realize. Jesus told us that we can't serve both God and *Mammon* (money). In Greek, the first letter of mammon is capitalized because Mammon was a foreign god of materialism and covetousness in ancient Israel. Even today, for many, money is a carefully disguised deity, that directs their lives, relationships, and decisions. Many would never admit it, but it's true.

Generosity is always a fruit of true repentance and a characteristic of a whole-hearted follower of Jesus. Generosity always breaks the grip of selfishness and opens the doorway for God to work in our lives. The apostle Paul encouraged us to be consistent givers, people who are content with our wages, and men and women who are learning to trust God in both the supernatural and the practical. Let's look for ways to live out the "generous and upright life" in our relationships and in the marketplace. When we do, we validate the message of repentance that we have chosen to embrace.

Luke Chapter 4

# ENDURING PROMISES:
# GOD'S WORD IN THE FACE OF TEMPTATION

*And Jesus, full of the Holy Spirit, returned from the Jordan and was led by the Spirit into the wilderness for forty days, being tempted by the devil. And he ate nothing during those days. And when they were ended, he was hungry. The devil said to him, "If you are the Son of God, command this stone to become bread." And Jesus answered him, "It is written, 'Man shall not live by bread alone.'" (Luke 4:1-4)*

## Jesus in the Wilderness

Full of the Spirit, Jesus is led into the wilderness where He is tempted by the devil for 40 days. He encounters three great temptations that each of us face in life:

1. The temptation to misuse our position or authority
2. The temptation to compromise our values for immediate gratification
3. The temptation to obligate God to our agenda

Jesus overcomes each of the three temptations by replying, "It is written..." and then quoting a passage of scripture from the Old Testament (Deuteronomy 6:13, 6:18, 8:3). Jesus stands on the enduring promises of God's word in face of demonic opposition and temptation. Once the 40 days in the wilderness are finished, Jesus successfully returns to Galilee by the power of the Spirit. He preaches His first sermon, from the book of Isaiah, at His local synagogue. He communicates His mission (proclaiming good news to the poor, giving sight to the blind, and liberty to the captives). One minute the people love Him. The next minute, they hate Him and want to kill Him. Miraculously, Jesus evades their mob-like assault.

## Jesus Heals

Jesus moves on to engage in the ministry of casting out demons in people and healing the sick. Some sickness and health issues have nothing to do with demonic power, but there are instances that do. The gospel of Luke describes 21 different miracles that Jesus performs. He then goes on to heal Peter's feverish mother-in-law by speaking words of healing. People are amazed at His authority. Jesus' fame begins to spread throughout the countryside. He continues to preach and teach the good news of God's kingdom (God's reign or rulership in our lives).

## Scripture is Like "Soul Food"

Whenever I read through this chapter, I'm always reminded of how Jesus handles temptation as it tries to hoodwink Him in a moment of opportunity. Jesus' response gives a snapshot of not only how He overcomes the devil, but how He spent His time on the front end of temptation: Jesus was a student of God's word.

Quoting a scripture is one thing in the face of temptation. Feeding daily on scripture as a source of "soul food" is another. Jesus did both. He was convinced that the Bible was God's revelation to man. It was the decisive "absolute authority" upon which He anchored His belief system. It was the foundation that fueled His values, goals, decisions, and purpose in life. It was also the place He looked toward when He was confused, troubled, or tempted. Jesus allowed the scriptures to shape and form every area of His life, and in a moment of trial it saved Him.

Later on, the apostle Paul tells us that the scriptures are God-breathed and God-inspired (1 Timothy 3:16). They are useful to teach, correct, rebuke, and train us in righteousness (which is being right before God and right in our relationships with others).

## Night Flying on Instruments

One of my friends, from Tucson, was an amazing A-10 fighter pilot in both Gulf Wars. He once described how pilots learn to "night fly" by reading and obeying what their instrument panel dictates rather than what their natural eyesight tells them. He said that they must learn to trust their instruments more than they trust their feelings of equilibrium. When flying in the black of night, it sometimes feels like you are upside-down when in fact you are right-side up.

So too, choosing to go by the truths and principles of God's word, in times of temptation, and trusting in what Jesus says is true in moments of weakness, can save our lives, families, relationships, careers, ministries, and legacies. The truest thing about you is what God says about you. The truest thing about your circumstance is what God says about it. That's why it's so important to not just agree with God's word, when it aligns with what we want to do anyway, but to obey it even when we don't "feel" like obeying. There is a difference between "agreeing" with God and "obeying" Him. Understanding the difference can save our lives in times of temptation.

## A Daily Diet of God's Word

My prayer is that we would have a healthy and daily diet of God's Word. I pray that we would hear it, read it, study it, memorize it, meditate on it, obey it, and share it. It has the power to change the trajectory of our lives and sustain us in dark times of temptation and trial.

Let me especially encourage those of you that find yourselves in an extreme season of temptation, discouragement, or confusion: Don't just agree with God. Trust Him. Obey Him. Fall into Him. Go by what you know God says is true, not by how you feel. Trust in God's enduring promises for your life and for your future. He is faithful even when we are not. He will carry you and sustain you by His Word. He did it for Jesus, and He will do it for you.

Luke Chapter 5

# SEARCH AND RESCUE:
# FINDING YOUR WAY HOME

*After this he went out and saw a tax collector named Levi, sitting at the tax booth. And he said to him, "Follow me." And leaving everything, he rose and followed him. And Levi made him a great feast in his house, and there was a large company of tax collectors and others reclining at table with them. And the Pharisees and their scribes grumbled at his disciples, saying, "Why do you eat and drink with tax collectors and sinners?" And Jesus answered them, "Those who are well have no need of a physician, but those who are sick. I have not come to call the righteous but sinners to repentance." (Luke 5:27-32)*

## The Call to Follow

Chapter five opens with Jesus calling His first disciples to follow Him. Jesus demonstrates that He is Lord by aiding the soon-to-be disciples in a supernatural catch of fish. They said "yes" to His invitation to become "fishers of men." The call to discipleship is more than just believing in Jesus; it's about putting that belief into action and actually following Him.

Jesus then cleanses a leper by a miracle of healing. His popularity spreads. His teaching ministry expands. Awe and controversy begin to brew. Jesus then heals a paralyzed man in a dramatic display of His supernatural power. He not only heals the man's physical body, but forgives His sins as only God could.

## A Matthew Party

Levi (Matthew) meets Jesus in the marketplace and is challenged to leave behind his old ways and follow Jesus as a disciple (the word *disciple* means a disciplined learner). He too says yes to God and leaves his old ways behind in order to pursue a new life with Jesus. Matthew celebrates his new decision to be a Christ-follower by throwing a party. He invites all his friends from the neighborhood. The religious leaders criticize Matthew for throwing such a party and inviting the kind of characters he did (and they criticize Jesus for attending). Jesus declares that He came for those who are lost, who find themselves far from God, and who are in need of finding their way back home (spiritually).

Questions arise about fasting. Jesus uses the question in such a way as to challenge the religious leaders in their thinking about the workings of God. He tells them through the analogy of "old wineskins" and "new wine" that a stubborn and brittle heart that refuses to let God do something new will miss out big time. Because God is gracious, He won't force Himself on anyone; He'll just move on to someone who is receptive.

Unfortunately, the Pharisees failed to recognize that the kingdom of God was in their midst. They were conversing with the Son of God face-to-face. The new covenant was emerging right in front of their eyes, but they rejected Jesus and what God was doing instead of welcoming them through honest repentance and spiritual regeneration.

Jesus' invitation to follow Him is extended to each of us as well. The disciples' call is still going forward. Although the ways God invites us are many, the call is the same: We're all invited to come home to Jesus.

## Lost in the Tucson Tunnels

When my three brothers and I were in elementary school, we would often go under the city streets of Tucson, in what we called the "tunnels," exploring with our flashlights. The tunnels were a complex underground water drainage system of huge pipes. City officials designed this interconnected system of metal and cement drainage piping to move the huge amounts of water that the summer monsoon storms would dump on the city streets in a matter of minutes.

Here's how it worked: The rain water on the city streets would enter the underground drainage system through openings that were located on the sides of all the streets. The water would flow into these openings and down into the drainage system tunnels. The tunnels emptied the water into area *arroyos* (huge gullies or desert-like creeks). The arroyos gathered the huge torrents of water and would then carry it away from the city. But when it wasn't raining, the underground "tunnels" were a playground for my brothers and me.

As rambunctious young boys, we would go on "exploring missions" during the summer. It was pitch black in the tunnels, and since there were no maps, it was easy to get lost. As a matter of fact, a few times we did and it was pretty scary. We ended up finding our way home by hoisting one brother up on our shoulders, positioning his head at street level so he could peer out through a drainage opening and get his bearings as to which way was home. I remember one time when that method didn't work. We were lost. Disoriented. Stranded. Terrified. We wandered and worried for what seemed an eternity. Our flashlights grew dim.

It was at that low point when, out of nowhere, one of our neighborhood friends appeared in the tunnel. He had come looking for us. We had been gone for hours and should have been home already. He shouldered up his daypack, flashlight in hand, and launched his own search and rescue mission to find us. He led us to safety that night and became our hero (at least for that summer).

## Search and Rescue Mission

Jesus said that's why He came to earth. He too was on a search and rescue operation. This was Jesus' mantra: searching for and seeking out those who were spiritually lost and leading them to God. Jesus has come searching for us, too. He's our hero and Savior. He came to lead us to the light and bring us to the truth. He is reality. He came to lead us out of our good intentions gone bad and our confusions that keep us going in circles. Even today, Jesus is on a full-out search and rescue mission for people who are lost, seeking, and spiritually disoriented. He invites those of us who are His disciples to join in on this rescue operation; it's called the Great Commission.

## Say Yes to His Call and Invitation

My prayer is that if you are one who finds yourself far from God, that you would reach out and accept His invitation to come home. He is searching for you, and anything Jesus would ask you to leave behind will ultimately pale in what He promises to add to your life. That's a promise you can count on. He's calling. He's willing to lead. Will you follow? Will you say yes to Jesus' call?

For those of us who are Christ-followers, will you again engage in the greatest search and rescue mission of all time? Will you enter the "tunnel" for a friend who is searching for the way out? Will you re-enter the marketplace this week with a renewed focus and passion to help those who are far from God, and those who are disoriented in a spiritual tunnel and aren't sure of the way out? They need our help. Together let's say yes to the greatest call of all time. Let's take out our flashlights and go. Let's keep an eye out for others who are searching for God, and let's help them. I'm sure glad someone came looking for me.

Luke Chapter 6

# HEAVEN INTERSECTS EARTH:
# A NEW KIND OF ETHIC

*And he came down with them and stood on a level place, with a great crowd of his disciples and a great multitude of many people from all Judea and Jerusalem and the seacoast of Tyre and Sidon, who came to hear him and to be healed of their diseases. And he lifted up his eyes on his disciples, and said: "Blessed are you who are poor, for yours is the kingdom of God. Blessed are you who are hungry now, for you shall be satisfied." (Luke 6:17-21)*

## Jesus on the Move

Through a series of events (plucking grain on the Sabbath, and healing a man's hand) Jesus teaches His followers that He is Lord above religious rules, rituals, traditions, and clergy. Miracles trail in His wake. Accusation and controversy follow. It's clear that God will not be bought, boxed in, or owned by religion. Jesus spends all night in prayer. In the morning, He selects His 12 apostles. He continues to heal people and teach them God's word. He delivers one of His most famous and memorable sermons of all time: the Beatitudes. His message contains "blessings" and "woes" that are tested, true, and timeless. It's a message that's counter-intuitive and filled with great paradox and spiritual power. It's a new kind of ethic that is sourced in heaven's value system.

Jesus turns people's expectations upside-down about what really produces happiness. He explains that true happiness comes from within and that it is independent of life's circumstances. Our English word "happiness" is anchored in the notion of chance or good fortune. As long as everything goes our way, we're good. But happiness, as Jesus describes it, is a joy that no person or no circumstance can take away from us. It's a joy that rises above our circumstances and troubles. It's tethered to a relationship with God and relating to others in a new way.  Jesus unpacks how people can experience this new God-life.

In chapter four, Jesus said He needed to go to other towns and preach the good news about the kingdom of God (the "kingdom of God" means a system of rule, governance, or rulership). This is exactly what He's doing here: He's teaching about the kingdom of God. He's explaining what God's value system looks like and how to allow this new ethic to affect our values and relationships. As we do, we'll experience a different kind of happiness because we experience a different kind of life. Jesus, in essence, is laying out a new ethical framework and foundation of how life really works in God's family.

## God's Heavenly Value System

As I'm writing this, I also imagine in my mind what it might sound like if God were to explain these principles of His "heavenly value system" to children or teenagers. He might phrase it differently. Here's one way it might go down:

"Kids, I know this new way of living that I'm describing is something counter-intuitive to the way most people think and act. What I'm describing is not normal on the playground at school, what you'll see on T.V., or what you observe in the culture. But I want you to know that this is normal in heaven. This new value system is the way life is really supposed to work. Guys, I want you to trust me on this and adopt this new way of ruling yourself, your thinking, and your actions as 'the family way.' This is how we do it in heaven, or 'at home,' so to speak. Heaven has come close to you. In some ways, it's like it has intersected with a part of where you live. Yes, I'm aware things are different on earth than they are in heaven. Nevertheless, what I'm telling you is the truth. The Holy Spirit lives in you. He will teach you. Let Jesus explain to you how We govern and how We want to lead you. Don't be shocked if other people don't think and act the way I'm describing. They don't know about Jesus yet. They think He's just a person from history. They haven't experienced His love and know Him as God, but they will. Keep praying for them. I love them too—very much. So listen carefully to Jesus' words. He explains how to handle problems, conduct your relationships, make decisions, and live life on this earth. This is part of what it means when you hear the phrase 'God's kingdom.' One day soon we will all be together. We won't be communicating through letters in the Bible, in prayer, or in impressions you feel in your heart. One day we'll see each other face-to-face and we'll all do life together just like it's being done right now in heaven. Don't' be afraid. I'll help you to live out this 'new ethic' here on earth. I love you. I'll help you. You'll have fun and grow lots as you apply what you are learning."

## Relationship Trumps

One last thing about living the God-life and embracing kingdom values before we're done. I think it's important to note that we don't adopt the value system first. We begin first with a genuine relationship with Jesus. We receive His love into our lives, which in turn allows us to love Him and to want to follow His ways. It's after we come into a relationship with Jesus, that we then focus on values. Why? Values are an expression of what we love, value, or prize. To attempt to sustain the Christian life (living God's way) without a relationship with Jesus becomes legalistic at best and miserable at worst. This is how Christianity degenerates into sterile religion: by only adopting the value system and not surrendering to Jesus. Yes, it's a noble ethical system all by itself, but it was never meant to be adopted without first having Jesus as Lord of our lives. Our values will naturally flow out of what we love most.

My prayer for us is that we reflect deeply on Jesus and His words of life. Heaven's value system is a current reality. It's active and taking place right now. We are invited to live that reality today here on earth. It's the way to happiness and a life of joy. Let's reflect on what we love most in this world, because more than likely, what we prize most will be reflected in our values and relationships. Let's rewind the videotape of our hearts to love, because love moves the heart, and our hearts dictate the rhythm and meter of our values. Our values write the lyrics of our life's song.

Luke Chapter 7

# FOLLOWING A DIFFERENT KIND OF JESUS

*The disciples of John reported all these things to him. And John, calling two of his disciples to him, sent them to the Lord, saying, "Are you the one who is to come, or shall we look for another?" In that hour he healed many people of diseases and plagues and evil spirits, and many who were blind he bestowed sight. And he answered them, "Go and tell John what you have seen and heard: the blind receive their sight, the lame walk, lepers are cleansed, and the deaf hear, the dead are raised up, the poor have good news preached to them. And blessed is the one who is not offended by me." (Luke 7:18-23)*

## Chapter Highlights

Luke wants the readers to know that Jesus is not just a great prophet, but that He is the Messiah, the Son of God. He records the details of two amazing miracles that Jesus performs:

1.  Healing the Roman centurion's servant
2.  Raising a poor widow's son from the dead

Reports of Jesus' fame reverberate throughout the Judean countryside like wildfire. In the middle of the chapter the disciples of John the Baptist emerge with a question for Jesus. John was troubled and in prison awaiting imminent execution. Jesus answers their question. They return to John. Jesus goes on to commend John and his powerful prophetic ministry. Jesus proclaims there is none greater in the land than John the Baptist.

## Dinner at Simon's Place

The chapter concludes with Jesus having dinner with a Pharisee named Simon. During dinner a woman unexpectedly enters the circle of people gathered around the table. She unashamedly and extravagantly anoints Jesus' feet with perfume. She spreads the aromatic ointment over His feet with her hair and then kisses His feet. All eyes are on Jesus, waiting for His reaction. Jesus then tells Simon a story of two moneylenders who forgave two debtors different sums of money, one large and one small. He explains that people who know they have been forgiven much love God very much. Those who think they have not been forgiven love God little. The Pharisees react. Jesus pronounces forgiveness of the woman's sins.

This is an amazing chapter with several notable stories that all highlight Jesus' status as the one true God. There are many spiritual lessons associated with each of the four stories (the centurion's servant, the widow's son, the disciples of John the Baptist, and the woman with the vial of perfume at Simon the Pharisee's dinner party). But there is one phrase that always sobers me as I read this chapter. It's the story of John the Baptist and it's found in verse 23: "Blessed is the one that is not offended by me."

## The Plight of John the Baptist

Let me give you some quick background information. When looking at this verse, it's important to remember that although John the Baptist was amazing, anointed, set apart for God's work, and singled out by Jesus as "great," he was still human. I should probably add "a little strange, too." Anybody who walks around in camel hair kilts and eats insects coated with honey isn't your average dude. Even in ancient times, his style of dress wasn't fashionable, so I'm sure he was a head-turner.

Remember, a few chapters earlier, John's fruitful ministry came to what appeared to be an abrupt halt. He was thrown in a dungeon for truth-telling about Herod and Herodias's immoral sexual escapade. The plan was to behead John, place the head on a platter, and bring it to Herodias as a gift. So, locked away, rotting in a cell, battling discouragement, and counting the hours until his head was to be severed, John sends word through his disciples to Jesus and asks Him one last time, if in fact, He really is the Messiah, the Christ, the Redeemer, God's Son. John is going through nothing less than a real-time faith crisis.

In his mind, John has a picture of who the Messiah was and what His ministry would look like, and the picture wasn't matching up with what Jesus was actually doing. John understood the scriptures to mean that the Messiah would overthrow the oppressive Roman government. He perceived the Messiah as one who would be Israel's rescuer and conqueror, and He would bring down God's judgment on sin and evil. But what does John actually see? He sees Jesus extending God's love, grace, compassion, forgiveness, healing, and mercy. He sees Jesus telling people to pay their taxes to the government. He hears about Jesus telling people to pray for their enemies. John's mental picture of "Jesus" didn't line up with the "Jesus" that everyone else was experiencing in Galilee. John is rightfully confused. So a question of clarification is sent via John's disciples to Jesus asking if in fact He really is the real deal—the Messiah.

Jesus replies with a staggering response. He doesn't answer with a "yes" or "no" to the question. Instead, Jesus answers through descriptive evidences of His miraculous workings. He declares that, "The blind see, the dead are raised, and the poor have the gospel preached to them." Then He says, "Blessed is the one who is not offended by me."

## A Sobering Side to God's Will

In essence, Jesus was saying something that goes against the grain of some of our popular Christian theology today. It's as if Jesus was telling John:

> "Yes, miracles are taking place left and right. Yes, God is moving and working. Yes, He is healing, delivering, and saving. The evidence of God's presence is profound and prolific. It's everywhere. But John, for you, God has chosen a different path. He's not going to work that way in your life this time. God is not going to rescue you from prison. In fact, God's plan for you is to die in the dungeon for your faith. So, John, you'll be blessed if you don't take offense at God for choosing this difficult path for your life. I know this isn't how you expected your life to play out. I know this is scary, painful, and maybe even confusing. I love you, but I won't be coming to save you in the palace dungeon. I hope you can trust God through this. There's a blessing for you in the end. Don't despise me. Trust me. Lean into me."

## The Truth About Suffering and Difficulty

As I reflect on this story, I'm reminded that God's plan for our lives isn't always about saving us from difficult circumstances, pain, and suffering. Following Jesus isn't about a life of comfort, security, and convenience. Somewhere along the line, we've picked up a theology that God would never allow us to experience difficulty, pain, and suffering. That's not in the Bible. I believe that for John, and for many of us, this is part of God's plan for our lives, at least for some seasons. That's why God tells us that we too will be blessed if we don't give up on Him, and don't give up on our faith, if, unbeknownst to us, God chooses to allow a painful season of life to be part of our storyline.

We forget too soon that the message of the gospel is not only about eternal life and God's generous blessings, but it's also a message about sacrifice, surrender, repentance, trusting God's sovereignty, and the cross. It's about choosing to "die daily" to our selfishness (1 Corinthians 15:31) with the help of God's grace. It's about laying down our lives in service to a great

God. It's not a faith that is preoccupied with trying to preserve our convenience and comfort.

## The Gospel is About the Cross

The gospel of Jesus challenges us to take risks, trust, contend, be fearless and courageous, and to move out of our comfort zones and the world of the familiar. The gospel of Jesus is about radical love. It's the kind of love where people pour out all they are in lavish worship at the feet of Jesus. It's about a God that has forgiven much and who thereby is loved very much. It's about full-on surrender to God. It's a gospel that declares a message that costs (and that cost Jesus His life). This is the side of the gospel that is often overlooked.

## Grace Triumphs Over Difficulty

My prayer for us is that we will not be hypnotized by a domesticated religious system that promises us a life of ease, safety, and pampering if we say just the right prayer to Jesus and rub the ribbons of our Bible just right, like you rub Aladdin's lamp hoping for a genie to pop out. My hope is that those of us who find ourselves in difficult circumstances, troubling situations, dangerous places of ministry, maybe even staring death in the face, would not let our hearts be offended at God for choosing and/or allowing these difficulties into our lives. For those of us, like John, who need a miraculous intervention to survive, be reassured today that in the end, God will prove Himself faithful.

Today, if you are in a place where God has chosen to be silent or slow to reverse your situation, know that He promises to walk alongside you through the fires of your trial and the agony of your pain, even though He won't intervene and bring change.

Don't give up. Don't be offended at Him. Don't cave in to the lies of the devil that tell you that you don't matter to God. You do. He loves you. Jesus went to the cross for you. He shed His blood on your behalf. He went to heaven to prepare a place for you. He will sustain you. His Spirit will walk with you and work in you. Contend. Trust. Be not afraid. Be assured that He who has called you will be faithful to see you and sustain your faith all the way through to the very end.

Luke Chapter 8

# BUMPING INTO JESUS VS. TOUCHING HIM

*As Jesus went, the people pressed around him. And there was a woman who had a discharge of blood for twelve years, and though she had spent all her living on physicians, she couldn't be healed by anyone. She came up behind him and touched the fringe of his garment, and immediately her discharge of blood ceased. And Jesus said, "Who was it that touched me?" When all denied it, Peter said, "Master, the crowds surround you and are pressing in on you!" But Jesus said, "Someone touched me, for I perceive that power has gone out from me." And when the woman saw that she was not hidden, she came trembling, and falling down before him declared in the presence of all the people why she had touched him, and how she had been immediately healed. And he said to her, "Daughter, your faith has made you well; go in peace." (Luke 8:42-48)*

## Jesus and Parables

Jesus continues preaching and teaching the "good news" of the gospel throughout different cities and villages. This chapter introduces the parable of the sower. Jesus explains that the quality of spiritual fruitfulness we experience in our lives depends on the quality of the soil of our hearts. Jesus mentions four kinds of soil. He goes on to explain that our fruitfulness in life is tethered to our relationship with Him, to the word of God, and how much (or how little) we receive and apply what we hear from God's word. It's Jesus' intention that we all flourish in the God-life.

Jesus often used parables to communicate spiritual truths. Parables are short allegorical stories that convey meaning using analogies or comparisons. They often contain hidden truths that require further explanation and discovery. Parables are a great learning methodology because they allow us to experience "self discovery," which all educators know is a great way to learn. Parables are also effective because they use familiar imagery from the current culture. This makes them easy to remember and apply. Jesus said that parables help spiritual seekers grasp spiritual matters.

## Unpacking the Cultural Context

Because our 21st century culture is so different from Israel's first century agrarian society, the parables that Jesus uses in the Bible are sometimes confusing to us at first glance. It's not that Jesus is confusing, it's that we don't always understand the culture from which He draws His analogies. If, from time to time, you find that to be true for you, let me encourage you to not get down on yourself for not understanding what Jesus is talking about. First, just take a few minutes to unpack a bit of the historical or cultural context. That will help a lot. This is where a good study Bible comes in handy.

The chapter finishes out with several other significant events involving Jesus: the parable of the lamp, an encounter with Jesus' mom and brothers, the miracle of calming a storm and demonstrating command over the atmospheric elements, healing a man with a demon, healing a woman in the crowd, and healing Jairus' young daughter. (Not bad for a day's work.) Jesus' fame continues to spread. People are amazed.

## Jesus Heals a Woman

There are so many gems in this chapter to choose from, but today I'm drawn to the story of Jesus, the crowd of people, and the woman with the discharge of blood. Here's the gem: There's a difference between bumping into Jesus and touching Him. Catch the scene with me in your imagination. Jesus is en route and on a heavenly assignment with His disciples. He's moving through a massive crowd of people who all want to get a look at Him. Villagers are patting Him on the back and waving their hands at Him. Shouts are rising. Children are cutting in and out of the crowd. There's pushing. Shoving. Smells. Sounds. People everywhere. In the midst of this backdrop, Jesus becomes startled and exclaims, "Someone's touched me!" The disciples respond, "Of course someone's touched you. People are clattering all around you."

Jesus is surrounded and bumping into everyone. Jesus explains that power has come forth from Him. He felt it go. A woman soon surfaces. She admits she's the one who touched Him. She explained that she just wanted to reach out and touch Him because she knew He had the power to heal her and change the trajectory of her life. As the story unfolds, Jesus not only heals the woman, but He makes her whole physically and spiritually.

## Experiencing His Presence

Certain things about life never change. Sometimes life can have a funny way of getting stuck on "fast forward." School, work, family, parties, schedules, homework, projects, responsibilities, deadlines, traffic, kids, chores, etc. You fill in the blank. It's in times like these that we can be tempted to be satisfied with just "bumping into Jesus" rather than experiencing His presence and "touching" Him in meaningful ways like this woman did. We can so easily settle for the superficial, rather than a true spiritual encounter with Jesus.

When we get caught up in the spin cycle of life, we can fall into patterns of just coming to church for an hour on Sunday or doing a quick devotional for the day, but in reality, we've yet to really "touch" Jesus. It's like we fit Him into our busy schedules like when we multi-task by exercising on the treadmill while catching up on the news.

Please hear this as an invitation to press through the crowd and over the busyness of life to experience Jesus and His love for you in an authentic, real, divine, and powerful way. Jesus desires for you to experience His presence in your life. The Bible says that God is jealous for you. He wants to be with you and desires to hang out with you. But we must make time and reach through the distractions. It's so amazing to see that Jesus was stopped dead in His tracks when just one person reached out to touch Him. When she did, it unleashed the miraculous into her life and changed her forever.

## Prayer

My prayer for us is that we would step beyond just bumping into Jesus this week and that we would reach through the press of the crowd, through the distractions of life, through the busyness of our schedules, and touch Him. Jesus' eyes are on you. He knows your thoughts. His embrace is open. He calls to you. Come. Press through. Experience. Be made whole. Together, let's make sure that we don't get so busy making a living that we never make a life.

## Luke Chapter 9

# PROBLEMS:
# STRANGELY WRAPPED OPPORTUNITIES

*"Send the crowd away so they can go into the surrounding vil-lages and countryside to find lodging and get provisions, for we are here in a desolate place." But he said to them, "You give them something to eat." They said, "We have no more than five loaves and two fish—unless we are to go and buy food for all these people. For there are about five thousand men. And he said to his disciples, "Have them sit down in groups of about fifty each." And they did so, and had them all sit down. And taking the five loaves and the two fish, he looked up to heaven and said a blessing over them. Then he broke the loaves and gave them to the disciples to set before the crowd. And they all ate and were satisfied. And what was left over was picked up, twelve baskets of broken pieces. (Luke 9:12-17)*

## Jesus and His Disciples

Jesus sends the 12 apostles out on a short-term ministry assignment into the surrounding cities. This assignment serves as a type of ministry internship in preparation for the great commission with which they will soon be charged. The apostles are given opportunities to apply what they were learning about God.

After they return, they huddle with Jesus for a time of reflection and debrief. The crowds discover that Jesus was in town and they flock to see Him. Jesus teaches them truths about God's kingdom and heals all the people that have needs. As night approaches, the disciples ask Jesus to send the people back into the villages to find food. Jesus uses this as yet another opportunity to apprentice His disciples. He tells them to feed the multitude themselves. Because there are over 5,000 of them, this assignment is daunting, but they rise to the challenge, step up to the plate, and trust God to intervene miraculously. God provides. Peter then confesses Jesus as the Christ (the anointed One sent from the Father). Jesus predicts His own death on a cross, and then extends the "disciples call" to all who were around. He challenges them to pick their own cross, die daily to their selfishness, and follow Him.

## Mountaintop Experience

About a week later, a few of Jesus' disciples are with Him on a mountaintop. Suddenly, they encounter a supernatural, bone-riveting experience of seeing Jesus' body illuminated with a brilliant white light. His face beams, holograph-like images of Moses and Elijah appear, and an authoritative voice speaks out from a cloud that Jesus is the Son of God. They witness a foretaste of Jesus' future glory and majesty that is talked about in the book of Revelation.

Crowds appear as they come down from the mountain. Jesus heals a boy possessed by a demon. People are astonished. Conversations about leadership and servanthood take place with the disciples. Jesus and the 12 move on to Samaria where they encounter other wannabe disciples. Jesus explains the cost and commitment necessary. Excuses are offered. Jesus asks for a full-life commitment. Nothing less will suffice.

## Mentoring Opportunities

I'm inspired to see how Jesus apprentices His young leaders along the way. He models exemplary leadership savvy by not just giving the disciples "information," but rather opportunity to "apply" what they are learning. We learn best when we are able to apply principles of truth into our lives.

As a great leader, Jesus seeks out mentoring opportunities for the 12 disciples. Jesus avoids a common leadership trap that many well-intentioned leaders fail to recognize, which is that leaders do not have to solve every problem they encounter. Some problems are actually wonderful opportunities that should be shared with those they are apprenticing. Why? Because we grow as leaders as we are allowed to wrestle with and find solutions to problems.

Problems are often the curriculum God uses to build capacity, faith, and spiritual growth in us. Some problems only God can fix. Other times, God uses us in His problem-solving process. Some of God's very best gifts in our lives have come as a result of working through a particular problem. When we share problems with those we are mentoring, we are, in essence, sharing strangely-wrapped gifts with them.

Another thing about Jesus' leader-building strategy is that leadership training is more than skill development, but faith development. As we encounter humongous challenges and work through them with God's grace, our perspective of who God is, and how God works, changes. We can only learn so much from a book. Sometimes we need to roll up our sleeves, get into the trenches of life, work through the mud and poop, call out to God ourselves, and engage in the drama of life. This is what Jesus was providing for His disciples in the feeding of the 5,000. If we let Him, God does some of His best work in these environments.

## The 4-Step Shadowing Process

Jesus trains, instructs, corrects, and re-directs His team in their ministry internship. He uses a familiar Hebrew apprenticeship model called "shadowing":

1. I do, you watch
2. We do together

3. You do, I watch

4. We debrief, celebrate, and where necessary, re-learn

This method of mentoring served as a strong foundation, enabling His disciples to be delegated with assignments and empowered with authority from on high. Too often, people are empowered without first being properly trained, which is a recipe for disaster. Jesus effectively trains His disciples and meets the needs of the masses all at the same time. Amazing!

My prayer for us is that we will see problems in a new light. My hope is that we will see them as strangely-wrapped gifts of opportunity. Who are the people that surround you? Who are those that you are mentoring, training, and apprenticing in the God-life? Don't solve all their problems. Allow them the opportunity to engage, grow, reflect, and learn. Provide the opportunity to increase their faith as they watch God work extravagantly in and through their lives.

## Luke Chapter 10

# THE JOY OF DOING LIFE WITH OTHERS

*After this the Lord appointed seventy-two others and sent them on ahead of him, two by two, into every town and place where he himself was about to go. And he said to them, "The harvest is plentiful, but the laborers are few. Therefore pray earnestly to the Lord of the harvest to send out laborers into his harvest." (Luke 10:1-2)*

## Declaring Good News

Jesus sends out 36 ministry teams (two people per team) into the surrounding cities and villages where He's preparing to go. Their assignment is to heal the sick and declare the good news of the gospel. We see a beautiful example of ministry being done in the context of relationships. Doing church as a team is God's design for effective ministry. It always has been. Jesus modeled it with the 12, and again in this chapter, when He sent forth these 72 disciples.

We were never designed to do life alone. God's plan is that every Christ-follower be involved and engaged in the work of the gospel alongside others in the context of community. We are created for ministry, gifted for ministry, authorized for ministry, and needed for ministry (Romans 12; 1 Corinthians 12; and Ephesians 4).

Jesus mentions the "harvest" and the need for workers. The harvest was always forefront on Jesus' mind. He knew that the harvest would not reap itself, but it would self-destruct. The harvest is dependent on us. Jesus was always thinking about people who were far from God and who needed to come into a loving relationship with Him. Why? Because everybody needs God. The French philosopher Pascal said, "There is a God-shaped vacuum in the heart of every man which cannot be filled by any created thing, but only by God, the Creator, made known through Jesus." Ecclesiastes 3:11 says, "God has placed eternity in the hearts of man." Even if we aren't cognizant of our need for God (to know Him and be known by Him), we are created to be in loving relationship with Him. Jesus longs for people to experience that "heavenly alignment."

Every human being that you and I have ever laid our eyes on, is someone for whom Jesus Christ has died for. Every person, Christian and non-Christian alike, is valuable to God. Because they are valuable to Him, they should be valuable to us as well. The apostle Paul said, "For God wants all people—every one—to be saved and come to a knowledge of the Truth" (1 Timothy 2:4). This was at the heart of Jesus' ministry, and what He was endeavoring to place into the souls of each of His disciples. I'm reminded again that we might not be able to reach the masses of humanity with the message of the gospel, but we can all reach out to a friend, neighbor, work associate, or a family member with the message of Jesus. It's no accident that some people are placed in our lives for such a time and reason as this.

As the chapter unfolds, the 72 return with stories of joy and the thrill of "doing ministry." They share their war stories with each other and Jesus about how they kicked the devil's butt. Young ministry apprentices are susceptible to getting caught up, or even led astray, because of an inordinate fascination with the topic of spiritual warfare, battling the devil, and their power over him. This is what was happening with the 72 and what happens sometimes even today. Jesus helps them to keep the main thing the main thing. He inserts a CliffNotes version of spiritual warfare and the devil. He reminds them that the devil is no match for God, but by themselves, they are no match for the devil. He then focuses their attention to the greatness and promises of God.

## Loving God and Loving Others

More questions of how to attain eternal life surface in their conversation. Jesus tells a young lawyer that the entire Old Testament can be summed up in what is called today the great commandment: loving God with all of your heart, soul, mind, and strength, and loving other people as you love yourself. In essence, Jesus tells him that all of the Old Testament prayers, rituals, laws, sacrifices, prophets, songs, writings, and poems are boiled down into the mantra of loving God and loving people. Jesus goes on to tell the story of the Good Samaritan to illustrate the "loving people" part of the commandment. He explains that the spirit of the law is as important as the letter of the law. Jesus raises the bar on the definition of "who is our neighbor." Great truths abound.

The chapter finishes up with a story about two sisters, Mary and Martha. Jesus encourages us to prioritize our relationship with Him in the midst of a busy world with lives full of chores and responsibilities. Sometimes, at the end of the day, we wonder what we accomplished and if it really mattered. Jesus reminds us that quality time spent with Him is something that no one can take away from us. It's always a good day, no matter what got done or what didn't get done, when some of our time was shared in intimate fellowship with Him.

## Keeping the Main Thing the Main Thing

My prayer for us is that we, like the 72, the lawyer, and Mary and Martha, will allow Jesus to guide us in such a way as to always keep the main thing the main thing. There are lots of things in life, good and bad, that want to sidetrack us from what's really important. The apostle Paul tells us that almost everything in life is permissible, but not everything is wise for us. Jesus tells us that we're wise if we make the thrust of our lives about loving God, and others, with all that we've got.

There are two things that are eternal and that will be in heaven: God and people. That's the heart of the gospel. We'll never go wrong if we dial in our hearts to that call and that assignment. If we keep our eyes on Jesus, we'll always be aiming at the bull's-eye. Let's aim wisely and allow His spirit to thrust us forward into a life with passion and with a laser-guided focus that zeros into Him.

Luke Chapter 11

# CONVERSATIONS WITH GOD

*Now Jesus was praying in a certain place, and when he finished, one of his disciples said to him, "Lord, teach us to pray, as John taught his disciples." And he said to them, "When you pray, say: "Father, hallowed be your name. Your kingdom come. Give us each day our daily bread, and forgive us our sins, for we ourselves forgive everyone who is indebted to us. And lead us not into temptation." (Luke 11:1-4)*

## Learning How to Pray

Chapter 11 of Luke begins with Jesus teaching His disciples to pray. He provides them with a relational blueprint that includes: worship, submission, provision, confession, forgiveness, and repentance. The disciples are encouraged to pray to God sincerely and specifically. Jesus promises to send the Holy Spirit to those who ask, because God's actions are always in compliment with His character. He never pulls a "bait and switch" on us. God is a good God and wants good things for His kids.

## Spiritual Authority

Jesus then casts out another demon. Eyes are raised and questions abound. Some accuse Jesus of having a demon Himself and working in cahoots with Beelzebub (traditionally thought to be the regional demonic authority of that area). Jesus explains how the supernatural world of spiritual authority works: a house divided cannot stand. Neither God nor Satan are divided or confused in how they work within their spheres of authority and rule.

The kingdom of darkness operates in a highly unified, hierarchical authority system, which moves downward from spiritual entity to that of a lesser spiritual entity. In short, the less powerful work under the more powerful. Both the Old and New Testaments describe bits and pieces of this hierarchal spiritual system. Often there is an "end goal" that is both a common denominator and a unifying force between the various entities within Satan's kingdom (steal, kill, and destroy - John 10:10). However, the strategies might be different due to differing roles, assignments, authorities, and responsibilities of each entity.

## Keeping a Clean House

Jesus warns that even though the devil is evil and a liar, he is not stupid. He studies our lives and desires to take us down. Jesus tells us to not just "sweep and clean up our house and get rid of sinful living," but to fill our house with God and with good. He reiterates the importance of not just kicking the devil and his vices out of our lives, but at the same time, filling our lives with God and engaging in the things that God loves. That healthy combination will catalyze spiritual health and growth in us.

When Jesus mentions "sweeping and cleaning our house" as well as "putting it in order," He's referring to removing things from our lives like dishonest business practices, getting drunk, doing drugs, pornography, and sleeping with our girlfriend or boyfriend, etc. God is also talking about the things that take place inside a person's heart. Things like pride, religious legalism, racism, materialism, and self-centeredness.

As Christ-followers, we're asked to "put away" those things and instead "put on" the new life that is available to us in Jesus. As we receive Christ into our lives by faith, and begin to apply His teachings, we begin to grow. As we begin filling our minds with scripture, talking to God in prayer, making new friends that support our new life in Christ, downloading wholesome materials onto our computer that are God-honoring, and building up our spiritual lives rather than polluting them, we will begin to flourish and come alive. Becoming "fully alive" requires that we "put away" certain things and "put on" certain things. And yes, it's about receiving and walking in God's grace, but at the same time, it's learning how to partner with His grace. I believe that the secret to success is knowing what things to say "yes" to and what things to say "no" to.

## Insights From Jesus

As the chapter continues, Jesus validates the story of Jonah in the Old Testament. He forecasts His impending death on the cross, His burial, and resurrection. Jesus calls the people to honest repentance and to a change in their way of thinking so they can walk in a new way of living.

Jesus uses the human eye as an analogy to initiate a conversation about self-reflection and honest evaluation concerning our lives. He suggests that the mental models, perspectives, worldviews, and truths we hold sacred have incredible power in our lives. The way we "see" and the "perspectives" that we embrace (both good and bad) influence our actions, behaviors, decisions, and relationships. He calls us to think deeply. To consider. To change where necessary.

Jesus finishes off His day having dinner at a Pharisee's house. Several lawyers and religious leaders join in. Cultivating a right relationship with God and loving people is the centerpiece of their conversation. Jesus explains that God is interested in having a genuine relationship with us, one with clean motives as the foundation. God is not interested in a "religious life" of robotic ritual and sterile ceremony with a heart that is absent.

## Connecting to God Through Daily Prayer

Jesus concludes the evening with some honest and direct words of rebuke for the Pharisees. It's always Jesus' intention that when He offers what appear to be "hard words" that they would be embraced in such a way that will produce "soft hearts." Jesus tells us the truth because He loves us. Learning to walk in God's ways is dependent on connecting with God in relationship. One of the ways we connect best with God is through honest and daily prayer. Whether we are battling sin, standing against the devil and his vices, seeking guidance or supernatural intervention in our own lives or for the lives of those we care about, genuine and honest communication with God is vital. Prayer is about listening, waiting, and reflecting as much as it is about asking and talking.

## The Disciples' Prayer

I love the prayer model Jesus teaches to the disciples in this chapter. At times, I enjoy simply saying this prayer back to God, word for word, just as it's written, thinking about each phrase as I pray it. I realize that it wasn't initially designed to be recited over and over and over again mindlessly. Rather, it was originally designed to be a healthy and balanced guideline on how to pray to God. Even though it's called the "Lord's Prayer," it should probably be called the "Disciples' Prayer" because it was for them.

As you pray the Lord's Prayer, let me encourage you to spend a few minutes speaking words of worship back to God. Thank Him for who He is. Speak words of appreciation for the privilege it is to be one of God's children and to have Him as our loving Father in heaven. Often, after I spend a few minutes personalizing the first phrase of the Lord's Prayer and speaking out loud the various words that come to my mind, I move on to the next phrase, which is about God's kingdom. "Your kingdom come and Your will be done on earth as it is in heaven." I again take another minute or so to personalize it.

I speak out words and thoughts that describe my desire to be submissive to God's ways and to the teachings of Jesus. When and where I'm aware that my life is off track, I admit it to God and ask to be forgiven. I make it right in my heart with God. I tell Him that I want Him to rule over my life and to be my leader. I pray for discernment to be able to recognize where I'm not following His lead, and that the Holy Spirit will show me so I can walk in alignment. After a few minutes or so, I move on to the next phrase: "Give us our daily bread."

When I come to the phrase about "daily bread," I obviously pray for my provision financially, emotionally, spiritually, etc., but I also pray for "daily bread" for those I love and for those I'm responsible for spiritually. Again, I use the Lord's Prayer as a guideline to pray for my needs as well as for the needs of others.

Let me also say that there are times when I just flat-out pray what's on my heart and I don't use any guidelines. It's raw and spontaneous. But sometimes guidelines help me, and I believe that they will help you, too. Then, as you've probably guessed, I move to the phrase about forgiveness, and then to "lead me not into temptation," and then protecting me "from evil."

## Start Small But Start Now

My prayer for you is that you would take time this week to memorize this powerful prayer (if you have yet to do so). Memorize one phrase a day. By the end of the week, you'll know it all. It's a very meaningful prayer. Jesus selected the words Himself when His disciples asked Him how to pray more effectively.

I would also challenge us to pray this prayer each day, in its entirety, for the coming week as a way to jump-start anew our prayer life and daily conversations with God. Use this guideline as a springboard to rejuvenate your relationship with Jesus in a deeper and more meaningful way. It worked for the disciples, and it'll work for us, too.

Luke Chapter 12

# WHERE HAS ALL THE MOXIE GONE...
# IN CHRISTIANITY, THAT IS

*Stay dressed for action and keep your lamps burning, and be like men who are waiting for their master to come from the wedding feast, so that they may open the door to him at once when he comes and knocks. Blessed are those servants whom the master finds awake when he comes. (Luke 12:35-37)*

## Kingdom Principles at Work

Jesus' audience has grown into the thousands at this point in His ministry. Talk of Him being the "Son of God" continues to spread. In this chapter, Jesus expounds on several "kingdom principles" of how life works in God's economy and value system. He tells several parables to unpack these truths. Topics that are discussed include: future judgment, death, fear, money, anxiety, God's provision, greed, contentment, eternity, spiritual alertness, correct priorities, commitment, faith, discernment, and right relationships. Threaded throughout these insightful teachings, Jesus calls for nothing less than full and total commitment to Him above anything and anyone. It's a radical invitation, one that is thrilling and frightening. It's an invitation that can only be received through the radical response to obey and follow.

## Brands of Christianity

We live in a culture that appreciates spirituality, but not in a way that labels anyone a radical. At first glance, that's puzzling because the majority of Americans consider themselves "Christian" when asked in survey after survey. Why the angst? It's because although the majority of our society claims to be "Christian," as you unpack what they mean through conversation, you'll discover that many people's brand of Christianity is something completely different than the brand that Jesus described in the New Testament.

For many people being a Christian means believing in Jesus as a historical figure, but no "Son of God" stuff. For others, "Christian" means doing good works (which we should do) or being a good person while at the same time discounting the Bible as God's inspired word to humanity. Therefore, they don't feel the need to obey it, just the parts in it with which they agree. To others, "Christian" means to go to a church as a family on Christmas and Easter and then off to open presents or collect multicolored eggs. For others, their brand of "Christianity" means believing in God as a higher power, divine force, or spiritual energy in the universe. That's why in my conversations with people about God I always like to use Jesus' name when referring to God because I want to be clear about the brand of Christianity that I'm coming from.

## Becoming a Radical

Please allow me to clarify what I mean when I use the word "radical Christian." I am not meaning "radical" to be someone who claims they are a Christ-follower (and has the bumper stickers to prove it), but outwardly is loud, angry, obnoxious, overly opinionated, listens only to talk radio for sermon material, slams homosexuals, and thinks everyone is going to hell if they didn't vote for the political candidates that they chose. You've met this person, haven't you? Let me be clear: That's not my definition of a radical.

Christians of the Millennial generation (young teens through late twenties) are sick and tired of this "brand" representing their faith and their God. They want full moxie in their faith, not a watered-down faith that speaks loudly and says all the right words but fails to act. That's decaf spirituality. It talks like espresso coffee, but it lacks the jolt, it doesn't deliver. Jesus told us to be the real deal. He told us in scripture to arise. To be awake! To get some oil in our lamps. Ask God to put some fire in our bones. Live a life that aligns with our words. Pursue goals in life that line up with your faith. Roll up your sleeves and get into the game. Don't just talk about it. Believe. Act. Love. Engage. Follow.

The word "radical" means "going to the root of origin," and doing whatever it takes to get there. This is what the young generation (as well as the rest of us) longs to see: people who love Jesus, who are passionate, and are sold out for Him, but in a way that incorporates a change of lifestyle. Yes, radicals are vocal, but they have the goods to back up their words. Radicals allow their faith to impact the core of their humanity. They live differently. They walk the talk with a radical lifestyle that represents Jesus accurately to the world of the skeptic.

## No More Decaf

My prayer for us is that we too would go back to the root of origin. It's *all* about Jesus. It's *only* about Jesus. It will *always* be about Jesus. Let's live a fully integrated God-life, one that walks the talk. God will help us to do that because that's what He wants to do in us. That is what Christian transformation is all about: letting God form Jesus in us. And as Jesus is formed in us, God will work through us in order to impact a watching world. No more decaf Christianity—only the real stuff.

Luke Chapter 13

# SECRETS OF THE MUSTARD SEED: DON'T DESPISE SMALL BEGINNINGS

*He said therefore, "What is the kingdom of God like? And to what shall I compare it? It is like a grain of mustard seed that a man took and sowed into his garden, and it grew and became a tree, and the birds of the air made nests in its branches." (Luke 13:18-19)*

## Jesus and the Kingdom

Jesus continues His journey toward Jerusalem and teaches about God's kingdom along the way. (The word "kingdom" means a system of rulership. Wherever the king is "ruling over" is where the "kingdom" is resident.) This chapter opens with a conversation about a local tragedy involving Pilate killing a bunch of people. Rumors circulate that this took place because those killed had "secret sin" in their lives, and God was supposedly judging them. Jesus tells the group that that's not true and He attempts to re-focus their thinking. He challenges them away from their apparent obsession with popular opinion and the chatter that is taking place in the town streets and cafés about this incident. It's not that Jesus didn't care about the people's loss, or that when horrific injustices do occur that we should just idly stand by. No, we must address those issues and stand up to them without fear and intimidation.

Jesus knew that as human beings we often like to discuss for hours on end the events and minute details about other people's lives (and misfortunes) rather than making sure we wipe the egg off our own faces and spend our time and energy on the things we can change and should change, starting with ourselves and our own relationship with God. Our lives tend to drift toward the things we focus on. Jesus suggests some "guard rails" that will aid us in the midst of life and all of the challenges that come with it. Learning to keep our eyes on the main thing is vital to our health, relationships, effectiveness, and influence as followers of Jesus.

## Spiritual Lenses

I wear progressive lenses in my glasses. When I look through the bottom half of my lenses, I can see up-close. This part of my lens focuses my eyes in such a way that I can read tiny print in a book. The top half of my lens allows me to see far away. It focuses my eyes so that I can read street signs hundreds of feet in the distance. I need both kinds of optical capacities built into my lenses if I want to function at my best.

I have a road bike that I like to ride in the streets of Boise. In order not to crash into cars, curbs, and kids, I had some prescription sunglasses made. There's only one problem: These glasses only have one kind of optical magnification built into the lens, unlike my other glasses. I can see far away, but not up close. This works just fine as long as I never need to read the instruments on my bike, find my water bottle, or look at my wristwatch! Jesus knows that the lens that we look through, like my sunglasses, affects our ability to move forward and navigate through the things in life both far and near. We must learn to see the big picture as well as the details. This plays off the old adage, "It's difficult to see the forest for the trees." Jesus helped these people see the "spiritual forest," so to speak.

## Juxtaposed Truths

Next, Jesus explains His contrarian wisdom by masterfully weaving two counterpoised values together as one truth in order to better explain the kingdom principles He was teaching. For example, Jesus explains the tight links between grace and truth, word and spirit, forgiveness and judgment, and patience and repentance. He illustrates these juxtaposed principles by explaining the parable of the fig tree, the mustard seed, and the narrow door, as well as finding time to heal another woman with a debilitating spirit.

## The Heart of Jesus

The chapter concludes with Jesus lamenting over Jerusalem. He demonstrates again His incredible love for all people. He sees past their busyness and preoccupation with daily responsibilities and pressures that many times shroud His presence. Just like looking out over a huge city from the balcony of a high rise hotel, where you can see thousands of cars lining the streets, the rising sounds of honking horns everywhere, and masses of people hustling and bustling along city sidewalks, Jesus also looks out and over humanity. He gazes over the city and feels deep compassion for people's searching, misplaced priorities, and lonely hearts. Jesus is stirred inside. He longs for people to be in loving relationship with the God who made them and redeemed them. We're reminded again that we enter into a relationship with God through the person of Jesus.

## Parable of the Mustard Seed

As I read this chapter, I'm drawn to the parable of the mustard seed. As you may know, the mustard seed is very small and seemingly insignificant.

It was the smallest seed used by Palestinian farmers and gardeners of the day. Under favorable conditions, it could grow quite high. So Jesus uses it as an "object lesson" to explain how God works.

In seed form, the mustard seed is nothing to brag about. Yet in full maturity, it becomes a stellar tree. When fully grown, birds build their nests in its branches and the branches provide shade for others. Jesus teaches us that this is one of the ways God works in our lives. Many things in life start off small. For example, some of the areas of fruitfulness in my own life today (and I'm sure in yours, too) first began with just a dream or a quiet decision that was inspired by the whisper of God. Big things usually start as little things. Some of the biggest areas of life-change occur because of a God-inspired decision to follow Him, to trust Him, or to love Him. Never think lightly of the things God sparks in your life when they are first introduced.

Looking back in my life, some of the most rewarding realities today first began as just a quiet thought, a simple impression, or an honest decision that was inspired by God. The danger of living in a society permeated with instant gratification, is that we can very easily overestimate what we think God should do in 30 days and underestimate what He actually does in 3 years. This is the secret of the mustard seed. The limitations of today are not always the realities of tomorrow. Give God time. God does the seemingly impossible.

## Moving to Boise, Idaho

I often think back to the very first time that I had, or what seemed to be at the time, "just a passing thought" about moving to Boise, Idaho, to start a church. I was living in Tucson, Arizona. It was a mustard seed thought, but it was placed there by God. I didn't realize it at first because it was so small, quiet, and seemingly so insignificant. At first I dismissed it, but it returned. My wife, Mary, and I began to talk and pray for several months about this whisper from God. Soon I acknowledged that this thought might be God placing an impression in my heart. We continued to pray.

I remember the day that we sat down with sets of people that we loved to tell them that we were going to move to a city that we had never been to and where we knew no one. No job. No house. No friends. We were going to sell our home, pack up a U-haul truck, drive from Tucson to Boise, and figure out specifics once we got there. Driving across the Utah desert at night with our three small children, I remember looking into the expanse of the night sky and thinking about the mustard seed dream becoming a reality. It was now not just a seed, but a germinated seed. It was by no means a tree, just a blooming seedling. I remember thinking that our only options were failure or success (we've experienced both). As of today, 18 years have passed since that mustard seed was placed into my heart.

## Small Beginnings

Let me encourage you to never despise small beginnings. Today, that seed (Grace Chapel of Boise) is an amazing church that is still growing and is filled with many wonderful people who love God and each other. It's been a wonderful journey to watch God conceive a thought into seed, a seed into a seedling, a seedling into a plant, a plant into a small tree, and a small tree into a maturing tree that teems with a spirit of servanthood as it gives shade to others and is a resource of God's blessing to the city of Boise and beyond.

## The Planting of the Lord

My prayer for us is that we will never discount the mustard seed beginnings that God places in our hearts. God plants these seeds in all kinds of ways: an impression, a dream, a conversation, a thought, or even a painful experience. He works in amazing ways. Always remember that God's timing is perfect. His power is limitless. His process is uncanny. Your mustard seed thought might actually be God's thought that He's placed in the soil of your heart. Guard it. Water it. Seek counsel about it. Pray. Search the scriptures. Who knows, it might just be God Himself working in you in order to do something extraordinary through you.

If you are one who finds yourself in a season of frustration because God's plan and process appears to be stalling and stuck in "seed mode," let me encourage you to not to give up. Don't give in. Stand. Pray. Wait. Watch. You'll see. God will come through because all mustard seeds that are His, always blossom in His perfect season and time.

Luke Chapter 14

# COUNTING THE COST:
# A HAPPY HOUR TO REMEMBER

*Now great crowds accompanied him, and he turned and said to them, "If anyone comes to me and does not hate his own father and mother and wife and children and brothers and sisters, yes, and even his own life, he cannot be my disciple. Whoever does not bear his own cross and come after me cannot be my disciple." (Luke 14:25-27)*

## Discipleship Unpacked

Chapter 14 begins with Jesus once again healing on the Sabbath. He continues to teach about the real cost of being a whole-hearted follower. He unpacks various discipleship principles centered on God's love and grace. He uses two parables: the wedding feast, and the great banquet, to make His point. Jesus gets specific. He clearly lays out what it takes to be a committed disciple. He tells His audience that it will cost everything; all the chips are out and on the table. Here are the highlights:

1. Disciples must love their family less than Christ. A disciple is one who loves Jesus more than anyone or anything. Yes, they are to love their families, but not more than Jesus.

2. Faith is about action. Disciples must move beyond "believing" and begin to "follow" and apply the teachings of Jesus in their lives. The scriptures tell us that even the devil "believes" about God (James 2:19). Discipleship has movement. It acts on what it believes. God's grace will help us as we take our first steps in our pursuit of God. His arms are open to us, but we are responsible for initiating action.

3. For the disciple, everything in life becomes secondary in comparison to Jesus. He is first and foremost in and around our relationships, finances, work, goals, sexuality, recreation, etc. Nothing takes precedence over Him or what He teaches us. Jesus must move to the front of the line in our priorities and pursuits.

Jesus then uses two illustrations (a building project, and going to war) to make His point about counting the cost up-front of what it will take to be successful in the faith journey. He's driving home the point that being a follower of Jesus will cost. In fact, it will cost everything. So don't make a hasty decision. Count the cost up-front. We live in a culture that wants to "add" Jesus to our lives rather than be the centerpiece of it. Jesus doesn't want to be added. He wants to be Lord over everything and everyone in our lives.

## A Happy Hour to Remember

Years ago when I was in Tucson driving down Pima Street, I drove by a happy hour sign advertising free cocktails. It caught my eye because a church was hosting the event. I pulled in to the parking lot and went inside to check it out. I was greeted by an attractive cocktail waitress who informed me where the bar was. She also told me that she was the pastor hosting the event. Others gathered around me and they asked who I was and where I worked. I told them I was a staff pastor at Grace Chapel Tucson (just up the road).

They offered to show me around this so-called church (it was actually a cult), as I must have seemed interested in the mission and vision statement that was on the brochure that they'd handed me. The waitress (I mean the pastor) led me into a large circular foyer that had doors in several directions. Each door led into a different room. Like an old game show hostesses, she said, "This door leads into our Buddha room." On the front of each door, there was a picture introducing what religion or teaching preference was behind the door. This door had a picture of the Buddha.

I looked at another door and glanced at the poster on it: Lord Krishna. This was the Hare Krishna room. Next to it was a door that sported an oversized sparkling turquoise colored gem: the crystal room. The next door had a picture of the universe: the EST room for trance-like mediation. Finally, at the far end of the room I saw a door with a picture of Jesus on it: the Jesus room.

## Gods of Choice

Talk about multiple options in an age of consumer satisfaction! There was a "god of choice" for just about everyone's preference. Later that night, I thought about how there are "lots of gods" and lots of options to "add on" to our lives. Our society applauds those men and women who possess a "balanced touch" or "sprinkle" of spirituality. It "rounds them out," so to speak. But in this chapter, Jesus isn't talking about "adding to" anything. He doesn't consider that an option. That's cousin to a spiritual fluff ball. Jesus knows that "adding," rather than "full surrender" to Him, doesn't really serve a person well in the long run. Why? Because when the first challenge comes their way, they'll be gone pursuing a new "add on" that doesn't cost.

They'll grab a martini and try a new door that doesn't challenge them too much.

## Captured By His Love

Jesus is talking about allowing God to have full-on rulership in every dimension and facet of our lives. He's talking about taking the loves of our lives (people, places, and things) and bringing them under Him (making them second). I don't know about you, but that doesn't sound like a "sprinkle" or touch to me. It sounds like becoming a "passionary" for God and the things that God loves. It sounds like someone who's been captured and arrested by God's love and call. It reverberates like someone who is becoming a force for God and for good in the world. It echoes like a message where Jesus is ruler and leader of every area of our lives.

You can see why, as Jesus shot straight like this with the crowds, they thinned out quickly. They chose other doors. His intention was not to discourage them. It was to be honest with them on how to not just get started in their faith but to finish well in it. The faith journey isn't always easy. Getting the right heart and perspective up-front is critical.

Heaven is a destination that all can enjoy. The disciple's call is a message the crowds turned their backs on. Salvation is free. Jesus paid the full price on Calvary's cross. He invites us to partake of His completed work by receiving what He did for us. But everything else in life costs. And that is what Jesus was getting at.

## No Regrets

My prayer for us is that we will consider the price Jesus paid for our salvation. Although He asks to be Lord above everything and anyone in our lives, in light of who Jesus is and what He's done for us, it's an honor to follow and a privilege to be known by Him. Let me ask you: Who's your Lord? What door have you chosen to go through? Have you "added" Jesus into your life, or have you responded to the disciple's call to love Him above anything and anyone? Have you chosen to move beyond believing and into following? Following Jesus will cost you but it's a decision that you will never regret. I pray that you will weigh the options wisely and choose the "Jesus door." Saying yes to Him is the most eternal decision you will ever make.

Luke Chapter 15

# PATHWAYS:
# A TALE OF TWO LOST SONS

*There was a man who had two sons. And the younger of them said to his father, "Father, give me the share of the property that is coming to me." Not many days later, the younger son gathered all he had and took a journey into a far country, and there he squandered his property in reckless living. And he arose and came to his father. But while he was still a long way off, his father saw him and felt compassion, and ran and embraced him and kissed him. But the father said to his servants, "Bring quickly the best robe, and put it on him, and put a ring on his hand, and shoes on his feet. Let us eat and celebrate." Now his older son was in the field, and as he came and drew near to the house, heard music and dancing. And the servant said to him, "Your brother has come, and your father has killed the fattened calf, because he has received him back safe and sound." But he was angry and refused to go in. (Luke 15:11-32)*

## The Lost Sheep, Coin, and Sons

Jesus is surrounded by a group of tax collectors, sinners, Pharisees, and teachers of the law. Once again, the religious elites are ticked off that Jesus has befriended the fringe subcultures. Jesus gives the Pharisee's a laser-guided look into the deep recesses of the heart of God. He presents a new way of seeing and understanding sin, lostness, and God's forgiveness. To make His point Jesus tells three short parables: the lost sheep, the lost coin, and two lost brothers.

Jesus directs the stories at the Pharisees and scribes as He sheds new light on how people become alienated from and found by God. The last story, the prodigal son, might actually be better understood if we referred to it as Jesus does: a story of a man who had two sons.

## Two Common Misconceptions

Jesus explains there are often two tragic paths people take when attempting to connect with God. First: the route of self-exploration. This is the path that the younger brother in the story took. It was an avenue of personal experimentation. He tried various pursuits, ideas, and pleasures outside the boundaries of what was considered safe, normal, and religiously conservative at the time. It was a perspective of wanting to "sow wild oats" in such a way as to experience "self-discovery" in regards to attaining spirituality, truth, happiness, and God. This proved disastrous for the younger son. But in the end, the son returns to the father and receives forgiveness and acceptance. The celebration begins as their relationship is renewed!

Second: the route of moralistic living. This is the path that the elder brother pursued. It's often missed by a cursory read of the parable. It surfaces at the end of the story when the elder brother argues with his father and won't come to the celebration for his younger brother. He's mad that he has lived morally and righteously all along and isn't getting anything special for it. He digs his heels in and defiantly refuses to walk alongside his father and celebrate that his younger brother has returned.

In the end, the older son doesn't find forgiveness, acceptance, or relationship with his father. The story ends, sadly, with the older brother refusing the father's invitation of community and relationship with him. In the final scene, the elder brother is alone and alienated from the father (God) because of his own self-righteousness.

## Keeping All the Rules

This second worldview (the elder brother perspective) is a path that "keeps all the rules" and maps a morally upright life with the expectation that salvation is earned through being a good person. There's a subtle "God owes me because I do what's right" mentality embedded deep down in this perspective. It's an "I earn my way to heaven" kind of thinking because "my ethics, morals, and decisions are better than other peoples." This "I should get something special from God" attitude is a form of self-righteousness (which means that I make myself "right and presentable before God" as a result of my own efforts and good deeds instead of Jesus making all things right as well as making me right by His shed blood on the cross for my sins).

Jesus teaches that both perspectives (the prodigal brother and the self-righteous elder brother) are misguided. In some ways they're the same in that these routes don't connect us or bring us close to God. Too often, we sentimentize this story and fixate only on the younger son. The point of the story is actually about the oldest son. Jesus was preaching to those who thought they were in right standing with God based upon what they knew and the moral and upright lives that they thought they were leading. This perspective is what many people in our culture think Christianity is all about: moralistic living, piety, being a good person, and doing good things. But having a personal relationship with Jesus, for many, is not even in the equation. Christianity, at its core, is not a set of moral behaviors, rules, or rituals to keep. It's not a "Golden Rule philosophy." It's all about Jesus and what He's done. Christianity is about a person—Jesus. It's about a relationship with Him. Both paths (self-experimentation and moralistic living) are attempts to connect with God without going through the cross and through the person of Jesus Christ. Jesus teaches that we will never find a genuine relationship with God by doing our own thing or by just doing the right thing. We experience relationship with God by accepting what Jesus has done for us on the cross. It's about admitting our sin and receiving His forgiveness, which allows us to be part of the family of God.

As you read the whole chapter, you'll notice that both sons are interested in themselves. Both are fixated on what they can get from the father, rather than on having a relationship with him. Both paths are dead ends.

## Finding Your Way Home

My prayer for us is that whatever path we are on today we would take time to consider, assess, and reflect honestly on our motives before God. It's possible to be lost "outside" the father's house as well as lost "inside" His house. It's so easy to develop a mindset that says, "God owes me" because of what I do for Him, and get angry when things in life don't work out like we hoped because we expected to be subtly rewarded for our good behavior.

My hope is that we will not serve God for what we hope to get from Him. Rather, we will pursue Him and love Him because of who He is and what He has done. I'm very much aware that inside of me there is a little Pharisee just waiting to flare up if left unchecked. So join me as I pray, "Search me, O God, and see if there is any unclean motive in my heart, and in the path that I am following in my pursuit to know You."

Luke Chapter 16

# LEVERAGING YOUR BLING:
# INFLUENCING OTHERS FOR ETERNITY'S SAKE

*"One who is faithful in very little is also faithful in much, and one who is dishonest in very little is also dishonest in much. If then you have not been faithful in the unrighteous wealth, who will entrust to you the true riches? And if you have not been faithful in that which is another's, who will give you that which is your own? No servant can serve two masters, for either he will hate the one and despise the other. You cannot serve God and money." (Luke 16:10-13)*

## Money, Power, and Influence

This chapter talks about money, power, influence, and eternity. Jesus tells the parable of the dishonest business manager to His 12 disciples and the Pharisees. He explains how the manager extends "business favors" by using his position to radically discount various "accounts receivables" for certain business owners with the expectation of receiving future kickbacks (once he's out of a job). Jesus praises the manager for his shrewdness (not for his dishonesty) as he leverages his influence and uses money in such a way that it positions him well for his uncertain future.

Jesus then spins the parable and applies it to His own followers and comments how they too should be forward-thinking in how they steward their money, possessions, and influence for their future life and the future life of others in regards to eternity. Jesus tells them that, unfortunately, people of the world are often more skilled at positioning themselves in this life than Christians are in positioning themselves in the world to come.

## Leveraging Money For Eternity's Sake

In essence, Jesus explains to the 12 that they should be generous in their use of money and with their stuff. He challenges them to use their bling in such a way that it helps those who are far from God come close to Him. When people who are in need experience genuine love through the generosity of others, it opens them up to consider the goodness of the Creator and the validity of the gospel message. When Christians use their wealth strategically and with other people's eternal destiny in mind, Jesus is made famous, and the gospel becomes real. When non-Christians are the recipients of loving Christian charity, generosity, and financial provision in times of need, Jesus' teachings take on a whole new reality. Jesus then tells us that we can't serve both God and money. We must serve one or the other. This is a case of Either/Or.

## Lazarus and the Rich Man

Jesus finishes up the chapter with a gripping story of a rich man and a poor guy named Lazarus. Both guys die. The rich man wakes up in Hades. Lazarus wakes up in heaven. A sobering conversation takes place. Let me be clear: The rich man is not in Hades because he's affluent. As you'll note in the story, Lazarus is actually standing next to Abraham, who was one of the wealthiest people in all of the Old Testament. The rich man's problem was that he never responded to God and to God's purposes for his life. The rich guy thought he never needed anybody, other than himself, including God. That was his Achilles' heel.

## Heaven and Hell

This parable teaches us that when we wake up in eternity (either heaven or hell) we will be wide awake. There's no jet lag or time delay. Your spirit immediately goes to one place or the other as soon as you die. When we get there, we will either be filled with joy and gratitude or overwhelmed with regret. Jesus gives us no option in the middle. Once we are in eternity, we will be able to look back at our lives on earth with clarity. Heaven and hell are real places. Real people end up in one or the other. This is one of the reasons Jesus spends most of the chapter talking about leveraging everything (money, possessions, influence, and talents) to serve and influence other people in such a way that they too see how wonderful Jesus is, come to know Him, and ultimately end up in heaven.

## Reflections

My prayer for us is that we would honestly look at how we spend our money and use our possessions.

- Is our life about God or about money?
- Is our pursuit in life money and a little bit of God, or is it pursuing God and stewarding money as God directs?
- Are we leveraging everything we have, and everything we are, in such a way as to help others that are our friends, work associates, extended family, and classmates come close to God?
- Do we have their eternity in our mind's eye?
- Are we stewarding our influence and talents in such a way that helps people discover Jesus?

These are tough questions. When we understand that other people are actually connected to the outcome, these questions move from being thought provoking to that of acting and intervening for the sake of others. Who is the "Lazarus" that God has placed in your path?

Luke Chapter 17

# RAISING YOUR T.Q.
# (THANKFULNESS QUOTIENT)

*On the way to Jerusalem he was passing along between Samaria and Galilee. And as he entered a village, he was met by ten lepers, who stood at a distance and lifted up their voices, saying, "Jesus, Master, have mercy on us." When he saw them he said to them, "Go and show yourselves to the priests." And as they went they were cleansed. Then one of them, when he saw that he was healed, turned back, praising God with a loud voice; and he fell on his face at Jesus' feet, giving him thanks. Now he was a Samaritan. Then Jesus answered, "Were not ten cleansed? Where are the nine? Was no one found to return and give praise to God except this foreigner?" And he said to him, "Rise and go your way; your faith has made you well." (Luke 17:11-19)*

## Chapter Highlights

Jesus begins this chapter with a warning about temptation and sin. He tells us that temptations are inevitable, but woe to the guy who becomes a source of stumbling to others, especially little children and the young in the faith. Jesus says it would be better for a person to wrap a chain around their own neck, anchor it to a 100-pound cement block, and drown themselves in the ocean, than be a source of destruction, sin, injustice, or violence toward a child (as well as those people who are vulnerable).

Jesus sets forth a pattern for relational health and harmony which includes: vigilant truth-telling, constant forgiveness, genuine repentance, and appropriate restoration. The disciples are taken back by how high Jesus raises the bar above the cultural norm of contemporary Judaism. Honestly, they're a bit freaked out and intimidated so they ask Jesus for an "extra shot" of faith.

## Healing of 10 Lepers

As Jesus and the 12 are on their way to Jerusalem they encounter a small company of 10 lepers. The lepers ask to be healed and Jesus grants their request. Now cleansed, the lepers head for town. One leper though, a Samaritan (a type of social outcast or fringe person), turned around, came back, and fell at Jesus' feet to say "thanks." Jesus converses with the guy and tells him that now he's not just healed, but made whole. The leper leaves cleansed, healed, forgiven, and fully alive.

Of course, it wouldn't be a full day of ministry unless Jesus takes on the Pharisees again. It's important to remember that Jesus puts up with so much of their guff, not because He delights in debating with people to prove them wrong, but because He loves them deeply. Jesus loved the Pharisees and wanted them to change their ways and connect with God (and some actually did). Jesus knows that many times it's in the midst of tough yet honest dialogue that we can experience self-discovery and "see the light" about many things. New insights can be the seeds of new growth that bring about change in our lives.

I'm grateful for the people in my life that love me enough to challenge me on the things that they don't think I'm seeing clearly on. There is an old axiom that says, "The eye cannot see itself." That's really true. We need people in our lives that love God and love us (and in that order), who will speak into our lives and into the perspectives that we hold dear. I've found that I come away from those conversations either strengthened in my current convictions or open to new ways of seeing because of their prodding and lovingly pushing back at me. It's always been beneficial and catalyzing for growth.

### Kingdom of God

The chapter finishes with conversations about the kingdom of God and when and how it will appear. The kingdom of God has two dimensions to it: (1) the partial current reality of Jesus' rulership, and (2) the future complete reality of Jesus' rulership, at the second coming, as described in the book of Revelation.

Jesus tells the group that God's kingdom is already among them (partially). Wherever Jesus is ruling, the kingdom is present. Jesus is already beginning to rule in people's hearts and lives throughout the region. So, in a very real sense, God's kingdom has already broken into the world. Jesus then shifts to explain the part of God's kingdom that will take place in the future: the second coming of Jesus. He tells the group that when that time comes, there will be no forewarning. It will be sudden, unmistakable, and witnessed by all.

### The Power of Thankfulness

As I reflect on the scripture concerning the 10 lepers, it's always caught my eye that only 1 out of the 10 ever came back to say thanks to Jesus. There's a difference between being appreciative and being thankful. Being appreciative means thinking thankful thoughts; thankfulness means speaking them out. Being thankful on a regular basis changes us from the inside out.

Thankfulness is more than an action. It can actually become part of your character if you do it enough. It's powerful. I wonder if those percentages are still true today? I wonder how many people are really thankful and grateful to God for His touch upon their lives and the gifts He's given them? I wonder what it would take to get the other 90 percent of the world to actually speak out words of thanks to God for who He is and all He's done. And, not in any way to take away from God, but there are people in our lives who also deserve to be thanked. There are lots of people who have contributed to our lives in both small and large ways.

## Prayer of Thanksgiving

My prayer for us is that we would be part of the 10 percent who speak words of thanks to God for who He is and all He's done. At the same time, I pray that we would also seek out those people in our lives that have contributed and invested in us as people. I've learned that any success we experience is because we stand on the shoulders of others who have lifted us up. Join me in making a list this week of some folks you could track down to say "thanks" to. Let's raise our TQ—Thankfulness Quotient—and be in that top 10 percent. Let's not just be healed; let's be made whole.

Luke Chapter 18

# LOOK UP:
# RECAPTURING A SPIRIT OF WONDER

*Now they were bringing even infants to him that he might touch them. And when the disciples saw it, they rebuked them. But Jesus called them to him, saying, "Let the children come to me, and do not hinder them, for to such belongs the kingdom of God. Truly, I say to you, whoever does not receive the kingdom of God like a child shall not enter it." (Luke 18:15-17)*

## Persistent Prayer

Jesus opens this chapter with the parable of the persistent widow. He teaches the disciples about prayer using a classic teaching method of logic and argument to make His point (If premise A is true, then premise B is even more true). Jesus explains that if an unjust officer of the court will eventually give in and take appropriate action when needed, how much more will a just and loving God intervene on behalf of those who are tenacious and entreat Him in prayer? We are encouraged to never give up in prayer. God hears us and will intervene in His perfect timing. He rewards persistence.

## A Pharisee and a Tax Collector

The next parable is one that highlights a Pharisee and a tax collector. Jesus selects two guys and two lifestyles that are on opposite ends of the pendulum to use as examples. Jesus hopes that those who are far from God will see their need for Him, humble themselves, receive His mercy and forgiveness, and come close to Him. Jesus contrasts using a guy whose life is in shambles, yet is humble and calls out to God for mercy, with a guy whose perception of himself is successful, morally upstanding, and self-righteous, and thereby someone who has no need for grace, mercy, or forgiveness. In the end, the guy with the messed-up life (the tax collector) actually ends up finding life because of his true humility toward God. The smug, self-sufficient Pharisee misses God completely.

Jesus dialogues about eternal life with the rich young ruler. He foretells His soon-coming death and resurrection for the third time. And once again, He heals a blind man on the road to Jericho.

## Cultivating Child-like Faith

In the middle of the chapter, a discussion about the value of children surfaces with the disciples and Jesus. The 12 were shooing kids away from Him and in so many words saying, "Jesus is too busy to be bugged by a bunch of rug rats." Jesus blasts the disciples out of the water and tells them that they could learn a lot about God through taking on some childlike qualities themselves (for example: faith, awe, wonder, trust, simplicity, curiosity, creativity, humor, and joy).

Even today, we are encouraged to be child-like in our faith. The apostle Paul differentiates between being child-like and being childish. As Christ-followers, we are to put away childishness but embrace childlikeness. (1 Corinthians 13:11)

## Rekindling a Spirit of Awe

I remember an old friend named Sam Sasser. I first met him in Texas when I was a young Christian. Sam was an older pastor and missionary to the Marshall Islands for many years. Sam had diabetes that was left untreated while he was in the mission field, and he had gone blind in one eye. Once back in America, he had a glass eye made to fit.

Sam told me of a time when he was back in the United States preaching. He quickly went to the bathroom before the worship service started. While he was in the bathroom, back in a stall, his right eye somehow fell out from its socket, hit the ground, and rolled on to the floor over by the sink. He panicked, but couldn't do anything at that point (if you know what I mean).

Just then, two nine-year-old boys burst into the bathroom, looked down, and saw Sam's glass eye rolling on the floor. "Whoa, dude. Check it out!" said one of the boys. Sam couldn't see them, but he heard them as they spontaneously made sounds of awe and gasps of amazement over his glass eye. They picked it up and held it three inches from their faces, twisting it in their hands.

By this time, Sam had made it out from the bathroom stall and approached the youngsters. He watched the boys for several seconds without saying anything. To make a long story short, Sam got his glass eye back. The boys bolted out the doors as fast as they could to tell their friends about their amazing discovery in the men's bathroom. Sam chuckled to himself.

As Sam was washing his hands, the Holy Spirit whispered to his heart, "Sam, you used to be just like those two boys." Sam responded, "What do you mean?" The Lord whispered in his heart, "You used to be in awe of Me all the time. Don't you remember how you used to think about Me when you first became a Christian? Do you remember when you would seek Me in prayer or read the scriptures when you were young in the faith? Sam, you were just like those young kids. You could walk out in the backyard and look up at the night sky and you would talk with Me. Gasps of awe would escape from your mouth. Words of praise and thankfulness were your common vocabulary. Sometimes you didn't have words to describe what was going on in your heart, except those same childlike feelings of awe, amazement, wonder, joy, and astonishment—just like those young boys when they saw your eye. You seem to have lost your awe and wonder about Me. Those were some of the best times. Sam, I wish we could go back to that time in our relationship."

Sam said he was stunned. He was so shook up deep inside that he could barely finish his message that morning. He told several of us later that the encounter in the bathroom changed the condition of his heart forever. It altered the trajectory of his ministry until the day he died. He pursued God until he recaptured the child-like qualities of wonder, awe, and passion and placed them back into his relationship with Jesus.

I think this is why Jesus knew that possessing a child-like heart was so powerful and necessary for His disciples. It gives us strength for the journey and joy for the present. It's a non-negotiable for healthy Christian living.

## A Prayer of Wonder

My prayer for us is that we too would recapture those child-like qualities of awe and wonder in our relationship with Jesus (if we've lost them). These are kingdom qualities, not just little kid qualities. These are "spiritual vitamins" that keep our relationship with God bubbling, alive, strong, and healthy.

My hope is that you will take time to go out in your backyard and look up at the expanse of the night sky once again. Gaze across the horizon. Look deeply into the spray of stars that fills the heavens. Reflect on our amazing Creator and the words He used to make them (Genesis 1). Let gasps of awe and whispers of wonder escape from your lips as you treasure anew how great and awesome is the God of the universe, and how marvelous is God's amazing Son, Jesus Christ our Lord.

Luke Chapter 19

# LOST AND FOUND:
# UNNAMED YET SIGNIFICANT

*And Jesus said to him, "Today salvation has come to this house, since he also is a son of Abraham. For the Son of Man came to seek and to save the lost." (Luke 19:9-10)*

## Mission-Minded

Jesus was on a mission from God. His life's mantra was "seeking and saving people who were lost." Even during His final days on the earth, Jesus was on an all-out search and rescue mission for people who were far from God.

In this chapter, Jesus encounters a guy named Zacchaeus, a hated tax collector and a man who had lost his way in life. Jesus befriends him and helps him connect with God. Jesus goes on to explain the parable of the 10 minas. We're reminded that we are called to be both fruitful and faithful.

Jesus makes His triumphant entry into Jerusalem. The crowds worship Him. The Pharisees hate Him. As Jesus enters Jerusalem, He weeps for the people who have rejected Him and for those who still remain lost in themselves and in their differing pursuits of self-salvation. God's loving heart for people bursts forth once again. Once inside the city of Jerusalem, Jesus goes righteously ballistic and cleanses the Temple. He's absolutely sick and tired of religious systems that are self-serving and that alienate people from God by classism, racism, and elitism. Jesus wants men and women everywhere to experience the love, forgiveness, and acceptance of God the Father. He's serious about tearing down barriers and making level paths for lost people to come home to God.

## Spiritual Lostness

Whenever I think of the term "lost," lots of images come to mind: lost keys, lost T.V. remotes, and lost cell phones. But for Jesus, the word "lost" meant only one thing: people. He knew that spiritual lostness (to not be in a personal relationship with God) is a universal human condition. The prophet Isaiah said, "We all are like sheep, have gone astray, each of us has turned to his own way; and the Lord has laid on him the iniquity of us all." (Isaiah 53:6)

Spiritual lostness takes place in a plethora of ways. Some of us get lost in life and unintentionally from God. For example, maybe we start to drift in our teenage years or in college. Then one day we wake up and realize, "I'm lost." It's not that we intended for it to happen. It just did. Others, like myself, chose to get lost. It wasn't an accident. I consciously turned my back on anything that smelled like God, and went the other direction pursuing a life of self-exploration, while attempting to figure out the meaning of life and obtain a sustainable measure of happiness.

The point is that we all get lost. Sometimes it's by accident, and sometimes it's by choice. When I was young, I got lost in drugs and alcohol. Others got lost in good careers and making money. Some of my friends even got lost in church and in trying to be good people. Some, like me, were over-the-edge, full-blown train wreck sinners. Others were nice, respectable, suburban sinners. Either way, lost a little or lost a lot, we're all lost and need to be found by God. Jesus has come searching for all of us.

Throughout the scriptures, Jesus was after people who found themselves alienated and disconnected from the God of the universe. He knew these folks were deeply aware inside themselves that whatever path they were pursuing really wasn't working for them. It didn't bring them lasting happiness. It didn't solve their deepest problems like they had hoped it would. Real meaning and peace were still missing from their lives. Their relationships were struggling. These were (and still are) the people Jesus was searching out. This is why the gospel is called "good news."

## Search and Rescue

I remember the first search and rescue mission I was on as a kid. It was on a sweltering hot summer day in the desert of Tucson, Arizona. My dad, three younger brothers, and I were hiking to see a waterfall in Sabino Canyon. We came upon a woman who was trapped under a several thousand-pound Saguaro cactus. Somehow, the 20-foot cactus had fallen on her and pinned her to the desert floor. Crying, moaning, and writhing in pain, she laid on her back with this massive, spike-covered trunk pressing on her stomach and thighs. She was in a state of shock.

Other hikers had found her first, stopped, and were trying to free her from the clasp of the cactus. Three guys took off their belts, fastened them together to make one longer belt, slid it under the huge Saguaro, and then tried to lift up the cactus so the woman could be pulled out to safety. It didn't work. There was horror in the woman's eyes.

My dad had all of us boys combine the drinking water from our canteens to give it to this woman to drink. She was quickly becoming severely dehydrated under the desert sun. My dad asked the leader of the group what we could do to help. The man said, "Go for help as fast as you can." (This was in the 1960s, way before cell phones). My dad rallied us young boys together (ages eight, seven, six, and four) and we hiked back out of the canyon without any water or rest along the trail. The good news of the story is that we were able to hike out of the canyon and call the Pima Country Search and Rescue team who ended up saving the woman's life.

The next morning, my dad showed all of us a small newspaper clipping from the *Arizona Daily Star* that said, "Woman rescued in Sabino Canyon by search and rescue operation with the help of an unnamed group of area hikers." That was our claim to fame: unknown yet significant in helping to save someone's life.

## The Great Commission

Jesus has passed His search and rescue mission over to us. He said, "As the Father has sent me, I am sending you." (John 20:21) After we have "been found" and "rescued" from our sins, Jesus wants to enlist us in the greatest search and rescue operation of all time. It's called the great commission: "Therefore go and make disciples of all nations, baptizing them in the name of the Father and of the Son and of the Holy Spirit, and teaching them to obey everything I have commanded you. And surely I am with you always, to the very end of the age." (Matthew 28:18-20)

The great commission is a mission statement for both individuals and for churches. Archbishop William Temple said, "The church is the only organization in the world that exists for people who aren't in it." Luis Palau said, "The church is like manure. Pile it up and it stinks up the neighborhood; spread it out, and it enriches the world." God has called us to go out into the world and love people like Jesus loves them. We're commissioned to live out the teaching of Christ in such as way that it causes non-Christians to see the validity of Jesus and accept His invitation to "be found" and thereby enjoy and live the God-life.

## Invitation to Consider

My prayer for us is that we will all honestly consider our paths and pursuits. If you say, "My life really isn't working for me," I invite you to consider the ways of Jesus and accept His invitation to experience His life in and through your life. If you are one who has "been found" by Christ, let's join in on the greatest search and rescue mission of all time. Let's partner with Jesus and what He is doing on earth: helping people who are lost and far from God, come home to Him.

Luke Chapter 20

# WE OWE YOU EVERYTHING

*"Is it lawful for us to give tribute to Caesar, or not?" But he perceived their craftiness, and said to them, "Show me a denarius. Whose likeness and inscription does it have?" They said, "Caesar's." He said to them, "Then render to Caesar the things that are Caesar's, and to God the things that are God's." (Luke 20:22-25)*

## Conversations with the Pharisees

This chapter opens with the Pharisees challenging Jesus' authority. They ask a rigged question in hopes of trapping Him. Jesus responds with a question of His own instead of an answer. Jesus asks them, "Is John the Baptist a fake, yes or no?" At first glance, it appears that Jesus is trying to outsmart the Pharisees and make them look dumb in front of the crowd. But that's not it at all. Jesus is asking about John the Baptist because the answer to that question actually answers their question.

In essence, Jesus is asking them if they thought John was a true prophet or false prophet. Remember, it was John who said that Jesus was the "Lamb of God who takes away the sins of the world." If John was in fact a true prophet, then the obvious conclusion was that Jesus was the one true God: the Messiah. If John was a phony, then so too was Jesus. The Pharisees refused to answer Jesus for fear of the people turning against them.

## The Parable of the Tenants

Jesus teaches the parable of the tenants. He declares that throughout Israel's history, many Old Testament prophets tried to call the nation of Israel back into a vibrant and genuine relationship with their Creator. Israel was obstinate and disobeyed God's laws and values. Jesus asserts that He is sent by the Father to fulfill everything the prophets of old proclaimed. Jesus explains that He's now the centerpiece and bridge for God's plan, and to reject the Messiah is to bring about God's judgment. Jesus extends another gospel invitation. Tempers flare. In the end, Jesus is rejected and crucified.

## The Resurrection of the Dead

The chapter ends with Jesus explaining the resurrection of the dead to the Sadducees. The Sadducees were an affluent, priestly sub-group of Judaism. They believed mostly in the Pentateuch, the first five books of the Old Testament. They did not believe in the resurrection of the dead like the Pharisees and the rest of the Jewish people of the day. Not only did the first century Jews, the apostles, and Jesus think differently than the Sadducees regarding the resurrection of the dead, but they also thought differently than many Christians do today. For many Christians, the resurrection of the dead is synonymous with life after death. To many, the resurrection happens when you die and go to heaven. First century Jews, the apostles, and Jesus didn't actually teach that at all. Although the patriarchs like David, Abraham, and Isaac were believed to be alive and present with the Lord in heaven, their bodies were not yet physically resurrected like Jesus describes throughout the gospels, as Paul does in 1 Corinthians 15, and as John does in the book of Revelation.

The resurrection of the dead was a future event where a person's soul and spirit would re-enter their newly created spiritual/physical body. The Bible teaches that the resurrection of the dead will happen when Jesus returns to the earth at His second coming (Revelation 19-22). So a better way to describe the resurrection of the dead might actually be to say "life after life after death."

## Give God What's His

In the middle of this chapter, questions are posed about paying taxes to the Roman government. Jesus tells the scribes and chief priests to pay Caesar what's his and to give to God what belongs to Him. What actually does belong to God? That's a good question for us to wrestle with today as well. What does He have exclusive rights to? Are we really giving those things to Him each day?

I think the short answer is that everything about us belongs to God. The scriptures teach that we are made in the image and likeness of God. His divine stamp is on our lives. He purchased us with His shed blood on the cross. The apostle Paul says, "Do you not know that your body is a temple of the Holy Spirit within you, whom you have from God? You are not your own, for you were bought with a price. So, glorify God in your body." (1 Corinthians 6:19-20)

## Owe You Everything

God made us, Jesus redeemed us, and the Holy Spirit lives within us. Jesus Christ gave up His life for us so we could have this "new life" in Him. My wife, Mary, and I wrote a song with this very theme. It's called "Owe You Everything."

## "OWE YOU EVERYTHING"

*Jesus my Redeemer, I love you precious Lamb of God*
*Called me out of darkness, life-giver to my soul*
*Oh most treasured Jesus, You gave your life so I could live*
*Your love is a mystery, my life is yours alone*
*King of all creation, I bow my heart before you now*
*Everything is yours, Lord, I worship you alone*
*I will give my heart in worship to you only*
*No other way to say how much I love you, Lord*
*For all you are I can be nothing else but grateful*
*Upon the cross you paid for all that I have done*
*Jesus my King, I owe you everything*

## Understanding Stewardship

As Christ-followers, we are no longer "owners," but "stewards." Too often when the word "stewardship" is used, people only think of finances. Yes, it does encompass finances, but it's much more. When Paul says that "we are not our own" and that we are to "glorify God in our body," he's talking about glorifying and worshiping God in the complete totality of who we are as people: mind, soul, spirit, intellect, emotions, talents, giftedness, finances, personality, sexuality, relationships, decisions, and goals. It all matters to God because we now belong to Him. We are stewards of the array of resources that God entrusts to us for His purposes, not ours.

My prayer is that we would offer our lives completely to Jesus as living sacrifices. There's something powerful about living life with "open hands" that trust Him and bring Him the things that belong to Him. Sometimes I forget that the blessings and resources that find their way into my life are not always just for me, but also for others. Owners are always focused on what belongs to them. Stewards are focused on what belongs to God and how they can serve Him and live a life that glorifies Him. I need God to chisel more of His image even deeper into my heart. I've got a long way to go, but God is faithful even when we're not. I'm so glad God's committed to working in our lives with His amazing grace. How about you?

Luke Chapter 21

# DEVELOPING THE HEART
# BEHIND THE ACTION

*Jesus looked up and saw the rich putting their gifts into the offer-ing box, and he saw a poor widow put in two small copper coins. And he said, "Truly, I tell you, this poor widow has put in more than all of them. For they all contributed out of their abundance, but she out of her poverty put in all she had to live on." (Luke 21:1-4)*

## The Heart with Which We Give

Jesus is now in Jerusalem and inside the Temple. The scene opens with Jesus watching how different people place their offerings into the local offering box. If it's true that our eyes are the window to our souls, then I'm sure Jesus looked deeply into the eyes of the men and women who passed by Him that day on their way to give their offering. Jesus comments on one particular poor widow and the amazing heart behind her giving. She had very little money, but gave what she had with an overflowing spirit of gratefulness and generosity. The look in her eye must have caught Jesus' eye that day. As far as God was concerned, she gave more than anyone. God cares about our giving, but He cares even more about the heart behind our giving and the spirit with which we give.

## Mother Teresa

Our spirit is one of the most defining things about us. It's a gift we give to one another. Mother Teresa once said, "It's not the big things that are done for God that make something beautiful; it's the small things we do with a big heart that make them valuable. It's not about spectacular actions, it's about a spectacular heart that we put into our actions that make something beautiful to God."

Mother Teresa once told a story of a leper that she had met while she was in Calcutta, India. She said of this leper, "He stood straight up and in his arms was a basket of cabbage. It was in his arms because on his hands, not a single finger was left." Mother Teresa goes on to describe how he brought this basket of cabbage to her, and when he gave it to her, he said:

> "I have lost my fingers but I have not lost my courage. I want to be someone who serves, someone who works, someone who gives, and someone who sings, just as you've taught us. So I learned to help myself without my hands. One hundred times the tool fell to the ground. And 100 times I got on my knees and picked it up again. I have brought you my first vegetables. And I give them to you because you taught me that I was not someone who was unwanted. You taught me that I was valuable."

## The Gift of Your Spirit

This so beautifully illustrates the heart behind the giving that Jesus is describing in this chapter. In fact, this is what being a "people of the tithe" actually means. Sometimes we think tithing involves just dropping money in the offering plate. It means a whole lot more than that. Tithing means giving God our best. It means giving God the first vegetables of our crop, even if it's small, even if it's with no fingers, even if it's just a single cabbage. If it's the best that we've got, then God looks at it and sees something beautiful! Why? Because we brought God our heart and not just some cabbage. This is what caught Jesus' eye and moved Him when the widow gave her offering. She brought money, but she brought a whole lot more. She brought the gift of her spirit.

## Jesus and His Return

As the chapter continues, Jesus predicts the destruction of the Temple and of the city of Jerusalem. This was an unfathomable claim to many because Herod's temple was considerably bigger than the Acropolis in Athens and exceeded the majesty of many of the wonders of the first century world. Most biblical scholars believe this prediction was fulfilled in the year 70 A.D. Jesus lists specific signs and gives several warnings concerning future persecution, war, natural disasters and, for some of His followers, death by martyrdom. Jesus encourages His followers with an assurance of His continued presence that will go on with them. He challenges them to be strong and to endure.

Jesus ends the chapter and foretells His second coming to earth when human history as we know it will come to an end. Jesus' return will usher in the "final consummation" of heaven and earth as they become re-created and renewed. God's judgment will come upon the earth to right every wrong. The resurrection of the dead will take place. Jesus asserts that although heaven and earth may one day change in the way that we know them, His words and His teachings are divinely inspired and will outlast it all.

## Being Present with God

God's word will never change. It is tried, trustworthy, true, and reliable. Jesus concludes this episode with a hope-filled challenge to "keep watch" and "stay awake." Let us remain faithful. Pray. Follow. Trust. Give. Obey. This was applicable to the early church, and it's still timely today.

My prayer for us is that we will grow as men and women of prayer. Hearing from God and receiving clear instructions for living is very valuable. I don't know about you, but I still need to learn how to better converse with God and be present with Him. There are many things that we can't control in life, but we can all learn to be present with God in the now and offer Him and others the gift of our spirit.

Luke Chapter 22

# SERVANT LEADERSHIP:
# AMBITIOUS FOR THE SUCCESS OF OTHERS

*A dispute also arose among them, as to which of them was to be regarded as the greatest. And he said to them, "The kings of the gentiles exercise lordship over them, and those in authority over them are called benefactors. But not so with you. Rather, let the greatest among you become as the youngest, and the leader as one who serves. For who is the greater, one who reclines at table or one who serves? Is it not the one who reclines at table? But I am among you as the one who serves."*
*(Luke 22: 24-27)*

## Unpacking the Passover Meal

The plan is hatched to kill Jesus. Judas Iscariot, one of the 12, plots with the chief priests regarding the details of His false arrest. Jesus longs to celebrate His final Passover meal with His disciples. This particular meal was important because:

1.  It was a symbolic event commemorating the founding of the nation of Israel and its freedom from Egypt
2.  It was the fulfillment of God's promise to send the Messiah (the Lamb of God who takes away the sins of the world was actually at the table)
3.  The bread and wine would come to symbolize Jesus giving His own body and shedding His blood on the cross for the forgiveness of sin, inaugurating a new agreement between God and man
4.  This Passover meal was symbolic of the "future and final meal" described in the book of Revelation where the Lamb (Jesus) and the Bride (the followers of Jesus) will celebrate together after Jesus' second coming to earth

As Jesus shares His final meal with His disciples, He presents again the message of the gospel: that He will die for the forgiveness of our sins. On the third day, He will rise again from the dead. Those who believe in Him will receive everlasting life.

Today, Christ-followers around the world celebrate this meal. Jesus told His disciples to partake of the meal in remembrance of Him and in remembrance of what He did on the cross after He is gone. He wanted them to consider it's implications in their lives. Jesus' death, burial, resurrection, and second coming was and always will be the centerpiece of this special meal. (People often refer to this meal as Holy Communion, the Lord's Supper, or the Eucharist).

## Jesus' Final Evening

As the chapter unfolds, the Passover meal begins and conversations fill the room. Topics of greatness, status, leadership, power, authority, and loving servanthood are discussed and exampled. Jesus warns Peter, in front of the others, that a time is soon coming where Peter will actually deny Him three times. Peter says "no way" in disbelief. Jesus tells him to be a strengthener of the disciples and other believers when it's over.

At the conclusion of the meal, Jesus and the 11 (Judas was not present at this point), leave for the Mount of Olives which was a place where Jesus often prayed. While in the garden praying, a self-appointed posse arrives to falsely arrest Jesus. They beat Him. In the midst of the fighting, Jesus even takes the time to heal the severed ear of one of the aggressors.

Jesus then receives an all-night beating where He is stripped, blindfolded, mocked, spat on, whipped, punched, lacerated, brutalized, and tortured. He's then taken before the council and interrogated. They ask Him again if He is indeed the Christ, the anointed one sent by God; the Messiah. Jesus declares that, yes, He is the promised one of God. He goes on to assure them that His crucifixion is not the end; it's a bridge. In fact, He says He will not only rise from the dead in three days, but He will one day return to the earth to rule and reign over it (Revelation 20-22). The council members go ballistic when Jesus claims to be equal with God.

## Servant Leadership

As I read through this chapter, I'm once again inspired by Jesus' life, actions, and character. But I'm particularly drawn to the compelling words of instruction that He offers to His disciples in the midst of a conversation on leadership. Many people today think about leadership, just as the disciples did, only in terms of status, position, greatness, advantage, and power. Defining leadership like that is less than noble, a bit jaded, and self-centered. Nevertheless, it really is what goes on in many people's minds. Because the disciples felt safe in Jesus' presence, they just said what they were thinking. Jesus loved them dearly, so He told them the truth in order to expose the "Achilles' heel" that is so often at the root of most leadership nightmares and abuses.

Like a donkey that is pulling a cart while pursuing a carrot in front of its nose, sometimes well-intentioned leaders pull the "leadership cart" while pursuing the carrot of status, position, and greatness. Their pursuit is fueled by an insatiable hunger for approval and acceptance from others.

Many times they aren't aware of what's motivating them on the inside. Because many well-meaning leaders lack healthy self-efficacy and self-image, they look for ways to meet that need. We live in a culture that applauds those who have status, position, advantage, and power. So it's only natural that broken and needy people pursue the things that will either anesthetize their desires or, in fact, meet them. Gaining leadership position and advantage is one option that people take.

Jesus calls us to rise up and pursue a different kind of leadership altogether. He first calls us to a genuine and authentic relationship with Him, the Son of God. As we grow in our understanding and experience of His love for us, our human need for approval, applause, and acceptance is found in Him, rather than in the accolades of our culture or through leader status.

## A Twisted View of Servanthood

When I was growing up, my brothers and I played a game called "King and Servant." (I think we watched too many King Tut movies on summer break.) But here's how the game went: The king would lie on the living room couch with his feet propped up and his head on a large pillow. The other servant (brother) would feed him grapes, freshly-made cinnamon toast, and fan him with a newspaper. Sometimes we would even wear little outfits during the game (sheets wrapped around the brother who was servant). I don't think I need to tell you that this is a demented view of servant leadership. As kids, the role of a "servant" and a "leader" had nothing in common to us. They were opposites. The leader used the servant for his own benefit.

Jesus combines them and puts the word "servant" first in the phrase "servant-leader." Being a servant leader is good. Being a servant-leader who is first grounded in a loving relationship with Jesus is better, because now these leaders enter the work of leadership to serve others with their own relational and emotional needs already met (approval, love, and acceptance).

## Ambitious for the Success of Others

To be a servant-leader is to be ambitious for the success of others. Too often, leaders are only concerned about their own success. Sometimes they aren't even aware of why they do what they do, nor the subtle lures of culture. Love still is the single greatest core competency that a leader can ever possess. When the people that we lead know that the single greatest motive influencing our hearts, in regards to leading them, is love, and when they are convinced that our greatest ambition as a leader is their success, then that is the single greatest force which catalyzes change and truly empowers others.

Luke Chapter 23

# DEATH AND DYING:
# LIFE LESSONS FROM JESUS

*Then Jesus, calling out with a loud voice, said, "Father, into your hands I commit my spirit!" And having said this he breathed his last. Now when the centurion saw what had taken place, he praised God, saying, "Certainly this man was innocent!" And all the crowds that had assembled for this spectacle, when they saw what had taken place, returned home beating their breasts. And all his acquaintances and the women who had followed him from Galilee stood at a distance watching these things. (Luke 23: 46-49)*

## Jesus' Crucifixion and Death

Luke describes the final details of Jesus' suffering and death on the cross. Jesus is brought before Pontius Pilate. Pilate sends Jesus to Herod, who has wanted to kill Him for quite some time. They finally meet face-to-face. Jesus is questioned and found innocent of all charges. Jesus winds up back in Pilate's court. He's found innocent again. The chief priests and the scribes demand His crucifixion. The crowd jeers. Pilate is a people-pleaser and is concerned with public opinion more than he is about doing what is right. Pilate concedes. He relinquishes to the crowd's unjust demands and releases a convicted murderer in order to murder an innocent man. The crowd roars, "Crucify him!"

Jesus is led away to the "Place of the Skull" to be crucified along with two other criminals. Jesus forgives His accusers, executioners, and a repentant thief on the cross. Paradise is mentioned. Jesus praises His Father in heaven and then dies. The curtain in the Temple is torn in two, signifying that the Old Covenant (the Old Testament law and priestly sacrifices) has been fulfilled and the New Covenant (the New Testament grace that Jesus offers by forgiving our sins because of His once-and-for-all sacrificial death on the cross) has begun.

The chapter concludes as many in the crowd now believe Jesus was, in fact, the Messiah: God's one and only Son. Jesus' body is taken from the cross and undergoes a type of Israelite embalming process. He is buried in a tomb. Witnesses watch the process. His tomb is sealed.

As I reflect on this chapter, my heart is grateful for Jesus and for the amazing bravery He displayed as He faced His own death. Emotionally speaking, Jesus probably began His own death and dying process three years earlier. It's clear, in the gospel accounts, that He accepted His manner of death by crucifixion as inevitable in order to fulfill God's plan to redeem sinful humanity from its fallen and lost state.

Not only was Jesus fully God, but He was fully human. Embedded within His full humanity, Jesus' death continues to teach us not just about the way of salvation, but also about the dying process we will face as we deal with our own death and the deaths of those we love. Although we will probably never die on a cross, we will all die. Death is a part of life. Jesus models how to live, but he even teaches us as He dies.

## Death and Dying

Not all of us will go through a "process" of dying; God will welcome some of us home suddenly. But no matter how fast or drawn out death is for each of us, we'll all probably watch someone we love go through the dying process. God invites us to move beyond the fear of death and to embrace it (and to help others face death) with grace, strength, and with His eternal perspective.  Let me begin by sharing some things I've learned about death and dying from the life of Jesus:

**1.** As we face death, we must each place our lives into God's hands and trust His will. Yes, it's normal to want your will to be done and to have your prayers answered the way you want. Yet each of us must come to the place where we can give our lives over to God's care and plan. He is both the Author and the Finisher of life.

*"He went away a second time and prayed, 'My Father, if it is not possible for this cup to be taken away unless I drink it, may your will be done.'" (Matthew 26:42)*

**2.** As an angel appeared and strengthened Jesus, we too should pray for God's supernatural encouragement to help us walk through our own "garden of Gethsemane." Praying for strength and help is not only what Jesus did, but it's what we should do as we encounter the overwhelming and agonizing emotions and pains that accompany the dying process.

*"An angel from heaven appeared to him and strengthened him. And being in anguish, he prayed more earnestly, and his sweat was like drops of blood falling to the ground." (Luke 22:43)*

**3.** It helps to have friends praying with you rather than "sleeping" or relating to you in superficial ways when you are facing death (like the disciples). Dying, as a Christian, should mean that the biblically functioning community (church) that you are a part of makes an intentional effort to surround you and your family with prayer and comfort as you walk the finals steps of your earthly journey before entering heaven.

*"Then he returned to the disciples and said to them, 'Are you still sleeping and resting? Look, the hour is near, and the Son of Man is betrayed into the hands of sinners.'" (Matthew 26:45)*

## Do's and Don'ts

Here are a few "do's" and "don'ts" to consider when trying to help and encourage people who are in the process of dying, or for family members who have just experienced the death of a loved one.

- Don't avoid them. Talk to them. Let them know you are thinking about them. Let them know you love them and that you are praying for them. Be there!

- Don't offer advice, pat answers, or theological opinions on why a loved one's death has happened. They need to be heard and loved. Just "being" with a person speaks volumes.

- Do pray for them.

- Do write them a note, call them on the phone, or visit them in person (but get their permission on the last one).

- Don't be offended if they don't respond like you think they should. The grief stage varies from person to person.

- If you have gone through a similar experience, share your personal story of how God helped you through (not what *they* should do, but what God has done for you) the death of your loved one.

- Attend the funeral or memorial service for their loved one. Not only does God want us to do life together, He also wants us to experience "death" together by being there to support one another. Our presence alone brings encouragement.

**4.** When God's will (final outcome) is revealed about the dying process, don't fight it with last-ditch efforts that ultimately just postpone the inevitable. Jesus accepted God's decision about His death. His disciples did not. They were fighting all the way to the cross. Jesus refused to see

Himself as a victim of circumstances. Rather, He accepted His death with God's confidence.

*"When Jesus' followers saw what was going to happen, they said, 'Lord, should we strike with our swords?" And one of them struck the servant of the high priest, cutting off his right ear. But Jesus answered, "No more of this!"* (Luke 22:49-51)

**5.** People are valuable to God. Continue to bless others around you as you travel on your road to heaven. Jesus still took time to heal a man's ear in the midst of the chaos and trauma surrounding His own death. I've personally been greatly impacted by people who have reached out to me in their final weeks and days of their lives here on earth. I treasure their stories and cherish the things they've taught me. I carry their words with me. Some of my greatest education about life has come through what others have taught me through their process of dying. God can do some of His best work in our final days as we reach out to those that God places in our paths.

*"And one of them struck the servant of the high priest, cutting off his right ear. But Jesus answered, 'No more of this!" And he touched the man's ear and healed him.'"* (Luke 22:50-51)

**6.** Focus on the eternal outcome and heavenly reward. Jesus focused His dying process on the other side of the grave. He saw past the bridge of death. His spirit and soul reached out toward the place where He would ultimately end up.

*"Jesus answered, 'But from now on, the Son of Man will be seated at the right hand of the mighty God.'"* (Luke 22:68-69)

**7.** Jesus wept for the non-Christian who was far from God and who wouldn't go to heaven rather than crying for the one who had a relationship with God and would go to heaven. Jesus' eternal perspective colors His definition of reality.

*"Jesus turned and said to them, 'Daughters of Jerusalem, do not weep for me; weep for yourselves and for your children.'"* (Luke 23:28)

**8.** Even as we are surrounded by death, look for opportunities to lead others to the cross. As Jesus encountered His own death, He helped a non-Christian (the thief on the cross) find the reality of God (salvation through Christ). What a magnanimous heart of compassion and love for people!

*"There was a written notice above him, which read: this is the king of the Jews. One of the criminals who hung there hurled insults at him: 'Aren't you the Christ? Save yourself and us!' But the other criminal rebuked him. 'Don't you fear God,' he said, 'since you are under the same sentence? We are punished justly, for we are getting what our deeds deserve. But this man has done nothing wrong.' Then he said, 'Jesus, remember me when you come into your kingdom.' Jesus answered him, 'I tell you the truth, today you will be with me in paradise.'" (Luke 23:38-43)*

**9.** Lavishly offer forgiveness. Jesus goes through the death process with no grudges. He forgave those who, many could say, had some responsibility in bringing about His circumstances. It is important for us to completely forgive family, God, our past, doctors, and ourselves when we go through the death process, too.

*"When they came to the place called the Skull, there they crucified him, along with the criminals—one on his right, the other on his left. Jesus said, "Father, forgive them, for they do not know what they are doing." And they divided up his clothes by casting lots." (Luke 23:33-34)*

**10.** Sometimes suffering is part of the dying process.

*"About the ninth hour Jesus cried out in a loud voice, 'Eloi, Eloi, lama sabachthani?'–which means, 'My God, my God, why have you forsaken me?'" (Matthew 27:46)*

**11.** Grief is a normal and healthy emotion that needs to be expressed. Christians grieve like everyone else over death. The only difference is that we grieve with the hope of resurrection.

*"Brothers, we do not want you to be ignorant about those who fall asleep, or to grieve like the rest of men, who have no hope." (1 Thessalonians 4:13)*

**12.** God is ultimately in control of our lives. He is the great authority behind all circumstances that we face. Always seek to define God's actions in the light of His character. Jesus refused to allow Pilate to intimidate Him into thinking that someone or something other than God was ultimately in control of His life, death, and destiny.

*"'Do you refuse to speak to me?' Pilate said. 'Don't you realize I have power either to free you or to crucify you?' Jesus answered, 'You would have no power over me if it were not given to you from above.'" (John 19:10-11)*

**13.** It is important for the dying person to know that their loved ones will be taken care of. Even Jesus needed to know that His mother would be okay. He asked His best friend to look after her.

*"Near the cross of Jesus stood his mother, his mother's sister, Mary the wife of Clopas, and Mary Magdalene. When Jesus saw his mother there, and the disciple whom he loved standing nearby, he said to his mother, 'Dear woman, here is your son,' and to the disciple, 'Here is your mother.' From that time on, this disciple took her into his home." (John 19: 25-27)*

**14.** Death is not final. It is the preparation for the resurrection. Death never gets the last word. For the Christian, the resurrection of Jesus Christ is the ultimate triumph and victory over death. Because Jesus has risen from the dead, we will too.

*"Listen, I tell you a mystery: We will not all sleep, but we will all be changed—in a flash, in the twinkling of an eye, at the last trumpet. For the trumpet will sound, the dead will be raised imperishable, and we will be changed. For the perishable must clothe itself with the imperishable, and the mortal with immortality. When the perishable has been clothed with the imperishable, and the mortal with immortality, then the saying that is written will come true: 'Death has been swallowed up in victory.' 'Where, O death, is your victory? Where, O death, is your sting?' The sting of death is sin, and the power of sin is the law. But thanks be to God! He gives us the victory through our Lord Jesus Christ." (1 Corinthians 15:51-57)*

**15.** Christ-followers will be allowed to see Jesus face-to-face after leaving this physical world, and be welcomed and embraced into loving community and relationship with Him in paradise.

*"Now we see but a poor reflection as in a mirror; then we shall see face to face. Now I know in part; then I shall know fully, even as I am fully known."* (1 Corinthians 13:12)

*"(The apostle Paul) I say, and prefer rather to be absent from the body and to be at home with the Lord." (2 Corinthians 5:8)*

## Teach Me to Number My Days

My hope for us is that we will live with a spirit of gratitude and wisdom. There's an old proverb that says that there is more wisdom at 1 funeral than at 10 parties. Moses, the Old Testament patriarch, said, "Oh Lord, teach me to number my days that my heart may be inclined unto wisdom." (Psalm 90) When we understand the frailty of our humanity, when we comprehend the inevitable reality of our own death, and when we reflect on it from Christ's perspective, and not from a human reaction rooted in fear, but in the grace and goodness of God, the psalmist tells us that this "coming to terms" with this eventual reality (our death) actually fosters wisdom in us (the ability to make right choices).

Death is the secret fear buried deep down inside every human being. As we honestly face the inevitability of our own death, and as we accept Jesus' invitation to be Lord and Savior of both our life and death, we can get on with living life to the fullest and under the shadow of His truth and hope-filled perspective. No matter what season of life we find ourselves in, Jesus walks with us when we accept His invitation to be Lord of life and Lord over death. To choose life is to choose Jesus. His invitation is extended. His presence is available. His promise is sure. My prayer for us is that we will choose wisely.

Luke Chapter 24

# FULLY ALIVE!
# RESCUED FROM THE GRAVE

*But on the first day of the week, at early dawn, they went to the tomb, taking the spices they had prepared. And they found the stone rolled away from the tomb, but when they went in they did not find the body of the Lord Jesus. While they were perplexed about this, behold, two men stood by them in dazzling apparel. And as they were frightened and bowed their faces to the ground, the men said to them, "Why do you seek the living among the dead? He is not here, but has risen. Remember how he told you, while he was still in Galilee, that the Son of Man must be delivered into the hands of sinful men and be crucified and on the third day rise." And they remembered his words, and returning from the tomb they told all these things to the eleven and to all the rest. (Luke 24:1-10)*

## Jesus - Alive and Well

This is the final chapter in the gospel of Luke. Mary Magdalene, Joanna, Mary the mother of James, and some others arrive at Jesus' tomb. Astonished, they find the large stone rolled away from the entrance of the tomb. Jesus' body is gone. Angels are present in the garden area just outside the tomb declaring Jesus has risen from the dead. The women dash toward the homes of the disciples to tell them the startling news. Peter and the others run back to see for themselves. Peter goes inside and sees with his own eyes that Jesus was indeed gone and all that remained were the burial clothes that He was wrapped in. Jesus was alive!

Luke concludes the chapter by recording several post-resurrection sightings, conversations, and encounters with the risen Jesus and His disciples. Jesus' new resurrection body has unique physical properties that appear to not be limited by time or space. He can eat food and walk through walls! Finally, surrounded by His worshiping disciples, Jesus ascends to heaven. He tells them to wait for the promised Holy Spirit that will soon come upon them in great power. They do.

## Unequivocal Evidence

The resurrection of Jesus Christ is the single most significant event in all of human history. Sir Lionel Luckhoo, the most successful defense trial lawyer of all time, looked at the evidence surrounding Jesus' resurrection and concluded, "I say unequivocally that the resurrection of Jesus Christ is so overwhelming that it compels acceptance by proof which leaves absolutely no room for doubt." The evidence is overwhelming:

1.  There were a plethora of firsthand eyewitness accounts and testimonials by people who were still alive during the times of the apostles that had either seen Jesus or talked with Him after His resurrection. Jesus appeared to women, men, individuals, and groups. He was seen indoors and outdoors. He appeared to people who were both skeptics and faithful followers. Jesus appeared to the hard-hearted and to the tender-hearted. He talked, walked, and ate with people. Jesus even invited Thomas, the skeptic, to put

his finger in the nail holes in His hands and in the spear wound of His side. The apostle Paul mentions that more than 500 people said they personally saw Jesus alive after His resurrection.

2.   Not just Jesus' followers, but even Jesus' enemies and skeptics conceded that His tomb was empty on Easter morning. His opponents tried to bribe guards to say that the body was stolen. Neither the Roman authorities nor the Jewish leaders wanted Jesus' body. They wanted Him dead. No one had a motive to steal the body.

3.   Jesus' body was placed in Joseph of Arimathea's tomb, which was in a well-known location. The women who were at Jesus' tomb didn't make an honest mistake by going to the wrong tomb on Sunday morning. Everyone knew where the tomb was, including the soldiers guarding it.

4.   The story of the Resurrection contains the testimony of women. If anyone was trying to beef up the validity of a falsified story, they would not use the testimony of women. First century Jewish culture considered women's testimonies worthless.

5.   No one would suffer beheadings, be eaten alive by wild animals, be boiled alive in caldrons of oil, or stripped naked in the Roman coliseums and watch their children be fed to lions for a lie. The disciples were tortured and martyred for their belief that Jesus Christ did in fact rise from the dead.

6.   The birth and rise of the church.

My hope for us is that we would honestly consider not only the evidence of Jesus' resurrection, but the implications that it has for our lives.

## Rescued From the Grave

Alfred Hitchcock told a story in one of his books that has a great lesson. It's about a woman who is sent to prison for the rest of her life for killing her husband. There's no way she's ever getting out. She's received a life sentence. As she's arriving at the prison compound that will house her for the rest of her life, she notices that right outside the wall of the prison, there is an old man digging a hole to bury a casket of a dead inmate. This elderly worker's job in the prison was that whenever an inmate died, he would bury the inmate outside the walls of the prison.

Once inside, she is bent on escaping. The woman remembers the old man burying the inmate outside the gates, and she thinks, "I could escape with the help of the old man!" At once, she starts to make friends with him. As their friendship grows, the woman notices the elderly worker suffers from horrible cataracts on his eyes. She tells him, "I can help you restore your eyesight if you will help me escape from the prison." The woman goes on to tell the old man that she has lots of money in the bank and that she'll pay for him to have an operation to regain his sight. The two cut a deal. The old man tells her that the next time an inmate dies, she is to come down to the morgue and enter through the back door. Once she's in the morgue, she's to discreetly climb inside the casket alongside the dead inmate. The elderly man said, "I'll bury the casket outside the prison wall. Then later in the night, I'll come back and dig you up and set you free."

A few weeks go by. Then one day the prison bell rings, which means that an inmate has died. Later that night the woman sneaks out of her cell, goes down the dark prison corridor, and into the morgue through the back entrance. It's dark and quiet. She feels her way to the casket, opens it up, climbs in, and lies alongside the dead body. She closes the top of the casket over her. She waits.

After a few hours she feels the casket moving. Then she feels it being lowered down into the ground. The woman hears the sound of dirt clods hitting the top of the casket. She waits for sounds that the old man has come to dig her out and set her free, but nothing happens. She waits in total darkness under the ground. She thinks to herself, "Where is he? Why is he taking so long?" She begins to feel claustrophobic. "What's going on?" she thinks. The woman starts to panic. Finally, she lights a match to investigate, and finds that the dead body next to her is the body of the elderly man. He was the one that died that night when the prison bell rang. The woman's only hope was buried with her in the grave.

I've always remembered that story because to me it illustrates the truth of the gospel. The woman in the story placed her faith and trust in another well-meaning human being who she thought could rescue her from the grave. In the end, he couldn't come through on his promise.

## Jesus is Alive

Every founder of every religion is still in the grave: Confucius, Buddha, Lao-tzu, and Mohammed. Only Jesus claimed to be God and claimed that He would rise from the dead on the third day. Some people don't necessarily trust people to rescue them from the grave, but they trust philosophies or other belief systems. Some just choose not to think about it at all. Who are you putting your trust in to rescue you from the grave? Where is your hope invested? Do you have a plan to escape the grave? Jesus said, "I am the resurrection and the life. He who believes in me will live, even though he dies." (John 11)

## Getting Beyond Good Intentions

My prayer for us is that we would trust our lives to Jesus Christ. Jesus is not like the grave digger who worked in the prison and had good intentions, but didn't have the goods to back them up. The evidence of Jesus' resurrection is compelling and its implications have eternal ramifications to our lives. Jesus' resurrection guarantees our resurrection. He has conquered the grave. He's alive! Jesus promises that He alone is able to rescue us from sin and death. What a relief and what an indescribable joy it will be to "light the match" and realize we are not in the grave, but in heaven in the presence of Almighty God and His Son, Jesus Christ.

John Chapter 1

# THE WORD:
# GOD IN A BOD

*In the beginning was the Word, and the Word was with God, and
the Word was God. He was in the beginning with God. All things
were made through him, and without him was not any thing made
that was made. In him was life, and the life was the light of men.
The light shines in the darkness, and the darkness has not overcome it.
And the Word became flesh and dwelt among us, and we have seen his
glory, glory as of the only Son from the Father, full of grace and truth.
(John 1:1-5, 14)*

## The Beginnings

John presents Jesus to us by framing his introductory words upon the backdrop of the book of Genesis (The book of beginnings). John explains to us that Jesus actually goes all the way back to the beginning of time. He tells us that Jesus is actually self-existent and is part of the Trinitarian creation team (Father, Son, and Spirit) who formed the universe, the earth, and all of creation.

John presents Jesus as one who was with God from the beginning, is God, and is in loving relationship with God the Father and God the Spirit. This portion of scripture introduces the doctrine of the trinity (one God in three distinct persons). John uses the phrase "the word" to present Jesus to both His Hebrew and Greek audiences. To the Hebrew people, God's word (or speech) and His actions were one-in-the-same. Throughout the Old Testament, when God would speak with authority, something incredible would always happen (creation, 10 Commandments, miracles, etc.).

To the Hebrews, whenever God would speak, He would break into humanity and accomplish great things. God's divine words and His all-powerful actions were often mentioned in the same sentence. The prophet Isaiah said that God's words do not come back void. They always accomplish their purpose (Isaiah 55:11). To use the phrase "the word" was, in actuality, talking about the Lord.

## The God of Reason

At the same time, the Greco-Roman world of the first century was deeply influenced by Greek philosophy. They had a proud philosophical heritage that included Heraclitus, Socrates, Plato, Aristotle, Cicero, and a constellation of other philosophers, poets, academics, historians, and journalists.

These Greek philosophers taught that at the center of the universe was this eternal principle called "reason" or the "word" (*logos*). They believed that this force was the reality behind the universe and that it held everything together. Like the great Wizard of Oz, this "reason" or "word" was the intelligent principle and power that brought everything that was invisible, together as one. Even today, many in our culture base their views of truth from this same worldview: that God is a collection of eternal ideas, principles, and words. To the early Greeks, the notion of truth, reality, and God could only be found from this fountainhead of wisdom, because all knowledge, knowing, reason, (or the word), was one and the same thing as God.

So, to the Greeks, the "word" (in their philosophical definitions and understandings) was God. To the Hebrews, the "word" (the synthesis of Yahweh's speech and action) was God. John catches their attention in the opening verses by saying that the word is God (which they both agreed on). John then blows everyone's minds when he drops a bomb on them, saying that the word (or God) as they know it is incomplete and wrong. Rather, the word is actually Jesus!

## Jesus is God

John declares that Jesus is the true God of both parties (Greek and Hebrew). Jesus is the God they have been searching to know all along. He is the "pot of gold" at the end of the proverbial, philosophical rainbow that the Greeks were seeking. He is the God of the Old Testament who has come, in the flesh, for the Hebrews. To see Jesus is to see God.

## A Seeker of Truth

On a personal note, I remember when I was first seeking to know God. I wasn't necessarily coming from a Greek or Hebrew worldview, but I was searching and seeking to know truth. I wanted to know God, but didn't know what His name was, or how to find out about Him. My heart was on a secret search for Him, and at times, I didn't even know that I was searching.

Along the way, I did dabble a bit into some modern, Greek-like philosophy as a means to connect to a spiritual world. I soon abandoned it and pursued other philosophies, (I didn't call them that because that sounded too academic) like worshipping myself and pursuing a life that centered only on having fun.

These worldviews that I embraced led me to destructive and sinful behaviors. Along the way, I also tried some other whacko spiritual pursuits, and they too failed to deliver what I originally had hoped for: meaning, truth, peace, happiness, and purpose in life. But one day, my brother gave me a New Testament and told me to read the book of John. I started with this passage. About a year later, things finally came into focus, and for the first time I began to connect the dots of philosophy, God, the word, and Jesus. It became clear that Jesus was the God I was really searching for all along.

In the gospel of John, Jesus gives the Greeks and Hebrews an invitation into a life of grace, truth, and a relationship with Him. Jesus offered that to me in 1983 when I said yes to His invitation to follow and enter into a loving relationship with Him. Jesus still offers that same life and invitation to you today.

## Prayer

Dear God, thank you for sending Jesus, who is fully God and was fully human. Thank you for Your patient pursuit of each of us. Thank you for never giving up on us when we chose to follow different philosophies and worldviews that led us further from Your grace, rather than closer. Thank you that at the center of universe, You are there. Jesus, You are the self-existent one along with the Father and the Spirit. We direct our praise, appreciation, and gratefulness to You. Give us the grace and strength to live for You alone.

John Chapter 2

# MIRACLES IN THE MAKING

*On the third day there was a wedding at Cana in Galilee, and the mother of Jesus was there. When the wine ran out, she said to them, "They have no wine." His mother said to the servants, "Do whatever he tells you." Now there were six stone water jars there each holding twenty or thirty gallons. Jesus said to the servants, "Fill the jars with water." And they filled them up to the brim. And he said to them, "Now draw some out and take it to the master of the feast." So they took it. When the master of the feast tasted the water now become wine, and did not know where it came from (though the servants who had drawn the water knew), the master of the feast called the bridegroom and said to him, "Everyone serves the good wine first, and when people have drunk freely, then the poor wine. But you have kept the good wine until now." This, the first of his signs, Jesus did at Cana in Galilee, and manifested his glory. And his disciples believed in him. (John 2:1, 3, 5- 11)*

## Obedience-Oriented

John introduces us to Jesus' first miracle: changing water into wine. The story begins when an outdoor wedding party is encountering an unexpected glitch in plans: the possibility of the festivities coming to a complete halt! In first century Israelite culture, "good wine" (not drunkenness) was a sign of God's joy, provision, and blessing (Psalm 104:15; Proverbs 3:10; and Matthew 26:2). To run out of it at a wedding was not only a hospitality nightmare, but as some scholars have suggested it revealed a deeper meaning of a nation "on empty" in regards to spiritual matters.

Jesus steps up and begins a simple dialogue with the servants at the party. He gives them some strange instructions: fill up six huge pots with water! They oblige. Somewhere along the way, the water turns into wine and the party continues without a hitch. Beyond the cursory reading of this miraculous event, there are some incredible lessons on many different levels concerning God's love, character, and provision. Not only is God the Creator of the universe, but He also cares about our daily needs and plans. At times, His sovereignty intervenes in mind-boggling ways on our behalf.

## God's Blessings

Every time I read this story about water, wine, and water pots, I'm reminded of how God often chooses to powerfully work in my life through a simple process. This story provides an example of how genuine obedience to follow Jesus' commands always ends up becoming a blessing. To have Bible blessings, we have to do things the Bible way. The Bible way is God's way. God's way is always obedience. It's unclear when the water was actually turned into wine. We're not sure if it happened as soon as Jesus told the servants to fill up the pots, if it happened halfway through the process, or if it transformed into wine right as the head waiter lifted the ladle to His lips to test it. We really don't know. But I do know this: It's in the step-by-step process of walking with Jesus and following His commands that God does so many wonderful things in our lives.

## The Truth About Miracles

When we listen to what Jesus asks of us, and then trust Him, one day we'll look back and see where miracles have taken place. We discover that our lives have been intersected by a great God. Somewhere in the simple process of just loving Jesus and "filling up water pots" in the midst of the daily challenges we each face, one day, as we look back in the rear-view mirror of life, we realize that the ordinary has become extraordinary: water into wine.

Miracles often hide in the process of life. Not only do miracles happen, but character is forged within us. God loves to turn things around in our lives, but He also loves to build character in us at the same time. It's in the process of life itself that character is built. Our society struggles with impatience. We are often searching for the "keys" to the fast track of success. Sometimes we just want the "victory," but God wants to build the character in us that brings the victory. Always remember that some of God's best gifts often hide in the day-by-day steps of following Jesus in simple obedience to His commands.

## Prayer

Dear God, thank you for Your commitment to accept us just as we are and loving us too much to leave us where we are. Thank you that You are shaping us and transforming us into the image of your Son, Jesus. Give us the heart to trust You in the midst of life's challenges, and in the middle of the day-to-day struggles, when it looks like nothing is happening, and when the ordinary appears to be winning. Remind us how You turn water into wine, not only in water pots, but in our lives, through the simple yet powerful process of obeying Your words day-by-day.

John Chapter 3

# LIFE EVERLASTING

*For God so loved the world, that he gave his only Son, that whoever believes in him should not perish but have eternal life. For God did not send his Son into the world to condemn the world, but in order that the world might be saved through him. Whoever believes in him is not condemned, but whoever does not believe is condemned already, because he has not believed in the name of the only Son of God. (John 3:16-18)*

## The Bible's Most Famous Scripture

This portion of scripture is one of the most famous sections in the entire New Testament, in that it explains the core message of the gospel. Because God loves people, He desires to be in relationship with them. People are made in God's image and likeness. All people have sinned and fallen short of God's best for their lives. Even if people do not believe the words in the Bible that makes this case against them (that they are sinners), their own consciences agree with this truth to some degree. There's not a person alive who hasn't at least morally failed within his own thoughts and motives. Deep down, everyone knows this to be true.

God is loving and just and cannot tolerate sin. Sin must be addressed, dealt with, and removed, or God would not be just and fair. God chose Jesus to be the solution to our sin problem. That's why Jesus came to earth. He came with a mission on His mind and in His heart.

## Jesus, God's Only Son

Jesus, God the Son, lived a perfect and sinless life and died on a cross to pay off our sin debt before God. After three days in the grave, Jesus was resurrected from the dead and is alive today. He currently is in heaven. Jesus came to earth the first time in order to solve the sin problem for humanity (die on a cross as our payment) and model the character of God for all to see. Jesus is the promised fulfillment of the Old Testament. That's why getting to know Jesus through the teachings of the Bible, is to know the character of God.

The scriptures say that when God the Father is ready, He will send Jesus back to earth for a second and final time. Jesus' second coming to earth will be to initiate the resurrection of the dead (for all people), and to conduct the final judgment of humanity, (which is the separating out of two groups of people: those who have believed in Jesus and have chosen to follow Him, and those who have not believed in Jesus and have chosen not to repent of their sin and gone their own way in this life). Finally, He will host a huge party with His friends (Revelation 19:6-9).

## Spending Eternity with God

It's at that time that heaven and earth will become "one," of sorts. People who have loved Jesus will get new physical bodies, old friends will reunite, and all will experience a relationship with God in a new depth of intimacy like never before. It's a gathering filled with musical celebration, worship, eating, no bedtimes, no tears, no pains, lots of fulfilled work, joy, friendship, and life to the fullest. It's kind of like a killer family reunion where Jesus is the center of it all! This is the promise for all people who believe and follow Jesus with their lives: life after life after death. The good news is that it can begin today and continue on for eternity.

This is how the gospel ends, and this is why we are invited: God wants everyone to live with Him forever. That's why we are invited to repent of our sin, and by faith, accept God's free and valuable gift (the promise of forgiveness and eternal life because of Jesus' death on the cross) by believing in our hearts that Jesus not only came to earth and died on a cross, but that He did it for you and me, so we could be made clean and right before God. This decision to respond to Jesus welcomes us into God's family. Once you and I make the decision to give our lives (past, present, and future) over to Christ, then God the Holy Spirit comes into our hearts and helps us get to know God the Father and Jesus, God the Son, in a new and meaningful way.

## Understanding the Spiritual World

Earlier in this chapter, John records Jesus' words to a man named Nicodemus. He was someone who was seeking spiritual truth, and had questions about the things that didn't make sense to him. He wanted to figure out all of his spiritual questions before he was ready to trust Jesus with his life. Jesus told him that he couldn't "see or understand the kingdom of God" without being in an alive and dynamic relationship with God. Jesus was politely telling Nicodemus that he had it backwards.

Jesus told him that you first have to come to God and receive His forgiveness and experience a "do-over" in your spirit and heart. Once you've done that, you can start to make sense of everything spiritually. This "do-over" makes you morally acceptable before God and opens your "spirit eyes," so that you are able to perceive a greater awareness and understanding of the invisible reality of the supernatural world.

## Jesus' Invitation

Jesus extends the same invitation to us. The good news of the Bible is that God offers a new ending to everyone's storyline. I say it that way because we really can't have a new beginning; we cannot go backwards in our lives and start all over. Life doesn't work that way. I know we would all do some things in our past differently if we could, but we can't. But we can all go forward. We can have a new destiny of how things will turn out for us in the end. Jesus extends that invitation to us, but we must accept His offer. He wants to live with us forever, starting now. So what do we do?

1. Admit the truth about our condition as people: You and I are sinners.

2. Repent of our sins in both our human nature and choices: We stop being the leaders of our own lives and allow Jesus to be our new leader. We do a U-turn and trust Christ and begin to follow Him by living life with a new set of core values and goals. As you read the Bible, it will explain what those values are. God will change us from the inside out. Remember, the Holy Spirit will help us in this pursuit. That is one of His jobs.

3. Receive the invitation from Jesus to be born again and have a new ending to the storyline of our lives: We accept Christ's full forgiveness of our sins by grace (we can't earn it, it's a gift) and through faith (we believe this in our hearts even though we can't see it with our eyes).

4. Confess your desire to believe in Jesus out loud. Over the years I've thought about a lot of different things, people, and ideas, etc., but the things that I'm willing to literally speak out about and move forward on have affected my life differently than the things I've just thought about. Something powerful happens when Jesus moves from our heads, to our hearts, and then to our mouths and actions.

5.   Connect with other Christians regularly by finding a good church to join and become a fully contributing member.

## Get Plugged In

One of the first steps for a new Christ-follower is to get plugged into a church that loves Jesus and teaches the Bible (remember that no church is perfect). We grow best in the context of committed relationships in community. Even though churches have many problems (because they are filled with people who have problems and are at different levels of maturity, etc.), you will blossom and mature in your faith if you are part of a church. I've noticed that scads of people who don't connect with a church and try to grow as solo-Christians, turn out malnourished at best and spiritually dysfunctional at worst. So in summary: admit, repent, receive, confess, and connect. God will do amazing and wonderful things for you, in you, and through you. Just watch. Just wait. You'll see.

Dear God, thank you for Jesus, and thank you for the gift of eternal life. Thank you for the invitation to join Your family and live with You forever. Sin is our problem and Jesus is the answer. Help us move past the hindrances that get in our way. Help us by faith say yes to You and Your promises for a new kind of life and a joyous ending that takes our breath away!

# John Chapter 4

# AN ORDINARY DAY AT THE WELL

*Jesus said to her, "Woman, believe me, the hour is coming when neither on this mountain nor in Jerusalem will you worship the Father. You worship what you do not know; we worship what we know, for salvation is from the Jews. But the hour is coming, and is now here, when the true worshipers will worship the Father in spirit and truth, for the Father is seeking such people to worship him. God is spirit, and those who worship him must worship in spirit and truth." (John 4:21-24)*

## The Samaritan Woman

This story begins with Jesus passing through Samaria en route to Galilee. Jesus experiences a divine appointment that is orchestrated by God. He encounters a Samaritan woman (who was considered an outcast) at a local well. As Jesus and the woman talk, the conversation moves from normal chit-chat, to the topic of this woman's personal life. Jesus initiates a supernatural encounter with her by telling her explicit details about her past and present life. The woman probably experienced goose bumps, and was freaked out, to say the least. She starts nervously talking about the subject of spiritual things and religion as a way to get the attention off of herself.

Jesus introduces the Samaritan woman to the truth that God wants to have a personal relationship with her. He's interested in honest and authentic worship from the heart, not ritual-like, religious ceremonies.

As the story concludes, this woman has experienced a powerful encounter from the God of the universe, and the whole town hears her amazing story. Jesus' ministry impacts her deeply. She, in turn, is used by God to turn a town upside-down (or should I say right-side up).

Many in the village come to discover the truth about Jesus, that He is the Savior of the world, and that He loves them. Hence, many become Christ-followers and begin to worship the Messiah, Jesus Christ. An ordinary day at the well becomes the transformational turning point of one person who ended up affecting many others.

## One Sunday in Texas

I can relate to the woman at the well. I grew up around religion and doing religious things. My parents took me to church when I was young, so I had some ideas of what church and organized religion were about. Some of it was okay, but most of it was misguided. I believed that there was a God out there somewhere, although I didn't know Him.

I would also get nervous if people talked about "spiritual things" and "knowing God" rather than just "religion." I was both awkward and curious with the people I met along the way who claimed to know God. But one day, I too, had a divine encounter with Jesus Christ. My power encounter happened when I was 23. God came near to me, not at a well, but one summer in east Texas while I was selling books and encyclopedias door-to-door.

Long story short, I found myself in a church service (I thought by chance) hearing a sermon for the very first time in my life. The topic was actually this story from John. I can't explain what took place, but I connected with God in my heart for the first time. As the pastor was talking, I realized that the God who I thought was so far away was, in fact, searching for me. I started to trace back some events in my life over the past years, and realized that Jesus had been pursuing me all along. It all began to make sense.

I had been searching and experimenting with many different things in an attempt to try and find personal happiness, career fulfillment, individual identity, love, worth, and value. It was as if I had heard in my mind, "Chris, come home. You have found me. I, Jesus, am who you have always been searching for. This is it. You are home now. The striving, the searching, the confusion is all over. You are found." My heart exploded. I couldn't keep the tears inside my eyes. I knew it was true. I wept uncontrollably and fell out of my seat onto the floor in the worship service. As a matter of fact, I messed up the sermon because back in those days in East Texas, you didn't move until the end of the sermon! But I didn't know and I couldn't wait.

I dropped to my knees. The service soon ended. Somehow I made my way out of the aisle and up to the front of the church so I could get out of the way. My brother Mike and several friends were all present. Three other young men saw what had happened to me and fell to their knees as well. We were causing quite a ruckus. I stayed approximately an hour and a half after the service, on the floor, on my face, weeping. It was a special day for me, one that I'll never forget. I had experienced the love of Jesus in a way that I had never known. Today, 28 years later, I love Jesus more than anything in my life. I think about Him off and on all throughout each day. It's still an honor to tell my story about the day my life was changed forever. I can still hear Jesus speak those words to me.

## Say Yes to Jesus

My prayer today is for those of you who hear the Spirit calling you and inviting you into a relationship with Jesus that's beyond religion and ritual. Jesus desires for us to be honest and authentic in our worship of Him. God is spirit, and we can worship Him anytime and anywhere. He's not confined to one location. He can speak to you at a well in Samaria, on a back country road in East Texas, or off the page of this book. God is not limited to time and space like we are.

God, our Father, desires for us to accept His Son, Jesus Christ, as the savior of our lives. When we do, God the Spirit comes in and resides in our hearts. I'm convinced that deep inside each person is a genuine longing to know truth and to know God personally. Jesus promises that as we trust our lives to God, "living water" will become like a "spring of water" that wells up to eternal life inside of us.

My prayer is that when you hear Him knocking at the door of your heart, or recognize that God has come close and might be pursuing you, that you won't get nervous and talk the religious talk. Don't put Him off until next week. Respond to Him today. This might well be the most important day of your life. Today is the day of salvation! Reach out and receive His offer to enter your life and flood your soul with living water. It will be the most important and eternal decision you'll ever make.

John Chapter 5

# AWARE, CONNECTED, ALIGNED, AND ENGAGED

*So Jesus said to them, "Truly, truly, I say to you, the Son can do nothing of his own accord, but only what he sees the Father doing. For whatever the Father does, that the Son does likewise. For the Father loves the Son and shows him all that he himself is doing. Whoever does not honor the Son does not honor the Father who sent him. Truly, truly, I say to you, whoever hears my word and believes him who sent me has eternal life." (John 5:19-24)*

## Loving God is Loving People

This chapter begins with yet another miracle of Jesus: healing the lame man at the pool of Bethesda. Jesus enters Jerusalem during a Jewish feast and encounters a disturbing situation. Love and compassion move Jesus to action. He intervenes to reverse a man's life-long disability and heals him. Jesus then disappears into the crowd. The news circulates within the community about what happened, and because Jesus healed the guy on the Sabbath, controversy brews among certain Jewish opponents.

The Sabbath was understood to be a day of rest, and a religious law to be upheld. Unfortunately, some people misunderstood the letter of the law without the spirit of the law. Jesus sets things straight. He chose to honor people's welfare over religious tradition. Jesus modeled that loving God is demonstrated by how we love others. It wasn't that Jesus didn't believe that the Sabbath had its place, it's just that it's place wasn't above showing love, mercy, and justice to people—no matter who they were.

## God in the Flesh

As the story continues, Jesus resurfaces and a timely discussion beyond healing emerges. Jesus declares His equality to God. The pompous religious elites of the day have their chains yanked as Jesus explains how to hear the voice of the Spirit, as well as how to have a meaningful and daily relationship with God the Father.

Jesus goes on to not only introduce His divinity, but to set the record straight concerning His unique role, authority, and responsibility as God's own Son in the flesh. Jesus lays it all out on the table. He concludes with an explanation concerning eternal life, the resurrection of the dead, and the final judgment.

I love how Jesus' words cut through and clarify. He has an amazing way of taking the complex and making it simple. Jesus has an uncanny approach of calling our spirits heavenward and, at the same time, focusing our actions to fully engage and serve humanity in a spirit of love, mercy, compassion, and justice. At first glance, living the God-life appears to not be rocket science, yet it can't be fueled and sustained in us without the aid of the Holy Spirit.

## Jesus' Incarnational Ministry

Throughout His earthly ministry, Jesus was always showing people how to love God with all they've got and how to set their priorities straight in life. Sometimes to accomplish this, Jesus "colored outside the lines" of well-meaning tradition in an effort to reach out to people who were far from God or disenfranchised with the organized religion of the day. Helping people get in right relationship with God and getting folks into right alignment, concerning their responsibility to invest in the well-being of other people, was a core value of Jesus.

Today, Jesus, through the Holy Spirit, and through other Christ-followers, still engages humanity. That's what incarnational ministry is all about. Two thousand years ago, Jesus came to earth as both fully God and fully man. He was God in the flesh. Incarnational ministry still continues today through God the Holy Spirit, but He uses Christ-followers and His Church to be the hands and feet of the invisible God to a world searching for true north. Jesus' ministry continues, but He uses "human vessels" to get the job done.

Jesus still wants to reconcile lost people back to God. He wants to display love and compassion to the downhearted and under-resourced, both in our communities and abroad. Jesus is still passionate about raising the bar for justice on behalf of the marginalized and forgotten.

## The God-Life

Resurrection is on His mind. He wants everyone to experience eternal life (beginning now and into eternity). Jesus desires for people to engage in the God-life, which is a life of loving relationship and communication with God the Father, God the Son, and God the Spirit, while at the same time, living a life that prioritizes others. Living the God-life is about realizing that life is not about you, it's about others. The God-life is both heavenward and earthbound. The early Gnostics tried to separate one from the other, but it can't be done. To be heavenly-minded is to be of earthly good.

## Speak Lord

So, my prayer today is that I too want to hear the Father speak. I want to be one that is accustomed to His voice. God, please give us grace that when we do hear You speak, we understand what You want us to do. Help us be people of follow-through, commitment, passion, and engagement. Let us grow in mercy and compassion toward others. Help us to not just talk about the God-life, but to live it.

Jesus, please use us to represent, to a watching world, not just the things You say, but the actions that accompany them. Give us eyes to see what You are doing so that we might do the things You are saying.

John Chapter 6

# BREAD THAT SUSTAINS

*Jesus said to them, "I am the bread of life; whoever comes to me shall not hunger, and whoever believes in me shall never thirst. For this is the will of my Father, that everyone who looks on the Son and believes in him should have eternal life, and I will raise him up on the last day." (John 6:35, 40)*

## Miracles of Jesus

John begins this chapter by recording the feeding of the multitudes. This miraculous messianic sign is described in all four gospels and demonstrates the deity of Jesus as God's one and only Son. Jesus uses this miracle of generosity (providing bread and sustenance to thousands of hungry people) as a backdrop to an even larger spiritual lesson and invitation that is about to unfold.

Jesus explains the connection between the Old Testament "saving" events (Passover, Exodus, manna in the wilderness) to the larger salvation promises of God found in and through the person of Jesus Christ. Through Jesus, we are saved, not just from a particular event like those depicted in the Old Testament, but for all eternity. (The Greek word for salvation is *sozo* which means to save, heal, preserve, and make whole.) Because of Jesus, the crisis and sentence of sin is broken and paid for through His death and resurrection. Through Him, we can live forever with God.

## "I AM"

Jesus goes on to make the first of seven "I am" statements that are found in the gospels. He declares "I am the bread of life," which is a promise to not just provide for our physical needs, but to provide for our spiritual needs, too. Jesus is the only one who can truly sustain and satisfy our spiritual longings. He alone is the one who meets the deep cravings housed within our souls. Jesus then broadens this invitation of everlasting life beyond the nation of Israel to one that includes all people, all genders, all backgrounds, all ethnicities, and all ages who look to Jesus (past, present and future) as Messiah, Savior, Lord, and God. The only prerequisite of this invitation is to come to Him and to believe. Finally, eternal life is discussed. A promise to be raised from the dead is assured. Everlasting life is guaranteed to those who say yes to His invitation.

## Food for a Hungry Heart

As I meditate on this passage of scripture, I'm reminded of how our culture offers us an array of spiritual junk foods and an assortment of tainted forms of water. We live in a world that offers many "wells" from which to drink and many forms of "food" to eat. They promise long life, happiness, and fulfillment. In the short run, they sometimes quench our thirst and fill a need or desire. But in the long run, they come up short. They don't deliver what they promise. In fact, some fail miserably and leave us thirstier and hungrier than when we started.

The prophet Jeremiah suggested hundreds of years earlier that many people were drinking from broken cisterns that they had made with their own hands. They refused to drink from the fountain of God's living water (Jeremiah 2: 13; 17:13). Isaiah the prophet expressed his concern and used the familiar imagery of bread and water that Jesus draws upon. Isaiah said:

> "Come, everyone who thirsts, come to the waters; and he who has no money, come, buy and eat! Come, buy wine and milk without money and without price. Why do you spend your money for that which is not bread, and your labor for that which does not satisfy? Listen diligently to me, and eat what is good, and delight yourselves in rich food. Incline your ear, and come to me; hear, that your soul may live..." (Isaiah 55:1-3)

## Jesus Satisfies

Jesus' promises are not to be mistaken as Pollyanna-like hopes. Rather, they are grounded in the character of God, who cannot lie. His promises are based on the foundation of the crucifixion and Resurrection, which was foretold in Genesis. Through the person of Jesus, and by the working of the Holy Spirit within us, God sustains, fulfills, satisfies, and saves us. That is His promise. It's tethered to His character. God asks us to believe in His Son, Jesus. We are encouraged to receive His invitation to be loved and accepted. It's as we place our trust in Jesus that all things become new. It's as we drink from His well and eat bread from His hand that life takes on a new dimension—one that is renewed, sustained, and truly made whole.

What well are you drinking from? What kind of bread are you consuming? My prayer for you and me is that God will give us the grace to let go of the junk foods that may taste sweet, but in fact are working against His plan and promise for our lives. May we be able to discern the difference from the healthy and the unhealthy, the good from the bad, and the wise from the unwise.

# John Chapter 7

# LIVING WATER

*On the last day of the feast, the great day, Jesus stood up and cried out, "If anyone thirsts, let him come to me and drink. Whoever believes in me, as the Scripture has said, 'Out of his heart will flow rivers of living water.'" Now this he said about the Spirit, whom those who believed in him were to receive, for as yet the Spirit had not been given, because Jesus was not yet glorified. (John 7:37-39)*

## Jesus' Big Announcement

This story picks up in the midst of the Feast of Booths (Tabernacles), which was a commemorative national celebration of God's faithfulness to Israel during the 40-year stay in the wilderness centuries prior. Jesus is surrounded by an atmosphere of disbelief from His brothers. He encounters mounting opposition from the Jewish authorities; some even want to kill Him. Both faith and controversy collide among the masses.

Opinions about Jesus healing the lame man on the Sabbath are circulating. Everyone's talking. There is praise as well as criticism percolating about Jesus. "Messiah talk" surfaces at this citywide gathering. Emotions are running high. A plot against Jesus is hatched to frame Him. Local authorities want to take Him away and lock Him up. Temple police are soon deployed to arrest Him. Chaos is looming.

As was the custom of this particular religious holiday, the last day was the pivot point. It was the most important part in this annual gathering. Jesus seizes on this unique occasion. With all of these factors unfolding in the backdrop, Jesus steps up and heralds this prophetic and powerful declarative call and promise to the masses. Jesus succinctly and powerfully cries out to the crowd that anyone who thirsts for God should come. And not just come, but come specifically to Him. For whosoever believes in Him (Jesus) will be satisfied.

## A Water that Sustains

Jesus intentionally uses the analogy of living water to make His point. It was God Himself, in the Old Testament, who provided water from the rock to the Israelites during their arduous journey in the wilderness (Exodus 17). Every person listening to Jesus would have understood the connection He was making. Jesus was saying that He was God. He was "the Rock" from where the water flowed (back then and now). He was the one that sustained and refreshed their ancestors of old. Now, Jesus was offering "this water" to the masses, but the choice was theirs.

At that point, you probably could have heard a pin drop. Within seconds, the silent awe turned into a roar. A verbal explosion erupts within the crowd. Some believe a divine encounter has just taken place right before their eyes. They start talking excitedly about the coming Messiah once again. Others clench their fists in anger and disbelief. Many of the Temple police don't know what to do. They have witnessed, with their own eyes, a phenomenon that words fail to describe. They become paralyzed in their decision-making. They don't know what to do with Jesus. In confusion, the Temple police turn away and fail to arrest Jesus. The religious leaders are frustrated, and Jesus moves on through the crowd as He continues His mission.

## The Rock of Ages

I love this story. It's filled with high drama, conflicted characters, and multiple spiritual truths on many levels. But for me, it always comes back to Jesus. Just like to the ancient Israelites, He is our Rock. He's the one who provides living water to our thirsty souls. His water never runs out. Jesus promises to fill us with His Spirit and live inside of us if we trust Him with our lives.

Jesus desires an ongoing relationship with each of us. He wants to use us as "vessels" that pour forth His water (love, truth, compassion, justice, the gospel message, etc.) to others who are thirsty. He desires for us to be a source of blessing to people. Jesus' invitation at the Feast of Booths is a historic event, yet the call still goes out today.

The prophet Isaiah talked about water. Here's what he said, "With joy you will draw water from the wells of salvation." (Isaiah 12:3) He goes on to say, "And the Lord will guide you continually and satisfy your desire in scorched places and make your bones strong; and you shall be like a watered garden, like a spring of water, whose waters do." (Isaiah 58:11)

## Come and Drink

Today, I want to encourage you to receive this timeless invitation from Jesus. Put your own name in the context of this scripture and say it out loud to yourself as a way to personalize its application to your life. "If *Chris* thirsts, let him come to me and drink. *Chris*, if you believe in me, as the Scripture has said, 'Out of *Chris*' heart will flow rivers of living water.'"

Let me challenge you to dive in and drink from the well of salvation. It's a river than never disappoints. It's water that soothes, satisfies, sustains, saves, and empowers. It's a spring of water that produces everlasting life in us and through us. Lord, fill us. We're thirsty for more of you!

John Chapter 8

# AN ASTONISHING CLAIM

*Again Jesus spoke to them, saying, "I am the light of the world. Whoever follows me will not walk in darkness, but will have the light of life." (John 8:12-13)*

## Light and Darkness

Jesus shows up at the local temple teaching the gospel to everyone that came out to hear Him. Soon the Scribes and Pharisees join the gathering to cause trouble. They try and trap Jesus with misleading questions and jaded motives concerning a woman caught in adultery. Jesus refuses to play their game. Instead, He penetrates their calloused hearts with truth.

Jesus goes on to unpack gospel truths about light and darkness, judgment and grace, the cross and Resurrection, the Father and the devil, truth, freedom, and faith. The chapter ends with a mob of people picking up stones to throw at Jesus. And again, Jesus escapes unscathed.

But lodged in the middle of this chapter, Jesus makes an astonishing claim. He asserts that He is the light of the world. Upon a cursory reading, one might think Jesus is saying He's an insightful moral teacher. Far more was being said. The Israelites of Jesus' day new exactly what He was insinuating.

Remember that in John chapter seven, Jesus was attending the Feast of Booths (Tabernacles), which was one of the annual celebrations that commemorated the 40 years of wandering in the wilderness. This eight-day event was a kind of national holiday, thanksgiving feast, and family campout, all rolled into one!

## Illumination of the Temple

There were also special ceremonies in the Temple during this feast. One in particular was called the "Illumination of the Temple." This ceremony took place on the first day of the festival. It included the lighting of four huge candelabras. When the sun set, the candelabras were lit and would shine brightly. The light could be seen flickering and emanating all over Jerusalem's dark night sky. These four symbolic candelabras were to remind the nation of Israel that it was God's presence, manifested through the pillar of fire, that guided the Jewish people through the wilderness at night (Exodus 13). Many Jews of Jesus' day hoped that God's promised Messiah would soon be upon them to continue God's great story of blessing the people of God (the Hebrews), so they in turn, could be a blessing and a light to the whole world.

## Light of the World

It was at this festival, with the candelabras burning in the backdrop, that Jesus makes this incredible claim: "I am the light of the world!" Jesus suggests that just as the Old Testament Israelites followed the pillar of fire in the wilderness, that people should follow Him as well. This was an absolutely radical and shocking proclamation. Jesus is associating Himself with the very presence of God (the pillar of fire) in the Old Testament.

Jesus' declaration not only rattled the cages of many of His listeners, but it should get our attention today as well. Jesus makes claim to the fact that He is not just a "god" or a man with a sprinkle of divinity within Him. Rather, He asserts that He is the God of the Old Testament! He is the one true God who created the universe! He was the pillar of fire. All through the Old Testament, God is associated with light.

- The Lord is my light and my salvation-whom shall I fear? (Psalm 21:1)
- The sun will no more be your light by day, nor will the brightness of the moon shine on you, for the Lord will be your everlasting light, and your God will be your glory. (Isaiah 60:19)
- Do not gloat over me, my enemy! Though I have fallen, I will rise. Though I sit in darkness, the Lord will be my light. (Micah 7:8)

## The God Claim

As you fast-forward the video to today's culture, the "God claim" about Jesus still rattles cages. Today, a lot of people think that Jesus was a great man, a spiritual teacher, or a moral philosopher. He is often mentioned in the same sentence with other moral leaders such as Mahatma Gandhi, Martin Luther King, Jr., Mohammed, Buddha, Joan of Arc, and other historical human figures of social, political, and religious change. Although compared on a human level to many great people of antiquity, it's important to remember that Jesus was the only figure to claim that He was God in the flesh.

## The One True God

Others see Jesus as one of many gods. He's welcomed into the pluralistic philosophy of one god among many gods, ideas, and philosophies. But eyebrows still lift, and conversations fill with angst when it's suggested that Jesus is the only, one true God. C.S. Lewis, the great Christian author and professor at Oxford, wrote in *Mere Christianity*:

> A man who was merely a man and said the sort of things Jesus said would not be a great moral teacher. He would either be a lunatic, on a level with the man who says he *is* a poached egg, or else he would be the devil of hell. You must make your choice. Either this man was, and is, the Son of God, or else a madman or something worse. You can shut Him up for a fool; you can spit at Him and kill Him as a demon; or, you can fall at His feet and call Him Lord and God. But let us not come up with any patronizing nonsense about His being a great human teacher. He has not left that open to us. He did not intend to."

## No More Darkness

As you read the Bible, you'll soon discover that it's not just Jesus' followers who make the case for Jesus' full divinity, but Jesus Himself makes the same claim about Himself. He proclaims His own deity, clear and simple. He then goes on to invite people into a relationship with Him through the person of God the Holy Spirit.

Jesus really is the light of the world. He tells us the truth. We don't have to live our lives in darkness. In fact, when you follow Him, you will not walk in darkness. Jesus wants to guide us, lead us, and direct our paths. And as we let Him, He promises to illuminate our hearts and minds to truth.

John Chapter 9

# A SPECTACULAR DEED

*As he passed by, he saw a man blind from birth. And his disciples asked him, "Rabbi, who sinned, this man or his parents, that he was born blind?" Jesus answered, "It was not that this man sinned, or his parents, but that the works of God might be displayed in him. We must work the works of him who sent me while it is day; night is coming, when no one can work. As long as I am in the world, I am the light of the world." Having said these things, he spat on the ground and made mud with the saliva. Then he anointed the man's eyes with the mud and said to him, "Go, wash in the pool of Siloam" (which means Sent). So he went and washed and came back seeing. (John 9: 1-7)*

## Who's to Blame?

This chapter opens up with an age-old assumption regarding sin, suffering, and evil: Personal sin causes personal suffering. This was an accepted worldview in ancient Israel. Even today, many people fail to understand that suffering is a much larger topic than can be reduced to simple, quantifiable answers.

Jesus tackles this misconception head on. He explains that in this particular case, sin is not the issue of the man's disability. Rather, God wants to heal this man in order for God to be glorified. The blind man's disability wasn't his fault, it wasn't some hidden sin of his parents, nor a unique set of circumstances related to an environmental blunder. No. This was a God thing.

Jesus' statement introduces us to a perspective that is often hard to understand: God sometimes allows us to go through hard and painful situations in order to experience His healing touch first-hand, lavish mercy, and sustaining grace in our lives. So, after a quick theological straightening-out, Jesus gets down to business and creatively heals a man who had been blind from birth.

## Sight to the Blind

In this chapter, He gives sight to the blind. As the story unfolds, the religious elite are ticked off because Jesus again heals on a Sabbath, like He did in John chapter five. But in the midst of more criticism and disbelief from the Jewish leaders, the blind man's opinion of Jesus begins to evolve. First, he thought Jesus was just a man. Later, he stated that Jesus must be a prophet like Elijah (Old Testament prophets commonly performed miracles). Finally, the blind man professed that Jesus was the Son of Man, which was a title used of the Messiah. He ended up believing in Jesus and became a Christ-follower. The blind man saw the light—the light of the world!

## Wrestling with Pain

As I think about my own life and the lives of those I love, it's so easy to slip into a kind of "cause and effect" thinking. When things are going well, we sometimes think that we are doing well, and possibly, we might have a little something to do with our blessings and good fortune. On the other hand, when life implodes and suffering abounds, we sometimes think, "What have I done to cause this? My pain must be a result of God being mad at me for something bad I must have done." Too often, we drift into unhealthy deductions and conclusions regarding sin and suffering.

It's interesting to note that when the disciples saw problems, they wanted to blame someone or something. When Jesus saw these same problems and difficulties, He saw them as opportunities for God to work.

What do you see in the midst of problems? What do you see when you wind up short on money or experience troubles in your relationships? Do you only see problems? Or do you consider the possibility that God might be using difficulty, even suffering, as an opportunity to work deeply in your life? Maybe God wants to demonstrate His love, mercy, healing, or provision to you. Maybe He wants to do something awesome in the midst of all that is confusing, wrong, and painful.

## Eyes to See Anew

My prayer today is that you and I, like the blind man, will see Jesus in new ways, and that you and I will progress in our understanding of who Jesus is, and what He wants to do in our lives. Not only is Jesus the Messiah of the Bible, but He's our God, our Healer, and our Redeemer, too.

God, give us eyes to see the evidence of Your presence and the evidence of what You are doing, rather than the evidence of Your absence. Give light to our eyes that we may see You in the dark places and shadows of our lives.

# John Chapter 10

# THE LIFE GIVING SHEPHERD

*The thief comes only to steal and kill and destroy. I came that they may have life and have it abundantly. I am the good shepherd. The good shepherd lays down his life for the sheep. (John 10:10-11)*

## Jesus Leads, We Follow

Sheep, shepherds, sheepfolds, and pastures are common word pictures used in both the Old and New Testaments to depict the relationship between God and His people. In short, God is the Great Shepherd who loves and cares for His sheep (you and me). He leads us and we follow Him.

In ancient times, sheepfolds were often located right next to someone's home. Several families would share in its upkeep and use. As a way to keep the sheep contained and predators at bay, the pen would be surrounded by a large wooden frame or fortified by a stone covered wall. Many times, the official front entrance wouldn't have a door. So, either a hired gatekeeper or the shepherd would stand in the gap when needed.

In times of great conflict, the hired gatekeepers would run away and abandon the sheep. But the shepherd would bravely stay and protect them from theft or violence. He wasn't a hired gun looking for a quick buck. Rather, the shepherd was a loving provider and protector. If need be, a courageous shepherd would even fight to the death on behalf of his beloved sheep.

## Psalm 23

I'm so grateful that God is our Good Shepherd. He loves, leads, and protects us. He always has our best interests at heart. Psalm 23 paints a beautiful scene, through powerful word pictures and concepts, to describe the intimate relationship between sheep and their shepherds. Many words come to mind: provision, leadership, rest, peace, protection, renewal, soul care, love, relationship, accountability, correction, discipline, comfort, courage, healing, joy, goodness, mercy, grace, and eternal life. In this poetic song, David suggests to us that these relational qualities of sheep and shepherds apply to our relationship with God.

## Watching Out for Predators

Every sheep had foes and predators who sought them out. It was the shepherd's job to be on the lookout for the sheep's best interest and to protect them from harm and evil. The thief (the devil) only wants to steal, kill and destroy. Satan's strategy for every Christian is threefold.

1.   Steal - to take away what is rightfully someone else's
2.   Kill - to take the life out of something
3.   Destroy - to render something ineffective or useless

## Same Old Stuff

The devil's strategies are still being used today. Although his methods might look different in the 21st century, his threefold motives never change. In applying this analogy to the spiritual world, the devil desires to take from God's people what God rightfully wants for them. What God's people do possess (relationships, callings, ministries, marriages, leadership, etc.), the devil wants to suck the life and joy out of them, so we'll give up on each of those areas ourselves. Finally, the devil wants to render God's people and God's plans in and through His people useless, ineffective, and void. He wants to squash people's God-given potential.

But, in the midst of the devil's intentions, God has good news! Jesus is not only stronger than the devil, but He has come to offer us a new kind of life and a new way to live. He offers us eternal life, which is a life that is fully alive. It's a life that is sourced and sustained in and through Him. Jesus offers you and me both a new "quality" of life and a "quantity" of life.

## Abundant Life

The abundant life is one of joy, peace, freedom, and purpose. It's part of the "eternal life" that begins when we accept Jesus Christ as the Good Shepherd of our lives and turn from being the shepherd of our own lives and destinies. The Bible uses this metaphor of "shepherd" as another way of communicating to us that Jesus is our God, Leader, Lord, and Redeemer. This "fully alive" life is offered to us through the death and resurrection of Jesus.

## Eternal Life

This "eternal life" is also one that never ends. That's the second half of the meaning of this word. Eternal life is a life that is never-ending and everlasting. Although this life begins when we trust our lives to Jesus, it's a life that lives beyond the grave. It is this life that Jesus offers to each of us, by invitation, to receive Him as Lord, Savior, and Shepherd. Jesus is our Good

Shepherd. We are His sheep. He knows each of us by name. Jesus offers to lead us. He always loves us. In return, we listen to His words and follow.

## Taking Time to Listen

My prayer is that you and I will begin to listen to the voice of our Shepherd in new ways, who is the creator of our conscience. Jesus can't lead us until we commit to follow. My hope is that as we hear the whisper of His voice quietly calling our names, and as we sense His promptings and impressions inside our souls, and that you and I will each say yes to follow Him! That will be the most eternal response we can ever make.

# John Chapter 11

# LIFE AFTER LIFE AFTER DEATH

*Martha said to Jesus, "Lord, if you had been here, my brother would not have died. But even now I know that whatever you ask from God, God will give you." Jesus said to her, "Your brother will rise again." Martha said to him, "I know that he will rise again in the resurrection on the last day." Jesus said to her, "I am the resurrection and the life. Whoever believes in me, though he dies, yet shall he live, and everyone who lives and believes in me shall never die. Do you believe this?" She said to him, "Yes, Lord; I believe that you are the Christ, the Son of God, who is coming into the world." (John 11: 21-27)*

## Lazarus, Come Out

This story begins in the village of Bethany, which was a small town located about two miles outside of Jerusalem. This incredible miracle of Jesus raising Lazarus from the dead is recorded only in John's gospel. It not only sets the stage for Jesus' own resurrection that soon follows, but it seals His death sentence as the Jewish leaders bitterly resolve to arrest Him on bogus charges.

As the story unfolds, Lazarus gets sick. I'm sure he gets whatever medical help was available in those days. We don't know if it was a fever, a lump, or a cough. But he dies. In fact, he's dead for four days before Jesus shows up. The point John wants to make is that Lazarus was really dead; no vital signs, flat-lined, and six feet under with absolutely no hope of resuscitation!

When Jesus arrives, He encounters Martha, Lazarus' sister, at the graveside. She displays knowledge of the common first century Jewish theology (Pharisees) of the final resurrection of the dead that will take place at the end of time. But Martha fails to understand who Jesus really was and the promises He offered. Jesus asserts His deity and authority over both life and death. He goes on to explain that if Martha would place her trust in Him that He would raise her from the dead as well. Jesus then tells her that, in fact, He is the resurrection and the life.

## An Invitation to Believe

After extending an invitation to Martha to place her faith and trust in Him, Jesus walks over to the grave. He prays out loud and thanks the Father for always listening. The wailing of the grieving bystanders subsides. Everyone's gaze is fixed on Jesus and what He's about to do. The stone is rolled away. Then Jesus calls out, "Lazarus, come out." He does, the grave clothes come off, and the party begins!

It was the late Mel Blanc, the voice of most of the Looney Tunes characters, who was famous for saying at the end of every cartoon, "That's all folks!" In fact, his family actually had that saying chiseled on his tombstone! But that's not what Christianity teaches. As Christians, we believe that life doesn't end after we die. Rather, we will be raised from the dead.

But not like Lazarus who, because he was human, ended up dying again in this life. Jesus is our example that we look to. Because Jesus has been raised from the dead, and is alive in heaven, we too will be raised from the dead and given new bodies at the final resurrection.

## Resurrection From the Dead

The ultimate resurrection story is not Lazarus', but Jesus' story. This is where Christians' hope resides. When Jesus came out of the tomb, death was defeated once and for all (1 Corinthians 15). For those who love and follow Jesus, the grave is not the end. It's not, "That's all folks." For the Christian, death in the short term is just like a change of address. It's a new location. Of course, when Jesus comes back to earth for the second and final time, and the new heaven and earth come together, the Bible says that then the final resurrection and judgment will take place and we'll get glorified, resurrected bodies. That is the promise and hope for every person who trusts in Jesus. God's promises are sure and true. Remember, although death is real, it's not the end. Because Jesus is alive, we'll be alive together with Him forever.

## Set Our Hearts to Follow

My prayer for you and me is that while we still have today we will devote ourselves to following Jesus with all our hearts. As we put our hope in Him, Jesus not only makes promises to us, but He is the promise. Jesus will never fail. He will deliver on every promise. God, please remind us again that the same Spirit that raised Jesus from the dead, lives in us (Romans 8:11). Your Spirit will not only dwell in us, but will walk with us through death and into life everlasting.

John Chapter 12

# TRADING UP TO THE GOD-LIFE

*Whoever loves his life loses it, and whoever hates his life in this world will keep it for eternal life. If anyone serves me, he must follow me; and where I am, there will my servant be also. If anyone serves me, the Father will honor him. (John 12: 25-27)*

## The Final Week

This is around the time Jesus enters into the final week before His arrest, trial, torture, crucifixion, burial, and resurrection. This chapter begins with Jesus having dinner in Bethany. During the dinner, a woman honors Jesus by demonstrating lavish love and sacrificial worship toward Him. Criticism soon follows.

The next day Jesus makes His triumphal entry into the city of Jerusalem on a donkey. Palm branches are waving. People are shouting. Foreigners are questioning. Creation is groaning. Jesus is speaking. Heaven is thundering. Death seems imminent. Jesus departs. His disciples ask questions. The prophet Isaiah is quoted. Salvation is explained. Jesus and the Father are glorified.

## The Great Paradox

Located in the middle of this story is a portion of scripture where Jesus explains the secret of how to have a meaningful and satisfying life. His thoughts run counter to what surrounds popular thinking within our society. He introduces a great paradox.

Jesus talks about loving and hating life. He selects words that are the antithesis of each other to emphasize a point. The phrase, "loves his life," means delighting in the life of this world more than loving and delighting in God and the things God loves. When Jesus uses the phrase, "hates his life," He means that a person thinks less of his life in this world compared to his love toward God and for the things God loves.

When a person loves God, as Jesus is suggesting, and understands that life is not all about the "self," but about God, and when a person is willing to sacrifice the things of this world for God, they in fact will find a life that is fully alive, meaningful, and eternal. Jesus teaches us that if we want to protect and save our lives, we will lose out. If we want to go our own way, do our own thing, and live for our own purposes, we will ultimately lose our lives and miss out on the God-life that is available to each of us.

On the other hand, if we lose our lives for Jesus, and prioritize Him first, then we will in fact find our lives. If we seek to discover God's purpose for our lives, live for God, and understand that there is more to this life than just being focused on our own wants and desires, then we will find life. George Bernard Shaw once wrote:

> "This is the true joy in life: being used for a purpose recognized by yourself as a mighty one; being thoroughly worn out before you are thrown on the scrap heap; being a force of nature instead of a feverish selfish little clod of ailments and grievances complaining that the world will not devote itself to making you happy."

## Finding the Good Life

So, how do you lose your life? Simple. Do your own thing. Be your own selfish pig! Be your own "selfish little clod of selfish grievances." Live life as if you are the center of it all. How do you find your life? Live the God-life! Love God and people. Love the things God loves. Understand that it's not about you, but that it's about God and others. The God-life is about living for God's purpose and pleasure rather than just for your own.

Jesus' words ring as true today as they did 20 centuries ago. God wants the best for each of us. He's not as some media purveyors portray Him: a celestial killjoy wanting to rain down on everyone's parade. Instead, God wants us to live and enjoy a life that is fully alive and teeming with meaning and fulfillment.

My prayer for you and me is that we'll remember that life isn't about us; it's about God and others. Our lives are not our own. We've been bought with a price (1 Corinthians 6:20). As we set our hearts and minds to love and serve God with all we've got, and when we choose to live for His purposes, we'll find the God-life: a life of righteousness, peace, joy, and true, meaningful fulfillment.

John Chapter 13

# SERVANTHOOD TAKES GUTS

*Jesus, knowing that the Father had given all things into his hands, and that he had come from God and was going back to God, rose from supper. He laid aside his outer garments, and taking a towel, tied it around his waist. Then he poured water into a basin and began to wash the disciples' feet and to wipe them with the towel that was wrapped around him. He came to Simon Peter, who said to him, "Lord, do you wash my feet?" Jesus answered him, "What I am doing you do not understand now, but afterward you will understand." Peter said to him, "You shall never wash my feet." Jesus answered him, "If I do not wash, you have no share with me." (John 13: 3-8)*

## Staying Close to Jesus

After being despised by the Jewish leaders, Jesus focuses in on His disciples for the last time. They are going to share a meal together and hear some of the most profound insights and final thoughts up to this point in their relationship with Jesus. With the Crucifixion in the back of His mind, Jesus models loving servant-hood to the 12 by washing their feet, which was considered a low-class task in their culture. What's amazing is that Jesus not only washes the feet of His friends, but also the feet of His betrayer, Judas Iscariot. The 12 had heard Jesus teach about loving God and loving your neighbor, but now Jesus takes love to an entirely different level: loving your enemies.

Jesus tells Peter that if he wants to be close to Jesus, then he must allow Jesus to wash his feet. Some believe that this foot-washing was a symbolic gesture speaking of the forgiveness of sins that would soon be available through Jesus' death and resurrection on the cross. It could also be another way of saying that once a person becomes a Christ-follower, there will be many times in their walk with God in which they will need spiritual "cleansing and washing" to keep their hearts, souls, and consciences clean before God. That's why repentance is not just a one-time thing—it's a daily decision. Repentance, or lack of it, affects our spiritual sensitivity and closeness in our walk with God. I'm sure as the disciples remembered this event, after Jesus' death and resurrection, they were gripped with respect and adoration as they pondered the humility and love Jesus displayed that evening.

## Servant: The Greatest of All

Whenever I think about Jesus washing feet, I remember as a kid having all kinds of aspirations and dreams of what I would like to become when I grew up: a cowboy, a professional athlete, a musician, an astronaut, or a heart surgeon. (I was never short on ideas.) But one thing that never entered my mind's vocabulary was the word "servant."

Leonard Bernstein, the world-renowned composer, once was asked, "What do you think is the most difficult instrument to play?" Without a second thought, he quipped, "The most difficult instrument? Second violin." Leonard went on to say, "There's plenty of folks who want to play first violin. But not so with the one who plays second. To find a person who plays second violin with the same level of passion, dedication, enthusiasm, and excellence as a first chair violinist, now that's a challenge. But if you don't have a second violin, you can never play harmony."

## The "Mini-Me" Generation

Those are wise and insightful words and they give us a clue about God's value system. We live in a culture that is all about "me" and "mine." Today's culture looks down on the concept of being a servant. To many, servanthood is perceived as something demeaning and weak. It's a way of living (attitude and actions) that is misunderstood, and even feared. When you mention the word "servant," it conjures up images of people groveling in the dirt, the lowest of the low. Jesus said the greatest in God's kingdom are the people who serve. In God's economy, servanthood is a high commodity. Servants are the greatest of people. Jesus teaches us that serving others is not only an expression of love, but guts. Of all the ways Jesus could have expressed His authority and heavenly position, He chose to express it through servanthood (Philippians 2).

## Guts, Grit, and Honor

Servanthood requires guts. It requires lots of character. Why? To be a genuine servant, you have to possess humility, self-control, endurance, compassion, and love. It takes guts to hang in there when credit passes you by. It takes backbone when no one applauds you, but you keep going anyway. It takes fortitude when no one gives you accolades, but you keep on serving. Being a servant takes grit when you are humiliated and refuse to drop out. Servanthood is for the strong of heart and the spiritually mature. The scriptures say, "The Son of Man did not come to be served, but to serve, and to give His life as a ransom for many." (Mark 19:34)

## Called Into Greatness

My prayer for us is that we will walk close to Jesus and that we'll allow Him to wash us, cleanse us, convict us, forgive us, heal us, speak to us, and empower us to serve. God has called us to be great. No, not necessarily great in the world's eyes, but great in His eyes. Greatness is always tethered to servanthood. God, please build in us a heart to love and to serve.

John Chapter 14

# A HOME, THE HELPER, OUR HOPE

*Let not your hearts be troubled. Believe in God; believe also in me. In my Father's house are many rooms. If it were not so, would I have told you that I go to prepare a place for you? And if I go and prepare a place for you, I will come again and will take you to myself, that where I am you may be also. (John 14: 1-3)*

## Going Home

John shares, in great detail, the conversation that took place between Jesus and His disciples the night before His crucifixion. It began with the washing of feet, a communion meal, and a new commandment (love). As the evening progresses, Jesus zeros in on the reality of His departing from earth and going home to the Father in heaven. Confusion, insecurity, questions, and fear rise up in the hearts of the disciples.

Jesus promises that God the Father will soon send the Holy Spirit (the third distinct person in the Trinity) to the disciples. God, the Holy Spirit, will act as a Divine presence that will dwell in them (and us, too). He will serve as a helper who will guide, teach, empower, shape, strengthen, and comfort them as they continue on as followers of Jesus.

## To Love is to Obey

Jesus then connects two commandments together: the new commandment of love that He has just introduced, and the commandment of obeying His teachings. Jesus explains that to love God is to obey God. Heart and soul are tethered to body and action. Love must not exist only in a mental concept. Love is a verb. It must be lived out in action for it to really be love. Jesus promises that the Holy Spirit will help us to love and obey in this new capacity.

Whenever I read John chapter 14, I think of our future home in heaven. Heaven, in this portion of scripture, is compared to that of an eternal dwelling place, a mansion that has many rooms. Heaven is the place where we go to be with Jesus after we die. It's the new community and location of where the presence of God and Jesus reside (along with other Christians). Heaven is the place where Christ-followers go until they are resurrected from the dead. Even though there's a lot of mystery surrounding heaven, the scriptures do share bits and pieces of what heaven is, and what is going on there.

## Thoughts of Heaven

My daughter, Megan, currently lives in Los Angeles, where she is working and attending college. Her bedroom is empty in our home. When

I say empty, I mean she currently doesn't live in our home. She lives in temporary digs in California.

Here at the house, Megan's room has some furniture in it, along with pictures and memorabilia sprinkled up on the wall. So yes, in one way, her room is empty; yet in another, it's prepared and waiting for her return during Spring Break. When I walk down the hall and see her bedroom door, I think of her. When I open up the door and go inside her room, I really think of her and long to see her face-to-face.

In some funny sort of way, that reminds me of heaven, of God, and His love for us. Jesus and the Father think about us in the midst of our busy lives. Hours and days can go by, and although we aren't necessarily thinking about our bedroom in heaven, God is.

Our eternal rooms have been individually prepared for each of us and they are waiting. Jesus tells us about heaven, not for logistical concerns, but so we will know how much we matter to the Father, and to demonstrate how much He loves us and thinks about us.

## Life Beyond the Grave

Part of the ministry of the Holy Spirit is to remind us that we are not alone here on planet Earth just slugging away at life and trying to make a living. The Holy Spirit wants to remind us that this life (earth) is not our home. Heaven is our home. Life beyond the grave is our destination. As God walks down heaven's hallway, so to speak, He smiles when He thinks about you and me. God feels emotion as He longs for us.

That's one reason why I love Jesus so much: Because He went to the cross and died for us, we now have a room in heaven. The scriptures say that for the joy set before Him, He endured the shame and pain of the cross (Hebrews 12:2). What was the joy set before Him? I think it means the joyful anticipation and longing He has to be with us in heaven. The joy is the emotion that takes place in His heart as He's walking down the hall and anticipating being with us again, forever. All throughout the Bible, God's heart seems to be set on making a home for us. In fact, John, later says in the last part of Revelation:

"And I saw a the holy city, new Jerusalem, coming down out of heaven from God, prepared as a bride adorned for her husband. And I heard a loud voice from the throne saying, "Behold, the dwelling place of God is with man. He will dwell with them, and they will be his people, and God himself will be with them as their God." (Revelation 21:2-3)

## Morning is Coming

My prayer for you and me is that we'll be reminded of God's sacrificial love and unending care for us. Dear Father, thank you for Jesus and His selfless act of going to Calvary's cross to pay for our sins and extend His forgiveness to us. God, please remind us that life here on earth is temporary. It's a gift to be stewarded, even when it's hard. Thank you that there is a home in Heaven waiting for us among a new community and family already there. Fill us anew with Your Spirit and peace. Help us to remember the hope and the promise that is waiting for of each of us. The day will come when we open our eyes and it will be morning. We'll be at home with You, and once again, walking down heaven's hallway.

# John Chapter 15

# THE CALL TO ABIDE

*I am the true vine, and my Father is the vinedresser. Every branch in me that does not bear fruit he takes away, and every branch that does bear fruit he prunes, that it may bear more fruit. I am the vine; you are the branches. Whoever abides in me and I in him, he it is that bears much fruit, for apart from me you can do nothing. If you abide in me, and my words abide in you, ask whatever you wish, and it will be done for you. By this my Father is glorified, that you bear much fruit and so prove to be my disciples. (John 15: 1-2, 5, 7-8)*

## Language of Relationships

John records the last of the seven "I AM" sayings of Jesus in this chapter. Throughout the Old Testament, the analogy of the vineyard and the gardener is used to describe the relationship between the nation of Israel and God. Often in the Old Testament, Israel's sin and lack of fruitfulness in their walk with God evoked His just discipline and needed correction. Because most societies in biblical times were agrarian in nature, spiritual truths were often depicted in terms and images that the people could relate to as people of the land.

As you read through the Old Testament, you'll discover a common language that uses the analogies and metaphors of gardens, fields, and gardeners as well as plowing, planting, sowing, weeding, watering, pruning, and harvesting. These word pictures explain the cause and effect principles embedded in spiritual truths, which we call today "sowing and reaping." This form of communication is a way of using visible natural laws of the universe to understand the invisible supernatural realities of the spirit world.

## Connected

Jesus tells us that God has called us to be connected to Him in a loving relationship. The word He uses to describe that principle is "abide." Jesus likens God the Father as the master gardener, Jesus as the vine, and you and I as the branches. He explains that fruitfulness is a natural by-product of staying close and connected in an honest and genuine relationship with God.

Fruitfulness can be described as that of a changed life due to the work of God's spirit inside a person. The Bible calls it the "fruits of the Spirit," or Christian character qualities (Galatians 5). Fruitfulness is also seen in the fruit of other changed lives. Christians are called to partner with God's Spirit and help produce other Christians. (Remember, inside a piece of fruit are the seeds that produce more of that same kind of fruit.) Jesus pours His life into us, and as His life flows through the vine and into the branches, so to speak, it bears seeds of change inside of us. These changes, in turn, affect other people, and in the process, glorify God.

Often, in Christian circles, we are challenged to go out and be fruitful. But Jesus doesn't ask that of us. Notice that instead, He challenges us to abide in Him. As we do, we will be fruitful. Why? It's because fruitfulness is a result of abiding in Christ. Attaining fruitfulness is not a result of pursuing fruitfulness. Sometimes we get it backwards. When we do, then it doesn't work right. Because we can't sustain it, we get discouraged and quit. But God wants us to be successful—so He tells us the truth.

## The Secret of Fruitfulness

The secret to a thriving and growing Christian life is learning to abide. Everything that really matters will flow out of that relationship with Jesus. It was Jesus who said that He only does the things that He sees His Father doing, and He only says the things that He hears His father saying. That's what abiding looks like.

Jesus tells us that if we (as the branches) stay attached to Him (the vine) then we'll bear fruit. If we don't, we won't. Fruitfulness happens when you and I stay attached to Jesus, just like a branch bears fruit if it's attached to the tree. The command isn't to get out there and try harder; it's about staying close to Jesus, and as we do that, we'll naturally bear fruit.

## Abiding is a Choice

One of the truths about abiding that I've learned over the years, is that it takes work. For example, if a marriage is to stay intimate and connected through the struggles of life, it takes work and commitment. It's not easy all the time. Great friendships are the same way. To maintain them throughout the years, it takes some grit. The same is true in our spiritual lives with Jesus. It will take intentional effort on our part. The natural proclivity, in all relationships (natural and spiritual), is that they drift if you don't invest in them. It's the same thing in our relationship with Jesus.

We stay connected to God by learning to trust Him and leaning on Him in our disappointments and setbacks, as well as in successes and victories. We stay close to Jesus as we cultivate a genuine and growing relationship with Him in prayer, reading the Bible, being obedient, and allowing Him to be our leader.

## Pruning

The good news is that God is committed to our fruitfulness more than we are, and He wants to help. That's where pruning comes in. Because God (the Master Gardener) loves us, He removes "the unwanted branches" from our lives. Some things in our lives must go, and other things just need to be pruned. But notice there's nothing in the middle. It either grows or it's pruned. Pruning is a vital part of the growth process, maturity, and spiritual formation.

Remember: The secret to fruitfulness is not adding, but pruning. We live in a society that applauds people who can spin 50 plates at one time and run themselves into the ground by living a life with no margins and boundaries (like wild and overgrown gardens). On the other hand, I've watched people overcompensate in the other direction, too. For example, when they sense they must prune some things out of their lives, instead of pruning, they go ballistic and hack away more stuff than is necessary. They throw the baby out with the bathwater. They become hermits and bail out on life altogether.

Pruning is an indicator that we have been fruitful. It's a good thing and should be celebrated. Pruning sometimes feels like "cutting off" in the initial stages. It may be painful, but the things God prunes grow back stronger and healthier. Pruning is a sign that you and I are loved by God. The Bible teaches us that God disciplines who He loves. God's shaping in my life indicates son-ship.

## Stay Connected to the Vine

My prayer for us is that we will stay connected to Jesus and that we'll do the things (private and public) that help us come close and stay close to Him. Be it a walk in the forest or a run in the park, let us choose the avenues that help us sense God's Spirit. Be it reading the Bible and having a solitary and daily devotion, or launching out into the community and serving the poor, let us obey the quiet promptings in our hearts that is from God. Be it surrounding ourselves with the beauty and serenity of art and music, or sharing our faith in the schoolroom with others, let us move forward when we hear the voice of God. Be it in your prayer closet pouring out your pain and heartache to God, or in church boldly lifting your voice in song, let us engage with God. Offer your whole self to Him in loving worship and surrender. However we do it, and whatever it is we do, we must put in the effort to stay close and remain connected with Jesus.

Finally, if you are reading this and you have yet to connect yourself to Jesus, I encourage you to trust Him with your life. Allow Him to connect you to Himself (the Vine). Tell Jesus that you are ready to start a relationship with Him. He knows your thoughts and discerns the intentions of your heart. Go for it: He's listening.

John Chapter 16

# THE HOLY SPIRIT: GOD'S LIVING PROMISE

*Nevertheless, I tell you the truth: It is to your advantage that I go away, for if I do not go away, the Helper will not come to you. But if I go, I will send him to you. And when he comes, he will convict the world concerning sin and righteousness and judgment. When the Spirit of truth comes, he will guide you into all the truth, for he will not speak on his own authority, but whatever he hears he will speak, and he will declare to you the things that are to come. He will glorify me, for he will take what is mine and declare it to you. (John 16: 7-6, 13-14)*

## Farewell Address

Jesus' farewell address to the disciples continues in this chapter. He gives more details about His impending death, resurrection, and ascension to heaven. He warns them about the intense persecution that lurks just around the corner. He gives some specifics to watch out for:

- The disciples themselves will scatter because of confusion and fear.
- Some of the persecutors will think they are doing God a favor, when in fact they will be instruments of Satan (the apostle Paul before his conversion was one).
- In the short run, the circumstances will appear to get worse before they get better. Jesus advises the disciples to pray, not panic.
- The disciples will not be left alone. A long foretold promise is about to appear.

## The Holy Spirit

Jesus assures His followers that He has overcome the world, and that their deep sorrow will soon turn into joy. He goes on to explain the work of the Holy Spirit a bit more. He tells them that, as of now, although He is God in the flesh, He is also subject to and limited by the natural laws and physics of earth's time and space in regards to His physical body. He tells them that when the Holy Spirit comes, He will not be limited by these earthly restrictions. In fact, He will be able to be in all places, with all people, at all times.

Jesus explains that the Holy Spirit will come as soon as Jesus goes. The Holy Spirit will continue the earthly ministry and mission of Jesus by inhabiting Christians and empowering them for service. The Holy Spirit will be free from physical limitations and the laws of nature. Through it He will teach and guide us into all truth. Therefore, they were (as are we) to rejoice because, in reality, they are not abandoned and left alone. God's Spirit will live in them (and in those of us who receive Christ) 24/7.

## The Promise From On High

Jesus concludes this chapter on a high note by encouraging the disciples to see the big picture of what God has promised, what He has done, and what He will do. Therefore, they can have joy, confidence, and peace in the midst of suffering and persecution.

The Bible extends many promises to Christians through what Jesus made available by His death and resurrection. One of the most amazing promises, is the promise of the Holy Spirit coming to dwell inside of us. But sometimes we're hesitant in receiving God's promises.

I think one reason is that we live in a society that doesn't always make good on its promises. Promises are more like hopeful wishes and good intentions. So, when we hear the word "promise" in the Bible, we're often skeptical, even if they are God's promises. We hold back. We develop backup plans in case it all falls through, because throughout the course of our lives, many people (including ourselves) have failed to make good on their promises.

It's important to remember that God is not like us. His ways are not our ways. He's perfect, faultless, and immutable. There's a verse in Joshua that says, "Not one of the good promises which the Lord had made to the house of Israel failed; all came to pass." (Joshua 21:45)

God's promises are not just nice sayings. They are bonds, covenants, and guarantees that are just and true. Every single promise God makes comes to pass. Every promise that God declares about your life, your future, and your job is trustworthy. Every promise of what God wants you to become as a person is not just a nice thought or optimistic intention, but a sacred and eternal pledge that is signed by the blood of Jesus through His death and resurrection.

God is committed to His promises. He cannot lie. His actions are always in compliment and alignment with His character. Fulfilling His design in you and me is a vow He takes seriously. Do we have any responsibility when it comes to God's promises? Yes, we do. We are to receive them in faith and obey when He speaks. He promises, we follow.

The Holy Spirit is God's living promise. He will be our Guide, Mentor, and Helper. He'll correct us when we get off course and comfort us when we're down and want to give up. He will transform us and shape us into the image of Jesus.

## A Prayer to Receive

My prayer is that we'll give our lives fully to Jesus. We'll listen to the whisper of His voice as He calls us to repent of our sin and turn towards God. As we do, we'll receive forgiveness, grace, and a promise: the Holy Spirit. Let me encourage you to welcome the activity of God's Spirit in your life. He promises not only to be with you, but to guide you into His truth, His plans, and His purpose for your life. That's a promise that Jesus died for and that you and I can live for.

# John Chapter 17

# THE POWER OF UNITY

*Holy Father, keep them in your name, which you have given me, that they may be one, even as we are one. Sanctify them in the truth; your word is truth. As you sent me into the world, so I have sent them into the world. I do not ask for these only, but also for those who will believe in me through their word, that they may all be one, just as you, Father, are in me, and I in you, that they also may be in us, so that the world may believe that you have sent me. The glory that you have given me I have given to them, that they may be one even as we are one, I in them and you in me, that they may become perfectly one, so that the world may know that you sent me and loved them even as you loved me. (John 17: 11, 17-18, 20-23)*

## The Triune God

Jesus prays His final prayer in this chapter. It's sometimes called His high priestly prayer. He prays for Himself, His disciples, and those who will later come to faith and believe in the gospel. Jesus once again asserts His deity by stating that the Father and He are one. He explains that the core ingredient for eternal life is about having a genuine relationship with God, through the person of Jesus. He goes on to talk about His earthly mission and how it's God's plan that it continues through the disciples, and other believers who will later come to faith in Christ.

## Power of Unity

Jesus introduces the power of unity (being one with Jesus and one with each other). He explains that unity of spirit and purpose, coupled with a shared gospel mission, if it is built upon a genuine relationship with God, and if it's under-girded with a spirit of loving servanthood toward one another, has the possibility to catalyze extraordinary supernatural results. It's a spiritual domino effect. Believers will be filled with joy. Non-believers will see an authentic and compelling witness of the love of God in action, which will help lead them to the reality of the gospel message. God will then be glorified.

Jesus concludes His prayer and asks that the love of the Father overtake the disciples. He prays they will know the depth and breadth of both the Father and His love. To know God's love is to know God's power, because God's love is His power, and His power is His love.

Be it in the story of the people's unity of giving for the Tabernacle (Exodus 35-36), the unity in dedicating the Temple (1 Kings 8), or the singleness of purpose exampled in the gathering and praying at Pentecost (Acts 2), when certain kinds of God-inspired togetherness happens, God promises to respond in powerful ways.

## Teamwork

Even today, if teamwork has played a key role in most of the major advances and breakthroughs of science and technology, then it shouldn't surprise us that God would use unity in powerful ways in the spiritual world as well. Especially if the end goals are unselfish and God-honoring.

"How good and pleasant it is when brothers live together in unity! It is like the precious oil poured on the head, running down on the beard, running down on Aaron's beard, down upon the collar of his robes. It is as if the dew of Herman were falling on Mount Zion. For there the Lord bestows his blessing, even life forevermore." (Psalm 133:1-3)

The psalmist tells us that God commands blessing where there is unity. "Grace Like Rain" is currently a popular worship song that is a great picture of this truth. When unity (not uniformity) exists, God "rains His presence" on barren places (which is what Mount Zion was like). This is part of what Jesus was getting at when He was talking about unity with His disciples. There is a "cause and effect" relationship to human unity with the purposes and presence of God.

Jesus suggests that walking in unity can influence people who are far from God in a mysterious, yet compelling fashion. Witnessing unity can unlock gospel revelation in non-Christians. (John 3:16—that God is real and loves them and wants to have a relationship with them.)

## The Devil Fears Unity

Maybe this is one of the reasons why the devil fights hard against us in our relationships and in our churches. He delights when we misunderstand each other and fail to resolve disputes in our families and friendships (Matthew 18). He's going after unity because he knows what unity can do.

In regard to the subject of relationships, we live in a world where people bail rather than resolve. We make excuses about why we can't resolve a relational problem or tell a person the honest truth. It's uncomfortable and awkward for most people.

## Garnering Unity

Because we're fearful and sometimes don't understand the principles associated with unity, we miss opportunities to lead and we create more layers of relational complexity, which fuels lack of trust. For example, in the work place, managers often resort to creating new policies for the masses because they lack the courage and fortitude to confront a difficult individual issue with an employee. Rather than sit down with that one person and tell the truth, even if it's awkward, we often create policies that affect everyone, when in reality, we only have one or two people in mind. The solution, in this example, is telling people the truth. Even if it is difficult, it's the right thing to do. It pays big dividends in more ways than one might imagine.

## Corporate Responsibility

Yes, unity costs. Yes, it requires courage. And yes, to sustain unity is not for the faint of heart. But when we understand that unity is everyone's responsibility, and that it's a core element of true success, we can garner up the courage and contend for it.

The apostle Paul challenges us to "make every effort to keep the unity of the Spirit through the bond of peace." (Ephesians 4:3) Cultivating and protecting unity is everyone's responsibility. Unity inspires and galvanizes vision.

The devil knows that human energy and financial resources will not be brought to a visionless and un-unifed church or Christian organization. This is important to understand because the accomplishment of every vision is dependent upon the goodwill of the people and the human resources and energies that are sown into it.

## Contending for God's Best

My prayer for you and me is that we will courageously contend for unity in our families, friendships, work teams, and churches. God wants to unite us in spirit and purpose in order that joy abounds, that lost people find Christ, and that God is glorified. The choice is ours.

My prayer is that we will protect the unity of our church communities by acting in love toward one another, by refusing to gossip, and by trusting and following the loving leadership God has placed in our lives.

"So let us concentrate on the things which make for harmony, and on the growth of our fellowship together." (Romans 15:19)

John Chapter 18

# CHOOSE YOUR ROLE WISELY

*When he had finished praying, Jesus left with his disciples and crossed the Kidron Valley. On the other side there was an olive grove, and he and his disciples went into it. Now Judas, who betrayed him, knew the place, because Jesus had often met there with his disciples. So Judas came to the grove, guiding a detachment of soldiers and some officials from the chief priests and Pharisees. They were carrying torches, lanterns and weapons. Jesus, knowing all that was going to happen to him, went out and asked them, "Who is it you want?" "Jesus of Nazareth," they replied. "I am he," Jesus said. (And Judas the traitor was standing there with them.) When Jesus said, "I am he," they drew back and fell to the ground. (John 18:1-6)*

## The Passion of Christ

This chapter begins with Jesus being betrayed by Judas Iscariot. It contains three main sections: Jesus' nighttime arrest, His rigged hearing with Annas, and His unjust Roman trial before Pilate. All four gospels summarize the major events surrounding Jesus' arrest, trial, crucifixion, burial, and Resurrection. Each of these accounts corroborate the unique details, subtle nuances, and rich narrative in such a way as to create a beautiful mosaic of the Passion of Christ. The author of this book, John the Beloved, wants us to see how God's providential and grace-filled plan is being fulfilled in the person of Jesus, and how the Old Testament prophesies and promises are now coming true in Him.

As we read on, we find the rooster crows and, as predicted, Peter denies Jesus three times. Jesus goes on to discuss with Pilate the question people around the globe 20 centuries later are still asking today: What is truth? Jesus responds and gives Pilate (and us) an answer and a glimpse of the spiritual reality of the God-life (the Kingdom of God). As we'll soon see, Jesus is sentenced to death on a cross, and is ultimately executed by Pilate's soldiers. He is buried, rises from the dead, and is seen by multitudes of people.

## Lessons From Judas

As I reflect on this chapter, I'm drawn to one of the most unlikely and infamous people in the whole Bible: Judas. I've often told my children that if they can learn from the bad, as well as the good, then they can increase their learning by 50%. Life is made up of both good and bad. Too often in life, people only choose to learn from the good (good teachers, good experiences, good friends, good past, good feelings, etc.). But if we can hone the art of learning from the bad in any and every situation in life, we leverage our learning and growth in such a way as to glean gems of wisdom from the most unlikely sources. Often, there are sunken treasures buried in the land of heartache, disappointment, betrayal, and failure.

## Learn From the Bad

It's been said that we must make a conscious choice to get better and not bitter in life. Judas offers us some life lessons in the most contrarian of ways. Wisdom can be obtained from not only our own experiences (good and bad) in life, but also from the experiences (and failures) of others. Judas, although low on the relational totem pole of most people, still can be a source who imparts learning.

## Early Warning Signs

The ramification and consequence for Judas' decision to betray Jesus was suicide. I'm sure if Judas could live his life all over again, he would do it differently. As you follow the progression of Judas' domino-like fall, you see interesting patterns and warning signs beginning to emerge early on in his life as a disciple. He wasn't a betrayer in the beginning, but he was a rebel and a person who harbored ill will against those God placed in authority over his life (Matthew 26:6-14, John 18:1-6). He didn't love people, but he sure loved money (John 12:3-5). He didn't love Jesus, but he really liked looking spiritual and religious in front of others (Matthew 26:25, John 13:29-30). Judas only cared about the short-term, and not the long-term (Matthew 27:3). Finally, he wasn't forced into his "betrayer role," he chose it (Luke 6:16).

## Choose Your Role

Yes, God is sovereign and has a plan and purpose for each of our lives, but at the same time, God allows each of us to choose what role we want to play in His kingdom. Both truths (predestination and free will) exist in harmony from God's perspective. It's like two children who both have their own unique individuality yet belong in the same family. So too do God's sovereignty and the choices humans make belong in the God-life and under the banner of our heavenly Father.

## Free Will

Just because I can't always understand how these truths overlay and relate doesn't mean they aren't true. It just means that I'm (we're) not God! Although our Creator has a master plan, we are not marionette puppets reacting to the pull of His strings. We are given free will from a loving and sovereign God. Yes, God has written a grand story, but we get to choose what part we will play in His story. Some people will choose to follow Him; others will choose to run from Him. Some will choose to support Him and care for His body (church); some will reject Him and the apple of His eye (the body of Christ). Some will slander and plot His death; others will pray, serve, and give. We are all given time and opportunities while on earth (Ecclesiastes 9:11). It's what we do with our time and opportunities that really matters.

## It's Your Choice

Let me ask you what role you want to play. It's your choice. You can choose to have a great part in God's kingdom, or a neutral one. You can choose to be a spectator or a participant. You can choose to play a large role, or a small one. You can be a person who walks through life kicking stones saying, "I hate God. I hate church. It's hard to be a Christian." Or you can be a person that makes choices that provoke God to say, "As is your faith, so shall it be unto you." (Matthew 15:28) Decisions...Choices...Roles. It's our call. What will you do? If the grave could speak, I believe Judas would say, "Choose the best roles. Make the wisest choice. Make a decision to play a great part in God's kingdom."

## Play a Big Part

My prayer for us is that we would choose to come out of the grand-stands of life and out onto the playing field of God's kingdom. We have only one life to live. God created us to do good works. And we are created to be in an alive relationship with the God of the universe and His son, Jesus Christ.

Let's live life with intentionality and passion. Let's live large with great faith and a desperate dependency on Christ. Let's allow God's Spirit, that lives in us, to develop and shape us in such a way that we can play the parts that make His story a stunning masterpiece to a watching world. His call and invitation has gone forth. It's now our opportunity. All of heaven watches with great anticipation. What role will you play in God's kingdom?

John Chapter 19

# PREPARATION FOR RESURRECTION

*After these things, Joseph of Arimathea, who was a disciple of Jesus, but secretly for fear of the Jews, asked Pilate that he might take away the body of Jesus, and Pilate gave him permission. So he came and took away his body. Nicodemus also, who earlier had come to Jesus by night, came bringing a mixture of myrrh and aloes, about seventy-five pounds in weight. So they took the body of Jesus and bound it in linen cloths with the spices, as is the burial custom of the Jews. Now in the place where he was crucified there was a garden, and in the garden a new tomb in which no one had yet been laid. So because of the Jewish day of Preparation, since the tomb was close at hand, they laid Jesus there. (John 19: 38-42)*

## Brutal Execution

Jesus is delivered up to the authorities to be crucified. He's beaten, given a crown of thorns, and a purple robe. He's mimicked, mocked, and falsely judged. He carries His own cross through the city streets and is followed by His mother and a few close friends who watch in horror. They arrive at the Place of the Skull (*Golgotha* in Aramaic) for His execution. Jesus is stripped naked and sadistically nailed to the cross. In the midst of His suffering, Jesus speaks some final words to His mother and then dies. A Roman solider pierces His side just to make sure He is dead.

## Two Courageous Guys

Joseph of Arimathea, a member of the ruling Jewish council, and a secret follower of Jesus, appeals to Pilate for Jesus' body. He and his friend, Nicodemus, take the battered body of Jesus, prepare it for burial in the Jewish customs of the day, and place it in an empty tomb.

I've always been intrigued with the ending of this chapter, where two regular guys (let's call them Joe and Nick) prepare Jesus' bruised and bloodied body for His coming resurrection. I've often wondered what would have happened if these two friends had not stepped up to the plate and helped to write the history of their generation. There's a story within a story packed into the verses.

## Incognito Christians

When I was a kid, "Secret Agent Man" was a popular song from a hit TV spy show of the same name. The show began with a guy in a black suit and shaded glasses slithering sideways in the shadows and peeking around the corner of buildings. It had all the makings of what a secret agent adventure should be.

Over the years, I've noticed that not just secret agents, but many human beings have had a tendency to go "undercover," too, especially when it comes to identifying publicly with Jesus Christ. Being unafraid to claim Christ and walk in His ways is a timeless call for every man and woman who has been touched by the Savior. Joseph of Arimathea and Nicodemus were two such guys who encountered the truth about Christ in their personal lives. When you first hear about them in the Bible, they are introduced as "nighttime spiritual seekers" of Jesus (John 3). These guys were drawn to Jesus and His teachings, but at the same time, they pursued Him in secret for fear of what others might say. They were afraid to go public with their faith. They were incognito Christ-followers.

I had a friend, growing up in Tucson, who had a pet chameleon. I remember watching how it turned different colors when my friend added different colored shrubs and backgrounds. I watched this lizard turn multiple shades of green, yellow, brown, and orange right before my eyes.

We can be like that, too. I know at times, I've succumbed. Surroundings can influence the color of our actions if we let it. Environments can hamper the tone of our Christian testimony if we're not vigilant. It's like we can become incognito secret agent Christians if the situation is just right.

## God Loves Our Humanity

The good news is that God understands our human frailties, fears, and insecurities. He's compassionate and loving. He speaks to us with words of acceptance and invitation. God invites us to approach Him just as we are: with our warts, foibles, and weaknesses. We're summoned by the Holy Spirit to come close to a God who loves. We're invited to bring Him our many unanswered questions about God, life, and faith as we lean into Him by faith.

We have a tendency to overestimate what God will do in one month, and underestimate what God can do in three years. These two guys are perfect examples. Approximately three years into the discipleship process, we see something amazing has transpired in the lives of Joe and Nick: No more secret agent man!

## Courageous Leadership

After Jesus' death on Calvary's cross, these two incognito Christ-followers become bold proponents of the Christian faith. Indecision converts into resolve. Weakness becomes strength. Timidity transforms into courage. Unanswered questions turn into convictions. Joe and Nick go public with their faith and love for Jesus. They become timeless examples of courageous leadership, but this is just the beginning of their inspirational story. I'm aware that what I'm going to propose is not necessarily the primary interpretation of this portion of scripture, but I do think there are some powerful truths within it that can inspire us even today.

## Truths that Inspire

First, I can't help but notice that as everyone is running away from the beaten, broken, and crucified body of Christ on the cross, these two guys are running toward it. Everyone has fled except them. They risk their lives and go right into Pilate's court to ask for Jesus' body, so they can prepare it for burial with spices that they purchased with their own resources.

Even today, there is something special about men and women who see the body of Christ (the local church) in all of its possibility rather than in its shortcomings and brokenness. Too often, I hear people critique and criticize the body of Christ pointing out how it is filled with so many problems and imperfections. They are masters at pointing out every spot, blemish, and wrinkle (which by the way, isn't too hard to do because it's filled with imperfect people). I sometimes tell these neatniks that if they're looking for a perfect church to not go to church. (If they go, it won't be perfect anymore!)

## The Apple of God's Eye

I love to be around people that can see past a church's imperfections, bruises, and dead spots. These people understand that the church, even in its weakness and humanness, is the apple of God's eye. He died for it. He loves it. The church is Jesus' bride (Revelation 21). Any husband I know can only take so much of others picking on his bride before he reacts.

The apostle Paul finally understood this truth while on the road to Damasucs en route to harass and hurt the Christian community (Acts 9). He understood that hurting Christians was the same as hurting Jesus. This epiphany exploded in Paul's heart (understanding the connection between Jesus and the church) and changed the trajectory of the great apostle's life, work, and legacy.

The story of Joseph of Arimathea inspires me. He understood that for the resurrected body of Jesus to come forth, it would require His body to be prepared for burial. Today, if the church is to come forth in resurrection power, it will take men like Joseph and Nicodemus who will both invest in it and prepare it behind the scenes.

## Love What God Loves

My prayer for you and me is that God will renew our love and commitment for the things God loves, and for the things to which He is committed. I'm praying that God will raise up men and women who possess the heart and spirit of Joseph of Arimathea. God wants to develop people's perspectives in such a way that they can look past the imperfections and brokenness of the local church and help prepare it for resurrection power in the 21st century.

## Fully Engaged

Where are the men who will step up and run toward the body of Christ while the vast majority remain lulled by distractions and fears? Where are the folks that will use their gifts, talents, and financial resources to prepare Jesus' church in order that the gospel message, coupled with spiritual power, can come forth and impact a lost and dying world?

Always remember: You will always find in life what you are looking for (Proverbs 11:27). No, I'm not suggesting that when we see problems we should bury our heads in the sand and ignore them. I'm suggesting that we learn to see problems (and life, for that matter) differently.

## See What God Sees

Together, let's learn to see the evidence of God's presence and not His absence, especially in the local church. Why? Because you'll always find in life what you are looking for. There could be 100 right things in a church, but if you have the disposition which is always looking for the one thing that isn't working right, you'll always find it. I invite you to engage with your church (the body of Christ) with a spirit like that of Joseph of Arimathea: a spirit that is fearless and focused on the future. See challenges in a new way and run in a direction that is counterintuitive to our culture. Help be part of the solution. It's when we are willing to lose our life that in the end we actually find it (Luke 9).

John Chapter 20

# SEEING JESUS IN OTHER FORMS

*But Mary stood weeping outside the tomb, and as she wept she stooped to look into the tomb. And she saw two angels in white, sitting where the body of Jesus had lain, one at the head and one at the feet. They said to her, "Woman, why are you weeping?" She said to them, "They have taken away my Lord, and I do not know where they have laid him." Having said this, she turned around and saw Jesus standing, but she did not know that it was Jesus. Jesus said to her, "Woman, why are you weeping? Whom are you seeking?" Supposing him to be the gardener, she said to him, "Sir, if you have carried him away, tell me where you have laid him, and I will take him away." Jesus said to her, "Mary." She turned and said to him in Aramaic, "Rabboni!" (which means Teacher). Mary Magdalene went and announced to the disciples, "I have seen the Lord" and that he had said these things to her. (John 20:11-16,18)*

## The Empty Tomb

John describes the empty tomb, Jesus' resurrection, the encounter with Mary Magdalene, the faith challenge to the wavering Thomas, and the commissioning of Jesus' disciples with the good news. Jesus is God and He can forgive ours sins and grant us eternal life if we believe and follow Him. There are many people mentioned in this chapter: Jesus, Mary Magdalene, Simon Peter, the other disciple (probably John), the remaining disciples, Thomas, two angels, and a gardener. A lot is happening with a lot of people. What an incredible moment it must have been to be part of this post-resurrection, life-altering, historic event.

I've always found interesting the encounter that took place with Mary Magdalene and the supposed gardener. As Mary arrives, early Sunday morning, to Jesus' tomb (some scholars believe to complete the burial preparation), she is overcome with emotion as she discovers that the stone in front of the tomb has been moved. Jesus' grave clothes are neatly folded and put off to the side and, worst of all, Jesus' body is missing.

## Eyes to See

Then, out of the blue, a gardener appears. Mary asks him if he knows where Jesus' body has been taken. A short dialogue follows. Mary is distraught and she fails to recognize that the gardener is Jesus. Then it happens! "Mary," said Jesus, and she snapped out of it. Mary recognized, that in fact, it was Jesus with whom she was conversing. (His resurrected body had changed in some physical form from the brutalized and disfigured form it took on a few days earlier at the Crucifixion). In the midst of Mary's grief, Jesus was present all along, but she didn't recognize Him. Even though Jesus was right there with her, Mary could only see her grief, not Jesus.

Mary's not alone. There's another encounter, in the gospel of Luke, where two disciples are walking on the road to Emmaus after Jesus' death and resurrection. Jesus shows up and walks with them in their trek across town. They too fail to recognize that this "fellow traveler" is in fact Jesus.

"As they walked along they were talking of Jesus' death, when suddenly Jesus himself came along and joined them and began walking beside them. But they didn't recognize him. As they sat down to eat, he took a small loaf of bread and broke it and was passing it over to them, when suddenly-- it was as though their eyes were opened-- they recognized him!" (Luke 24:14-31)

## Recognize His Voice

As I think through this story, I see a lesson to remember about Mary's encounter with the gardener. Mary was frustrated, confused, disillusioned, and afraid. The life she had hoped for was abruptly put on hold. Her hopes were completely dashed. In some ways, it was like it was raining stones instead of raining blessings. For Mary, just a few days prior, things had moved from bad to worse, but everything changed when she recognized Jesus' voice in the midst of her circumstances.

When I responded to the voice of Jesus calling my name, things changed for me, too. Although I didn't hear a literal voice calling out to me, I did sense a very clear and strong impression in my heart and mind. I was 23 and had many questions and unresolved issues surrounding my thoughts and beliefs about God. Nevertheless, I did know with certainty that God was in fact speaking to me and that He was real. I knew God was calling me into relationship with Him to believe, to be forgiven, to be loved, and to be used by Him.

Looking back on all of this, I realize that the "gardener" had actually called my name many times over a several-year period, but I didn't recognize it. God orchestrated many opportunities for me, but I failed to recognize His voice in the midst of them. I only saw a gardener and not Jesus.

## The Reality of Faith

God can use all kinds of people, situations, and phenomena in ways that call out to each of us and invite us into the reality of faith through the person of Jesus Christ. Having faith in God is not an illusion or self-help mechanism, as some philosophers and psychoanalysts might have us believe. Jesus is not a philosophy or good feeling or a Rocky Mountain high. He is not a coping methodology for a stress-filled life. He is reality. Jesus said, of Himself, that He is the Way, the Truth, and the Life (John 14).

## See the Evidence of His Presence

My only regret in life is that when I first heard my name being called that I would have recognized it was really Jesus, not the gardener, calling out to me and inviting me into relationship. My prayer for you is that you will recognize and seize the moment when Jesus uses "gardeners" in your life. At first glance, you might not see clearly, but look with new eyes and hear with an open heart what's taking place all around you.

Let me ask you, what might God be using in your life to speak to you? Who or what has God placed in your life to be used as a gardener? Has it been a friend or family member? Has it been a work associate, a feeling, a book, or a blog? Is it a problem, a failed friendship, or a discouraging season in your life? "Gardeners" come in all shapes and sizes. They call out to us when we least expect it.

Let me encourage you to assess your life accurately. Look carefully, discern deeply, and consider honestly that what you see, hear, or feel might be more than what it appears to be. Oh yes, there's always the possibility that it might be a figment of your imagination. Yes, that happens, but it also might very well be Jesus, by the Holy Spirit, coming to you in another form. There might just be something happening under the radar of your life. Speak Lord, we're listening!

John Chapter 21

# CHOOSING A NEW ENDING FOR YOUR LIFE

*When they had finished breakfast, Jesus said to Simon Peter, "Simon, son of John, do you love me more than these?" He said to him, "Yes, Lord; you know that I love you." He said to him, "Feed my lambs." He said to him a second time, "Simon, son of John, do you love me?" He said to him, "Yes, Lord; you know that I love you." He said to him, "Tend my sheep." He said to him the third time, "Simon, son of John, do you love me?" Peter was grieved because he said to him the third time, "Do you love me?" and he said to him, "Lord, you know everything; you know that I love you." Jesus said to him, "Feed my sheep. Truly, truly, I say to you, when you were young, you used to dress yourself and walk wherever you wanted, but when you are old, you will stretch out your hands, and another will dress you and carry you where you do not want to go." (This he said to show by what kind of death he was to glorify God.) And after saying this he said to him, "Follow me." (John 21:15-19)*

## One Last Time

This final chapter of John's gospel begins on the beach off the Sea of Tiberas. Jesus appears for His third and final time (post-resurrection) before His ascension, which soon follows. While the seven disciples are in the midst of a lackluster night of fishing, Jesus aids them in a sudden and miraculous catch.

As the nets are breaking and their hearts pumping, the disciples soon realize they were not being helped by an on-shore local fisherman, but rather Jesus. Filled with joy, they immediately paddle to shore. Once on the beach, the seven have breakfast with Jesus and engage in a compelling and life-altering conversation. Peter is singled out. Jesus deals with his painful failure, assures Peter of His love, establishes a simple ministry team structure from which to operate, and re-commissions Peter and the others to God's purpose and calling for their lives. Faith, hope, and love once again triumph.

This is clearly one of the most gripping moments in the life of the disciples. These words still speak off the pages of the Bible today and apply to each of our lives. I think if we're honest, we can all relate to Peter more than we might think at first glance. We've all found ourselves in his shoes at least once. I know I have.

## Caught in the Middle

Have you ever been caught with a heart that loves the Lord but with a lifestyle that denies it? Have you ever found yourself with a desire to serve God and long for His best in your life, but at the same time, you feel unqualified because you feel your life doesn't measure up to what you think it should? I think this is what Peter might have been feeling that morning on the beach with Jesus. Always remember that Jesus doesn't confront our hearts about where they were yesterday, but rather where they are today. Sometimes we get stuck in "yesterday" and Jesus wants to forgive us and help us get on with our lives. I'm not trivializing Peter's failure. It was real, raw, and painful. But living in our failure is not God's plan for our lives. The way I see it, we have four options in regards to how we deal with our failure and sin:

1. Let the devil deal with it and interpret it for us.
2. Let our own conscience and emotions deal with it.
3. Ignore it all together.
4. Let Jesus deal with it and forgive it.
   (The right answer is behind door number four!)

## The God-Life

In this story, Jesus comes to Peter and deals with his failure up-front. He then talks about love and following. But here's the rub: We can't follow Jesus without His love as the impetus. God doesn't expect us to first get our lives together so we can serve and follow Him. No, the God-life doesn't work that way. Jesus knows that outside of His embrace and outside of His power, we can't get it together. To try to do so is called "religion." It's within God's embrace and within His love and power that we can change and thereby move forward into a bright future. That's why we call it the "good news." Jesus is alive and well. Billions of people over a span of 20 centuries will attest to that fact. Even today, many of your friends and work associates would tell you (if you asked them) that Jesus, through God the Holy Spirit, has transformed their lives as well.

## Will You Follow Jesus?

As we conclude the gospel of John, we're left to wrestle with life's most important question. Each of us must answer it. Even if we choose to postpone it, that too is an answer. Peter answered it and so did the other disciples on the beach that morning. We are asked to answer it as well. The question is simply, "Will you follow Jesus?" How you and I answer that question will determine our future and the final outcome of our lives more than we can ever imagine.

## Choosing a New Ending

I've learned that you can't have a new beginning in life. I don't care what people say, I believe that new beginnings are not possible. It doesn't work that way. You can't go back and undo the things that have happened in your past and start fresh. For example, if you are in a 100-yard dash and you jump the gun and come out of the blocks early, the fact is that you'll be penalized with a false start. You can't change that. You jumped the gun. It's a fact. But here's the good news about the God-life: You and I can have a new ending. That's what grace is all about. The way we finish the race can be different. We can still win. That's what happened to Peter, and that is a promise for you and me as well. With God's love and power we can edit the storyline of our lives. Yes, we can change the way our lives will end by receiving God's marvelous grace. Our endings are yet to be written. They are not governed by karma, but by grace through Jesus Christ. We're never too old or too young to have a new ending.

## Becoming a Follower of Jesus

Jesus calls us to follow Him. As we do, He will deposit His grace into our lives all along the way. You and I don't have what it takes, in our own strength, to finish strong in our walk with God. God promises that if we receive His forgiveness and love, and choose to follow Him today, He will build into us a greater capacity of wisdom, strength, hope, faith, and love all along life's journey. That's what happens when you are in relationship with Jesus. That's what He did for Peter and the others. God will do the same for us as well.

Historians tell us that, in the end, all of the remaining disciples became courageous martyrs for their Christian faith. Some believe Peter was actually crucified upside down because he didn't feel worthy to be compared to Jesus and the way Jesus was crucified (right-side up). Where did these once cowardly men gain such capacity and depth of character and courage? How did they finish out their lives so strong? It was building all along the way. They chose to trust and follow Jesus daily. The accumulation of those daily decisions changed the endings of their lives.

Where did the author of this book, John the Beloved, find such courage and joy in the midst of being exiled to an abandoned island when he was old, and where he eventually succumbed by being boiled alive in a cauldron of oil? It was built up all along the way. How about the apostle Paul, who penned some of the most powerful New Testament epistles while waiting to be beheaded in Nero's court? It was built up all along the way. The same can be true for you and me.

## Grace for Today

God will provide us with all we need for today and all we desire for the future. That's why the scriptures say, "'I know the plans that I have for you,' says the Lord. They are not plans for your calamity but for your welfare that you might have a future and a hope." (Jeremiah 29:11) Let Jesus deal with your past and your failure. Receive His love into your heart. Choose to follow Him today. Let God give you a new ending to your story.

## Life's Most Important Decision

If you have never received Christ, I challenge you to step forward with your heart and trust Him with your past, your present, and your future. God might be asking you to simply let your past be the past. Receive His forgiveness. Demonstrate your love to God by getting back on track and following Him once again. Love God by loving others.

My prayer for you and me is that we will choose today to write a new ending for our lives. Saying yes to Jesus is the most eternal decision we'll ever make. Choose well. And may God richly bless you!

# REFERENCES

Barker, K. General Editor (1995). *The NIV study bible.* Grand Rapids,: Zondervan.

Barna, G. (2009 ). *The seven faith tribes: Who they are, what they believe, and why they Matter.* Brentwood, TN: Tyndale House Publishers.

Barclay, W. (1975 ). *The gospel of john: Volume 1* (Revised ed.). Philadlephia, PA: Westminster Press.

Barclay, W. (1975 ). *The gospel of john: Volume 2* (Revised ed.). Philadlephia, PA: Westminster Press.

Barclay, W. (1975 ). *The gospel of luke* (Revised ed.). Philadlephia, PA: Westminster Press.

Barclay, W. (1975 ). *The gospel of mark* (Revised ed.). Philadlephia, PA: Westminster Press.

Barclay, W. (1975 ). *The gospel of matthew: Volume 1* (Revised ed.). Philadlephia, PA: Westminster Press.

Barclay, W. (1975 ). *The gospel of matthew: Volume 2* (Revised ed.). Philadlephia, PA: Westminster Press.

Barton, R. H. (2006). *Sacred rhythms: Arranging our lives for spiritual transformation.* Downers Grove, IL: Intervarsity Press.

Benenate, B., & Durepos, J. (Eds.). (1989 ). *No greater love: Mother teresa.* Novato, CA: New World Library.

Bonhoeffer, D. (1955). *Ethics.* New York, NY: Macmillian Publishing Company.

Bonhoeffer, D. (2005). *A year with Dietrich Bonhoeffer: Daily meditations from his letters, writings, and sermons.* San Fransico, CA: Harper-Collins Publishers.

Bray, G. (1996). *Biblical interpretation: Past and present.* Downers Grove, IL: IVP Books.

Brown, D. A. (1999). *What the bible reveals about heaven: Answers to your questions.* Ventura, CA: Regal Books.

Cloud, H. (1992). *Changes that heal: How to understand your past to ensure a healthier future.* Grand Rapids: Zondervan.

Clarno E. (Ed.). (1994). *A reader on healing and wholeness: Jesus, our hope for wholeness.* Los Angeles, CA: International Church of the Foursquare Gospel.

Colson, C. (1992). *The body: Being light in darkness.* Dallas, TX: Word Publishing.

Craig, W. L., & Gould, P. M. (2007). *The two tasks of the Christian scholar: Redeeming the soul, redeeming the mind.* Wheaton, IL: Crossway Books.

Cordeiro, W. (2004). *Doing church as a team: The miracle of teamwork and how it transforms churches.* Ventura, CA: Regal Books.

Davis, S. T. (1997). *God, reason and theistic proofs.* Grand Rapids, MI: Wm. B. Eerdman's Publishing Company.

Deutschman, C. (2007). *Change or die: The three keys to change at work and in life.* New York: HarperCollins Publishers.

Diddams, M., & Daniels, D. (2008, Fall). Good work with toil: A paradigm for redeemed work. *Christian Scholar's Review, XXXVIII,* (1), 61-82.

Driscoll, M. & Breshears, G. (2007). *Vintage jesus: Timeless answers to timely questions.* Wheaton, IL: Crossway Books.

Driscoll, M. & Breshears, G. (2008). *Vintage church: Timeless truths and timely methods.* Wheaton, IL: Crossway Books.

Dyck, B., Neubert, M. J., & Wong, K. (2008, Fall). Unchaining weber's iron cage: A look at what managers can do. *Christian Scholar's Review, XXXVIII,* (1), 41-60.

Evangelical Environmental Network. (2009). *Worshipping God. Loving People. Caring for His creation.* Retrieved November 5, 2009, from http://creationcare.org/responses/faq.php.

George, B. (2007). *True north: Discover your authentic leadership.* San Francisco, CA: Jossey-Bass Books.

Gladwell, M. (2008). *Outliers: The story of success.* New York, NY: Hatchette Book Group.

Goleman, D. (2002 ). *Primal leadership: Learning to lead with emotional intelligence.* Boston, MA: Harvard Business School Publishing, Inc.

Gottman, J., & Silver. N. (1999). *The seven principles for making marriage work.* New York, NY: Three Rivers Press.

Grudem, W. General Editor. (2008). *ESV study bible.* Wheaton, IL Crossway Bibles.

Guinness, O. (2000). *When no one sees: The importance of character in an age of image.* Colorado Springs, CO: NavPress.

Gungor, M. (2008). Ancient Skies (CD). Atlanta, GA: Brash Music.

Hafer, T. (2007). *Faith and fitness: Diet and exercise for a better world.* Minneapolis, MN: Augsburg Books.

Hemfelt, R., Minirth, F., & Meier, P. (1989). *Love is a choice: The definitive book on letting go of unhealthy relationships.* Nashville, TN: Thomas Nelson Publishers, Inc.

Holy Bible. Barker, K. (Ed.). (1995). *New international version.* Grand Rapids, MI: Zondervan Publishing House.

Hull, J., & Hull, L. (1998 ). *Fully alive: Discovering the adventure of healthy and holy living.* Kansas City, MI: Beacon Hill Press.

Hybels, B. (2004). *The volunteer revolution: Unleashing the power of everybody.* Grand Rapids, MI: Zondervan.

Joiner, R., Lane, J., & Stanley, A. (2004). *7 practices of effective ministry.* Colorado Springs, CO: Multnomah Books.

Keller, T. (2008). *The prodigal god: Recovering the heart of the christian faith.* New York, NY: Penguin Group.

Kelly, T. (1941). *A testament of devotion.* New York, NY: HarperCollins Publishers.

Kolp, A., & Rea, P. (2005). *Leading with integrity: Character based leadership.* Mason, OH: Atomic Dog Publishing.

Lamott, A. (1999). *Traveling mercies: Some thoughts on faith.* New York: Random House.

Lawrence, Brother. (1895 & 2005). *The practice of the presence of God: With spiritual maxims.* Boston: Shambhala Publishers, Inc.

Lewis, C.S. (1940). *The problem with pain.* New York, NY: HarperCollins Publishers.

Lewis, C.S. (1943). *Mere Christianity.* New York, NY: Macmillian Publishing.

Lewis, C.S. (1947). *Miracles.* New York, NY: Harper Collins Publishers.

Malphurs, A. & Stroope, S. (2007). *Money matters in the church: A practical guide for leaders.* Grand Rapids, MI: Baker Publishing Group.

Manning, B. (1994). *Abba's child: The cry of the heart for intimate belonging.* Colorado Springs, CO: NavPress.

Mayo Clinic Staff. (2006). *Stress: Unhealthy response to the pressures of life.* Retrieved April 3, 2008, from http://www.mayoclinic.com/health/stress/SR00001.htm

Meade, C., & Meade, M. (2000). Tell the people (CD). Boise, ID: WorshipAlive.com

Meade, C., & Meade, M. (2003). Packin' up my sorrows (CD). Boise, ID: WorshipAlive. com

Meade, C., & Meade, M. (2007). Stronger than life (CD). Boise, ID: WorshipAlive.com com

Meade, C. (2008). *Leadership alive: Changing leadership practices in the emerging 21st century culture.* Boise ID: LeadershipAlive.com

Meade, C. (2010). *Christianity alive: Faith. love. action.* Boise ID: LeadershipAlive.com

McManus, E. (2005). *The barbarian way: Unleash the untamed faih within.* Nashville, TN: Thomas Nelson, Inc.

Murrow, D. (2008). *Why men hate going to church.* Nashville, TN: Thomas Nelson Publishers.

Noebel, D. (2006). *Understanding the times: The collision of today's competing worldviews* (2nd ed.). Manitou, CO: Summit Press.

Otis, G. (2000). *God's trademarks: How to determine whether a message, ministry or strategy is truly from God.* Grand Rapids, MI: Chosen Books.

Prichard, R. (2005). *Credo: Believing in something to die for.* Wheaton, IL: Crossway Books.

Rainer, T. S. & Geiger, E. (2006). *Simple church: Returning to God's process for making disciples.* Nashville, TN: B&H Publishing Group.

Rainer, T. S. (2005). *Breakout churches: Discover how to make the leap.* Grand Rapids, MI: Zondervan.

Sanders, O. J. (1994). *Spiritual leadership.* Chicago, IL: Moody Press.

Schaeffer, F. (1968). *Escape from reason.* Madison, WI: Intervarsity Press.

Schaeffer, F. (1968). *The God who is there.* Madison, WI: Intervarsity Press.

Schaeffer, F. (1971). *True spirituality: How to live for Jesus moment by moment.* Carol Stream, IL: Tyndale House Publishers.

Schaeffer, F. (1972). *Genesis in space and time.* Madison, WI: Intervarsity Press.

Schaeffer, F. (1972). *He is there and he is not silent.* Carol Stream, IL: Tyndale House Publishers.

Schaeffer, F. (1972). *Two contents, two realities.* Wheaton, IL: Crossway Books.

Schaeffer, F. (1976). *How should we then live? The rise and decline of western thought and culture.* Wheaton, IL: Crossway Books.

Schaeffer, F. (1981). *A christian manifesto.* Wheaton, IL: Crossway Books.

Schaeffer, F. (1996). *25 basic bible studies.* Carol Stream, IL: Tyndale House Publishers.

Senge, P. M. (1990). *The fifth discipline: The art and practice of the learning organization.* New York, NY: Currency Doubleday.

Sire, J.W. (1997). *The universe next door: A basic worldview catalog* (3rd ed.). Madison, WI: Intervarsity Press.

Smedes, L. (1993). *Shame and grace: Healing the shame we don't deserve.* New York, NY: Harper Collins Publishers.

Sproul, R.C., & Mathison, K. General Editors (2005). *Reformation study bible: English Standard Version.* Orlando, FL: Ligonier Ministries Publishing.

Stott, J. (1958). *Basic Christianity.* Downers Grove, IL: IVP Books.

Stearns, R. (2009 ). *The hole in our gospel: The answer that changed my life and might just change the world.* Nashville, TN: Thomas Nelson, Inc.

Strobel, L. (2000). *The case for faith: A journalist investigates the toughest objections to Christianity.* Grand Rapids, MI: Zondervan.

Sweet, L. (2007). *The gospel according to starbucks: Living with a grande passion.* Colorado Springs, CO: WaterBrook Press.

Waalkes, S. (2008, Fall). Money or business? A case study of Christian virtue ethics in corporate work. *Christian Scholar's Review, XXXVIII,* (1), 15-40.

Weld, C., & Eriksen, K. (2007). Christian clients' preferences regarding prayer as a counseling intervention. *Journal of Psychology and Theology,* 35, (4), 328-341.

Wilkinson, B. (2001). *Secrets of the vine: Breaking through to abundance.* Colorado Springs, CO: Multnomah Books.

Willard, D. (2005). *Renovation of the heart: Putting on the character of christ.* Colorado Springs, CO: Navpress.

Wright, N. H. (2003). *The new guide to crisis and trauma counseling: A practical guide for ministers, counselors and lay counselors.* Ventura, CA: Regal Books.

Wright, N. T. (2004). *John for everyone: Part one.* Louisville, KY: Westminster John Knox Press.

Wright, N. T. (2004). *John for everyone: Part two.* Louisville, KY: Westminster John Knox Press.

Wright, N. T. (2004). *Luke for everyone.* Louisville, KY: Westminster John Knox Press.

Wright, N. T. (2004). *Mark for everyone.* Louisville, KY: Westminster John Knox Press.

Wright, N. T. (2004). *Matthew for everyone: Part one.* Louisville, KY: Westminster John Knox Press.

Wright, N. T. (2004). *Matthew for everyone: Part two.* Louisville, KY: Westminster John Knox Press.

Wright, N.T. (2008). *Surprised by hope: Rethinking heaven, the resurrection, and the mission of the church.* New York: HarperCollins Publishers.

Wright, N.T. (2006). *Simply christian: Why christianity makes sense.* SanFranciso: HarperCollins Publishers.

Zacharias, R. (1994). *Can man live without God.* Dallas, TX: Word Publishing.

# ABOUT THE AUTHOR

Christopher Meade is the president of LeadershipAlive.com. He is an author, speaker, leader, pastor, educator, and musician. He earned both his bachelor's and master's degrees in Organizational Leadership from George Fox University. He earned a second master's degree in Christian Ministry from Northwest Nazarene University. He holds a Ph.D. in Education with a concentration in Leadership and Organizational Learning from the University of Idaho.

Chris is the lead and founding pastor of GraceChapel.com, an innovative, Christ-centered, multi-cultural church located in Boise, Idaho, where he has served for over 17 years. He is an ordained minister with the Foursquare Church International.

Chris is an Assistant Professor of Business at George Fox University's MBA graduate program. He is the Coordinator of Community Consulting Projects. Chris is also a Faculty Advisor in George Fox University's Semiotics and Future Studies Doctor of Ministry (DMin) program. Chris has taught classes in Executive Level Management, Leadership and Business Ethics, Transformational Leadership, Management and Organizational Behavior, Leadership Dynamics, Research Design and Methods, Statistics, Christian Faith and Thought, and various professional development seminars.

He has served as a consultant and a leadership coach to a wide range of non-profit organizations, individuals, and companies in the private sector. Chris has over 20 years of professional experience as an educator, entrepreneur, pastor, motivational speaker, and leadership and life coach.

As a motivational speaker, Chris's most popular talks include subjects on leadership, the emerging 21st Century culture, and personal and spiritual formation.

Chris is the author of *Leadership Alive: Changing Leadership Practices in the Emerging 21st Century Culture.* This one-of-a-kind book (print and audio) on leadership and the emerging culture was based on research interviews with 20 national Christian leaders from the East Coast to the Pacific Rim. Chris's second book, *Christianity Alive: Faith. Love. Action,* contains 25 insightful essays including the issues of faith, spiritual growth, wholeness, emerging culture, discipleship, and leadership.

Chris is a musician and songwriter. He and his wife, Mary, have composed over 50 original songs, 40 of which are listed with CCLI and/or Word Music® and can be found at WorshipAlive.com. He has produced three original worship albums: *Tell the People, Packin' Up My Sorrows,* and *Stronger Than Life.*

Chris enjoys running, playing the guitar, reading, writing, and eating sushi any chance he gets. Chris has been married to his wife, Mary, for 26 years. They have three children: Luke, Megan, and Allison, and a wonderful daughter-in-law, Rachel.

## CONTACT INFORMATION:

### Christopher Meade

### PO Box 4851 Boise, Idaho 83711

### Chris@LeadershipAlive.com